The Reorder of Things

Difference Incorporated

Roderick A. Ferguson and Grace Kyungwon Hong, Series Editors

THE REORDER OF THINGS
THE ROERDER OF THINGS
TEH ORERDER OF THINGS
TEH ORERDER FO NGITHS

The University and Its Pedagogies
of Minority Difference

Roderick A. Ferguson

Difference Incorporated

University of Minnesota Press

Minneapolis • London

The publication of this book was supported in part by an annual award from the University of Minnesota Provost's Office from the Imagine Fund for the Arts, Design, and Humanities.

Portions of chapter 7 were previously published as "Administering Sexuality; or, The Will to Institutionality," *Radical History Review* 100 (winter 2008): 158–69. Reprinted by permission of the publisher, Duke University Press.

Published by the University of Minnesota Press
111 Third Avenue South, Suite 290
Minneapolis, MN 55401-2520
http://www.upress.umn.edu

ISBN 978-0-8166-7278-3 (hc)
ISBN 978-0-8166-7279-0 (pb)
A Cataloguing-in-Publication record for this book is available from the Library of Congress

Printed in the United States of America on acid-free paper

The University of Minnesota is an equal-opportunity educator and employer.

20 19 18 17 16   10 9 8 7 6 5 4 3

In memory of FOCI (the Faculty of Color Initiative),

in gratitude to its other founding members
(Ananya Chatterjea, Jigna Desai, Vinay Gidwani,
Qadri Ismail, and Hiromi Mizuno),

and in acknowledgment of our efforts
to be in the institution but not of it.

Contents

Acknowledgments

I AM GRATEFUL THAT THIS BOOK has been the recipient of much good fortune. A generous line of people told me that this was more than a vagabond errand. David W. Noble, dear friend and treasured colleague, was the first to say to me, years before I started this project and in response to a conference paper that I wrote, "I think your next book should be on the university." I thank David Eng, who, in a moment of inspiration at a bar in Philly, came up with the title of this book. For the ways in which they inspire me, I am indebted as always to M. Jacqui Alexander, Kandice Chuh, Macarena Gómez-Barris, Gayatri Gopinath, Avery Gordon, Judith Halberstam, Grace Hong, Eng-Beng Lim, George Lipsitz, Lisa Lowe, Jodi Melamed, Chandan Reddy, Stephanie Smallwood, and Ruby Tapia: they are the ones I take with me as I go out to meet the academic world.

For the homes that were opened, the meals that were prepared, the conversations that were had, the wine that was poured, and the love that was bestowed, my everlasting gratitude goes to Hakim Abderrezak, Ananya Chatterjea, Lisa Cacho, Maria Damon, Gina Dent, Priscilla Gibson, Lynn Hudson, Leola Johnson, Regina Kunzel, Diya Larasati, Jodi Melamed, David Noble, Gail Noble, Lisa Park, David Pellow, Tony Peressini, Kavita Philip, Jane Rhodes, Ward Smith, Dara Strolovitch, Deborah Vargas, and Dag Yngvesson.

Special thanks go to those folks who managed their work lives to make the life of this project possible: Dr. Sydney Van Nort for her help with the archival documents at City College; Miglena Todorova for her extraordinary research assistance and for deep friendship and abiding conversations; and Colleen Hennen, my genius administrative assistant, for her protection of my writing time while I was chair of the Department of American Studies at the University of Minnesota. Special dispensation must always go to Richard Morrison—for his friendship, for his painstaking editorial work, and for his belief in this book.

In addition to the anonymous readers who helped me to refine and rethink this project, I must also thank those friends and colleagues who patiently and enthusiastically offered their services as readers and listeners: Kulvinder Arora, Lisa Arrastía, Davarian Baldwin, Lisa Duggan, Daylanne English, Leola Johnson, José Muñoz, Kevin Murphy, Alondra Nelson, Salvador Vidal Ortiz, Laurie Ouellette, David Serlin, Hoon Song, Suzette Spencer, Catherine Squire, Shaden Tageldin, and Michelle Wright.

All the friends and kin who are not academics but were good enough to ask about the health of this manuscript particularly warmed me. Special mention must go to my running buddy Jean Ann Durades, who nagged me with the same question whenever we talked: "Are you writing?" My cousin Tameka Boggs-Mejias always asked very sweetly, "So how's the book goin'?" I would be remiss if I did not mention Cheryl Jones, my dear friend of more than twenty years, and my goddaughter Cecelia Whettstone. During my sabbatical in 2008, they generously opened their home and gave me a room in which to write. Dr. Arlene Maclin's encouragement, counsel, and laughter have been constant since my days at Howard.

As a project that was both critical and contemplative, this book helped me to reactivate that wisdom that we often carried to our childhood rites of passage. No need to worry that a scraped knee and a bruised palm will result in defeat; there will be other chances to get up and try it again.

Affirmative Actions of Power

LET THIS IMAGE BE A LESSON TO YOU. In fact, think of it as an archive, but one that records what typical depositories refuse to document. It's called *Self-Portrait 2000*. The piece is a collage by African American philosopher and conceptual artist Adrian Piper. It's made up of two columns and a picture residing at the base. The left column is an excerpt of a letter that Piper, a professor in the Department of Philosophy, sent to Diana Chapman Walsh, president of Wellesley College from 1993 to 2007. Piper's letter reads:

> After having spent nine months at the Getty Research Institute in an environment supportive of my professional interests and respectful of the singularity of my professional needs, I am able to see anew Wellesley's longstanding hostility to both. I now realize that my inability to extend under these circumstances the record of *professional success and personal wellbeing* I had established before I arrived here is not due to my own failings, moral dereliction, or lack of motivation. It is the consequence of the paralyzing and punitive limitations Wellesley has repeatedly imposed, since the first year I arrived, on the anti-racism work I have done both on and off campus. Having chosen to hire me as Welleseley's only tenured black woman purportedly because of my high-profile anti-racism work in both art and philosophy, Wellesley has consistently refused me the institutional support necessitated by the high level of public visibility at which I am conducting these two careers. In consequence it has knowingly sabotaged both of them, by standing by and watching as I get buried in an unending avalanche of visibility-related demands that have made it virtually impossible to produce and publish the anti-racism work it purportedly brought me here to do. Wellesley has used my public visibility *to enhance its multicultured*

1

No more
one-up/
one-down
games,
God

No more jerk-offs
No more jerks
No more gun binge
  blood binge
  sex binge
  bucks binge
  head binge
  drug binge
  doze binge
  death binge
No more
  kick-me/
  pay-as-you-go /
  bad faith
  crap shoots
No more
  head/heart splits
No more
  do good/eat shit/
  think piss
  put-downs
No more wide-eyed lies

You fix that voice
  in there
Make it say what's right and
  turn the wheels
Or get rid of it and
Get the hell out of the way
  of my gut
You get on it *now*, God
You kick ass good
Or I'm out of here
(6/7/92)

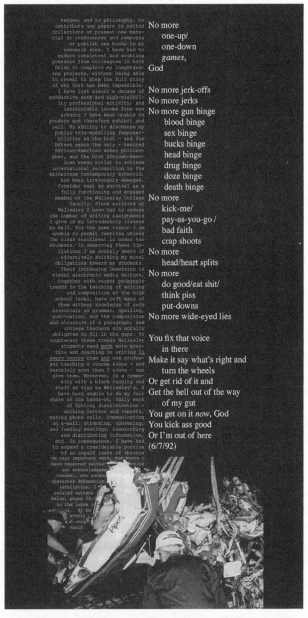

Lower portion of Adrian Piper, *Self-Portrait 2000*, 2000. Scroll-down Web site artwork. Copyright Adrian Piper Research Archive Foundation, Berlin. Collection of Adrian Piper Research Archive Foundation, Berlin.

public image while in reality actively preventing me from doing the multicultural work it publicly claims to welcome.[1]

The other column in the collage is a poem written to God. While the letter to Chapman observes the rhetoric and dispassion of a professional, the poem claims an emotional tone fit for more artistic genres:

> Hey, God!
> How come I get stuck
>   with this
>   dumb bunch?
> It sucks
> you goofed bad
>   on this sad batch, God
> and you know it
> Where do you think
>   you're off to?
> You get back to that lab
>   right now and
> shake up those test tubes
>   one more time
> Don't you dare
>   turn tail and run
> Screw that
> Big Bang shit, God
> You fucked up
>   big time,
> now you fix it . . .[2]

At the feet of the two columns lies a picture of a downed airplane. Barely distinguishable as a plane, the only element that saves it from anonymity is the word *Piper* written on the side. Two white men in hard hats inspect the wreckage. In the artist's notes for the exhibit, we learn that the letter to Chapman is part of a larger dossier of grievances, including legal documents against Wellesley as well as word of an appendicitis that Piper suffered, presumably because of her working conditions. We also learn that the felled plane named Piper is the one in which JFK Jr. died and that the Piper Aircraft Company—founded by Piper's great-uncle—owns the plane.

We are also informed that Piper's mother was the upstairs maid in Cape Cod for JFK Sr. during the early 1960s.

Several histories are "archived" in *Self-Portrait 2000*. There is the history conjured in that decade known as "the sixties," a period noted for its historic promise of minority incorporation into social, political, economic, and academic realms. Then there is the historical present evoked in the title. As *Self-Portrait 2000* is bookended by Piper's mother's employment in the Kennedy house in the early sixties and the letter to President Chapman in 2000, it constellates the features of the contemporary American academy by connecting them to the social formations of the sixties and seventies. Put plainly, we might think of the collage as presenting us with an arc that traces a line between past promises of recognition and present-day catastrophes. Indeed, by using the letter to Chapman Walsh, the poem to God, and Piper's portrait of her own wreckage, the collage seems to measure the failure of those promises. That failure—"archived" by the collage—goes somewhat like this: An academy that was reborn from the protests and agitation of the sixties and seventies was supposed to make good on its promise to minorities, in general, and to a black woman artist and intellectual, in particular. Humanity was supposed to keep faith with that promise and with the people of color to whom the promise was made; a life—Adrian Piper's—was supposed to land safely and come to intellectual and institutional fulfillment. How, then, do we explain this disfigurement that followed a promise and a chain of supposed-to's?

The pages that come after this question represent attempts to answer it. One of the questions that the piece raises is this one: in the context of the academy, how are modes of power exercised upon the daily lives of minoritized subjects and knowledges and how was that exercise prepared for in histories that are supposedly no more? One of the things that the piece points to in its letter to a college president, its poem to the divinity, and a picture of a minoritized life brought down to ruin is the ways in which that life is caught within a new configuration of power, a configuration whose climax is preceded by courtship, invitation, and acknowledgment.

Hence, I choose to read *Self-Portrait 2000* as a meditation on this new configuration. In it is a complex history of the ways in which technologies of power began to work with and through difference in order to manage its insurgent possibilities. When Piper writes, for instance, that Wellesley has "sabotaged" the antiracist artistic and philosophical work that the college "purportedly" brought her there to do, she engages the very chronology that this book is interested in—an insurgent articulation of difference begun in the sixties because of and with the U.S. student movements and the subsequent institutionalization of modes of difference and the undertheorized technologies that this institutionalization wrought.

Despite all that we think we know about difference and power via poststructuralism, *Self-Portrait 2000*—read as the archive of the attempts to manage the student movements and their outcomes—divulges a story not captured in the taken-for-granted analytics of Foucault, Derrida, Lacan, Lyotard, or their descendants. Typical poststructuralist and postmarxist theorizations leave out the student movements that yielded the interdisciplinary fields. As this book will illustrate, a theorization that takes seriously their historical and discursive impacts is crucial to understanding not only the changes within the American academy but also the ideological and discursive shifts that informed power's clutch on state, capital, and social life in the post–civil rights world.

The history of the U.S. ethnic and women's studies protests presents the transition from economic, epistemological, and political stability to the possibility for revolutionary social ruptures and subjectivities. For instance, the San Francisco State student strikes of 1969 advocated a "Third World revolution" that would displace and provide an alternative to racial inequality on that campus. That same year, 269 similar protests erupted across the country.[3] At Rutgers, black students took over the main educational building, renaming it "Liberation Hall." At the University of Texas at Austin, a student organization called Afro Americans for Black Liberation "insisted on converting the Lyndon B. Johnson Presidential Library to a black studies building and renaming it for Malcolm X."[4] Inspired by the black power movement, Chicano students would also form "the United Mexican American Students, the Mexican American Student Association, and MECha, Movimiento Estudiantil Chicano de Aztlán, while others in San Antonio founded the Mexican American Youth Organization, MAYO."[5] Those students would also begin to demand Chicano studies courses and departments. Similarly, in 1969 American Indian activists took over Alcatraz Island and claimed it as Indian territory, with hopes of building a cultural center and museum.[6] And in 1970, the first women's studies programs would be established at San Diego State University and at SUNY-Buffalo.

While the state governments in California and Wisconsin called out the National Guard on students advocating for ethnic studies, systems of power also responded to these protests by attempting to manage that transition, in an attempt to prevent economic, epistemological, and political crises from achieving revolutions that could redistribute social and material relations. Instead, those systems would work to ensure that these crises were recomposed back into state, capital, and academy. Whereas modes of power once disciplined difference in the universalizing names of canonicity, nationality, or economy, other operations of power were emerging that would discipline through a seemingly alternative regard for difference and through a revision of the canon, national identity, and the market.

This theorization of power converges with and diverges from Foucault's own observations, converging with him through an emphasis on the strategic nature of power relations. For instance, recall his argument about power in the first volume of *The History of Sexuality,* where he argues for power's "intentional and nonsubjective" nature.[7] According to Foucault, whatever intelligibility power relations may possess, it "is not because they are the effect of another instance that 'explains' them, but rather because they are imbued, through and through, with calculation."[8] Elaborating on the strategic but nonindividualized character of power, Foucault wrote that "there is no power that is exercised without a series of aims and objectives. But this does not mean it results from the choice or decision of an individual subject."[9]

The Reorder of Things builds on this element of Foucault's theorization by looking at how state, capital, and academy saw minority insurgence as a site of calculation and strategy, how those institutions began to see minority difference and culture as positivities that could be part of their own "series of aims and objectives." As formations increasingly characterized by the presence of minority difference, state, capital, and academy—in different but intersecting ways—began to emerge as hegemonic processes that were "especially alert and responsive to the alternatives and oppositions which [questioned] or [threatened their] dominance."[10] Hence, this book looks at the diverse but interlocking ways in which state, capital, and academy produced an adaptive hegemony where minority difference was concerned.

In keeping with Foucault, the book eschews an individualized notion of power, preferring instead to regard power as a complex and multisited social formation. Rather than being embodied in an individual or a group, power—Foucault says—is a set of relations in which "the *logic* is perfectly clear, the *aims* decipherable, and yet it is often the case that no one is there to have invented them, and few who can be said to have formulated them."[11] In this book, the impersonal nature of power is derived from the ways in which hegemonic investments in minority difference and culture are distributed across institutional and subjective terrains during and after the period of social unrest, terrains such as universities and colleges, corporations, social movements, media, and state practices.

The book also uses the category "power" in the spirit of Foucault's own implicit belief that complex situations deserve a name. Even though the name is ill-fitting, it is the "closest [we] can get to it."[12] Addressing the catachresis called power, Foucault says, "power establishes," "power invests," "power takes hold."[13] Furthermore, in his description of biopower, he writes, "Power would no longer be dealing simply with legal subjects over whom the ultimate dominion was death, but with living beings, and the mastery it would be able to exercise over them would have to be applied to the level of life itself."[14] For Foucault, power becomes like a character in a story, a code name for the "multiplicity of force relations."[15] Like Foucault, I use *power* as shorthand for a plurality of relations, arguing that if power is the "name that one attributes to a complex *strategical* situation in a particular society,"[16] then power in the age of minority social movements becomes the new name for calculating and arranging minority difference.

While *The Reorder of Things* attempts to rigorously attend to how dominant modes of power in the post–World War II moment utilized minority difference, the book does not reduce the "the political and cultural initiatives" of the social movements—those grand champions of minority culture—to the terms of hegemony. Indeed, as part of its own archival investigation, the book attempts to unearth those elements of the social movements that were antagonistic to the terms of hegemony, giving attention to how university and presidential administrations in the sixties attempted to beguile minorities with promises of excellence and uplift. Thus, as part of its investigation of the changing networks of power, the book analyzes how dominant institutions attempted to reduce the initiatives of oppositional movements to the terms of hegemony.

This book diverges from Foucault as it takes racial formations as the genealogy of power's investment in various forms of minority difference and culture while extending Foucault's emphasis on the productive—and not simply the repressive—capacities of power. From the social movements of the fifties and sixties until the present day, networks of power have attempted to work through and with minority difference and culture, trying to redirect originally insurgent formations and deliver them to the normative ideals and protocols of state, capital, and academy. In this new strategic situation, hegemonic power denotes the disembodied and abstract promotion of minority representation without fully satisfying the material and social redistribution of minoritized subjects, particularly where people of color are concerned. One of the central claims of this book, then, is that the struggles taking place on college campuses because of the student protests were inspirations for power in that moment, inspiring it to substitute redistribution for representation, indeed encouraging us to forget how radical movements promoted the inseparability of the two.

As such, this book attempts to revise a reigning assumption about the academy—that as a social institution, it is always secondary to and derivative of state and capital. Instead, I hope to demonstrate the ways in which power enlisted the academy and things academic as conduits for conveying unprecedented forms of political economy to state and capital, forms that would be based on an abstract—rather than a redistributive—valorization of minority difference and culture. As the book deploys the academy as a way to re-know state and capital as interlocutors with rather than determinants of American university life, the book does not look for power "in the primary existence of a central point, in a unique sovereignty from which secondary and descendant forms would emanate."[17] Instead, it discerns relations of power in their most dispersed associations with minority difference. As a text that understands oppositional formations as both critical and solicitous of power, *The Reorder of Things* understands the institutions that attempt to recycle those formations as contradictory ones that harbor the elements of their own negation.

To Reckon with Kant's Trickery: Materialist Critique and the Relocation of the Academy

The dominant means of approaching the question of the academy has been to read it as a derivation of capitalist economic formations. Hence, we talk about the academy in terms of the "corporate university," the "neoliberal university," the "knowledge factory," and so on. With all that these expressions tell us about the ways in which the academy understands and articulates its relationship to knowledge, students, and faculty, they presume a flow of influence that the student movements seem to contradict. Indeed, the diverse social formations that made up the U.S. student movements suggest that the academy is not simply an entity that socializes people into the ideologies of political economy. In many ways, those movements point to an institution that *socializes state and capital* into emergent articulations of difference. Framed as such, the antiracist and feminist movements and the changes that they inspired in the American academy constitute a history that compels us to once again think the limits of economic narratives in theorizations of power.

In *Eyes of the University,* Jacques Derrida locates the genealogy of this derivation within Immanuel Kant's *The Conflict of the Faculties.* Inspired by Kant, Derrida argues that the university has been constituted by a series of analogies, a constitution in which "one would treat knowledge a little like in industry . . . ; professors would be like trustees . . . ; together they would form a kind of essence or collective scholarly entity that would have its won autonomy."[18] The presumed autonomy of the university reaches its limit once the university has to transact with the public sphere. As Derrida states, "When, however, the issue is one of creating public titles of competence, or of legitimating knowledge, or of producing the public effects of this ideal autonomy then, at that point, the university is no longer authorized by itself. It is authorized . . . by a nonuniversity instance or agency—here, by the State—and according to criteria no longer necessarily and in the final analysis those of the scientific competence, but those of a certain *performativity.*"[19] Hence, for Derrida, the university must perform a certain degree of responsibility to students (i.e., "the young") and to the interests of the state. Derrida thus seems to reinforce the academy's subordinate relationship to the state and civil society.

While using his analysis of *The Conflict of the Faculties* to point to the university's historic identification with political and economic institutions, Derrida fails to unpack the full implications of the university's (and Kant's) performance of deference. While the university and Kant may perform an unadulterated responsibility to the state and the king of Prussia, that performance camouflages its manipulation of the state and the king in a veneer of sincere obedience and submission. This tension between sincerity and manipulation engenders a subtle contradiction within *The Conflict of the Faculties*. For instance, while Kant prominently argues for the university's role as the vassal of the state, he also theorizes the university as the indoctrinator of the future agents and architects of civil society. In his explanation of the "lower faculties"—that is, that division of the faculty that "looks after the interests of science"[20]—he writes:

> It is absolutely essential that the learned community at the university also contain a faculty that is independent of the government's command with regard to its teachings; one that, having no command to give, is free to evaluate everything, and concerns itself with the interests of the sciences, that is, with truth: one in which reason is authorized to speak publicly. For without a faculty of this kind, the truth would not come to light (and this would be to the government's own detriment).[21]

Kant's theorization of the lower faculties is deliberately full of ironies. To begin with, the lower faculties are simultaneously subordinate and independent, impotent and endowed. Throughout the passage and the text, one gets the sense that the lower faculties are the model of restraint and abstention—a faculty possessing "no command to give." Theorizing the lower faculty in this way was doubtless a reassurance to King Frederick William II, who was quite nervous about the teachings and arguments of Enlightenment enthusiasts.[22] To this argument about the lower faculties' restraint and impotence, Kant attaches what appears to be a contradictory pronouncement—the lower faculties' far-reaching powers of evaluation. While the higher faculties can issue commands to its agents—the clerics, lawyers, and theologians—the lower faculties ostensibly have no constituency to command, but they have an intellectual and ethical obligation to evaluate. In doing so, Kant hides the lower faculties' interpretative and evaluative prowess by strategically constructing evaluation and interpretation as modest and unobtrusive endeavors. As Kant says, "reason is by its nature free and admits of no command to hold something as true (no imperative 'Believe!' but only a free 'I believe')."[23] To submit to the lower faculty is to surrender to truth, and in this surrender there is no subjugation, only freedom.

We can see the contradictory and surreptitious articulation of the lower faculties in Kant's theorization of that ideal that comes to characterize this division—truth:

> But a department of this kind, too, must be established at a university; in other words, a university must have a faculty of philosophy. Its function in relation to the three higher faculties [medicine, law, and theology] is to control them and, in this way, be useful to them, since truth (the essential and first condition of learning in general) is the main thing, whereas the *utility* the higher faculties promise the government is of secondary importance.[24]

In keeping with the contradictory nature of the lower faculties, to be controlled by the lower faculties and regulated by the truth—a control and regulation that Kant must conceal—represents the horizon of what is useful and effective for the higher faculties and for government. This control and regulation will allow the higher faculties to produce students who are themselves so regulated, students who will go on to become the officials and agents of state and civil society and who will proceed to "create a lasting influence on the people." Contrary to the idea that the lower faculties internalize the elements of a preexistent and fully formed state, the lower faculties internalize the interests of government only *after* they have articulated those interests *for* the state and its constituents. Contrary to the presumption that the academy is a mere reflection and derivation of state and civil society, Kant suggests here that the academy—as the laboratory that produces truth and political economy's relation to it—is a primary articulator of state and civil society.

The student movements of the sixties and seventies represent both a portion and a disruption of this genealogy. They point to an academic moment that helped to rearticulate the nature of state and capital, a moment in which truth as the ideal of the university and the mediator of state and civil society was joined by difference in general, and minoritized difference in particular. Moreover, the academy became the "training ground" for state and capital's engagement with minority difference as a site of representation and meaning.

A historical *and* theoretical reconsideration of the interdisciplinary fields means displacing the economic and its thesis that the academy is a mere reflection or derivation of political economy. In terms of this narrative of reflection and derivation, we are the inheritors of a philosopher's deception, the children of a ruse. The extent to which we accept the academy and things academic as the designs of the economic is the measure of our dependence on this trick secured through a rhetoric of impotence and remove.

The modern Western academy was created as the repository and guarantor of national culture as well as a cultivator and innovator of political economy. As such, the academy is an archive of sorts, whose technologies—or so the theory goes—are constantly refined to acquire the latest innovation. As an archiving institution, the academy is—to use Derrida's description of the archive—"*institutive* and *conservative*. Revolutionary and traditional. An *eco-nomic* archive in this double sense: it keeps, it puts in reserve, it saves, but in an unnatural fashion, that is to say in making the law *(nomos)* or in making people respect the law."[25] The academy has always been an eco-nomic domain; that is, it has simultaneously determined who gets admitted while establishing the rules for membership and participation.

In the context of the post–World War II United States, the American academy can be read as a record of the shifts and contradictions of political economy. Indeed, with the admission of women and people of color into predominantly white academic settings, the eco-nomic character of the American academy did not simply vanish. The academy would begin to put, keep in reserve, and save minoritized subjects and knowledges in an archival fashion, that is, by devising ways to make those subjects and knowledges respect power and its "laws." Put differently, the ethnic and women's studies movements applied pressures on the archival conventions of the academy in an effort to stretch those conventions so that previously excluded subjects might enjoy membership. But it also meant that those subjects would fall under new and revised laws. As a distinct archival economy, the American academy would help inform the archival agendas of state and capital—how best to institute new peoples, new knowledges, and cultures and at the same time discipline and exclude those subjects according to a new order.

This was the moment in which power would hone its own archival economy, producing formulas for the incorporation rather than the absolute repudiation of difference, all the while refining and perfecting its practices of exclusion and regulation. This is the time when power would restyle its archival propensities by dreaming up ways to affirm difference and keep it in hand. Ethnic studies and women's studies movements were the prototypical resources of incorporative and archival systems of power that reinvented themselves because of civil rights and liberation movements of the fifties, sixties, and seventies. Part of the signature achievements of these affirmative modes of power was to make the pursuit of recognition and legitimacy into formidable horizons of pleasure, insinuating themselves into radical politics, trying to convince insurgents that "your dreams are also mine."

By excavating the social movements, we may be able to chart the emergence of this new kind of archival economy that transformed academic, political, economic, and social life from the late sixties and beyond. Moreover, focusing on the social movements and the denominations of interdisciplinary forms that emerged from them might allow us to produce a counterarchive detailing the ways in which power worked through the "recognition" of minoritized histories, cultures, and experiences and how power used that "recognition" to resecure its status. The histories of interdisciplinary engagements with forms of difference represent a conflicted and contradictory negotiation with this horizon of power. Seen this way, we must entrust the interdisciplines with a new charge, that of assessing power's archival techniques and maneuvers. As *Self-Portrait 2000* suggests, the involution of marginal differences and the development of the interdisciplines, broadly conceived, denoted the elaboration of power rather than the confirmation that our "liberty" had been secured. We must make it our business to critically deploy those modes of difference that have become part of power's trick and devise ways to use them otherwise.

The influence that the student movements had on institutional life within the United States points to a need to assess the streams of the academy within political economy. If state and particularly capital needed the academy to reorient their sensibilities toward the affirmation of difference—that is, to complete the constitutional project of the United States and begin to resolve the contradictions of social exclusion—then it also meant that the academy became the laboratory for the revalorization of modes of difference.

This changing set of representations, the institutions that organized themselves around that set, and the modes of power that were compelled by and productive of those transformations are what we are calling the interdisciplines. The interdisciplines were an ensemble of institutions and techniques that offered positivities to populations and constituencies that had been denied institutional claims to agency. Hence, the interdisciplines connoted a new form of biopower organized around the affirmation, recognition, and legitimacy of minoritized life. To offset their possibility for future ruptures, power made legitimacy and recognition into grand enticements.

In doing so, they would become power's newest techniques for the taking of difference. What the students often offered as radical critiques of institutional belonging would be turned into various institutions' confirmation.

As a critique of institutional belonging, *Self-Portrait 2000* grapples with the potential malignancies of recognition. Indeed, the collage narrates a transition—that is, the shift from the figure of Western man as the basis of agency and representation to that of minoritized cultures, subjects, and differences as contenders in the quest for acceptance, normativity and lawfulness. But through its substitution of a plane crash for an actual portrait of Piper, the piece refuses any humanist celebration of Man's minoritized replacements. Never giving us a picture of minoritized people or one of Piper, the piece withholds the visage of the very figures that the moment and the collage were supposed to represent. In *Self-Portrait 2000,* the institutional and artistic forms that are supposedly best equipped for representing people in general, and minoritized people in particular—the state, the academy, the portrait—are utterly incapable of representing those subjects and can offer only a wrecked depiction instead. In doing so, *Self-Portrait 2000* refuses the affirmations that constitute minority nationalisms.

We might contrast the absence of a biographical image in *Self-Portrait 2000* with revolutionary and cultural nationalisms' presumption that they can make institutional, state, and administrative forms in their own image. Indeed, we can think of various cultural and revolutionary nationalist projects as attempts to stamp their own visages upon institutional contexts. Such attempts are not idiosyncratic or insignificant but conventional and definitive for minority nationalisms. In the context of the sixties and seventies, such attempts were not only expressed in terms of the fabled takeover of the state form but in terms of epistemological, administrative, and institutional reflection as well—ostensibly launched by the actual takeover of academic buildings and the erection of departments, centers, and programs. The triumphant and anticolonial slogan of "Massa day done" applied, then, not only to the state but to other modern institutions as well, particularly the academy.

Self-Portrait 2000 refutes this fable of reflection that posits dominant institutions as potential mirrors for minority culture and difference. Instead, the collage seems to suggest that institutions—if mirrors at all—are ones that can offer only dim likenesses. In this way, we might read *Self-Portrait 2000* as a rebuttal to the boasts of institutions, that in their archival capacities they can adequately reflect minoritized cultures and differences. We may go even further and say that *Self-Portrait 2000* exhibits and expresses the critical possibilities of minority cultural forms, particularly in post–civil rights moments. By "critical possibilities" I mean the potential of those cultural forms to offer accounts of institutional modes—not simply the disfranchisements and betrayals of institutions, but also the rules of inclusion and the anatomies of recognition and legitimacy; not simply how we are entrapped, but also how we might achieve provisional forms of freedom and insurgency.

As a critical formation, powerful strains of women-of-color feminism have historically offered a critical suspicion to bourgeois, cultural, and revolutionary nationalist desires for recognition and institutional legitimacy. Indeed, women-of-color feminists have often theorized minority nationalisms not as formations insulated from state nationalism but as ironically entwined with its ideologies and discourses. Plainly put, such interventions have sought to discern the institutional models at play in minority nationalisms.

In a similar gesture, Jacques Derrida offers a reading of cultural forms as records and articulators of institutional practices and logics. Again, in *Eyes of the University,* he writes:

> with students and the research community, in every operation we pursue together (a reading, an interpretation, the construction of a theoretical model, the rhetoric of an argumentation, the treatment of historical material, and even a mathematical formalization), we posit or acknowledge that an institutional concept is at play, a type of contract signed, an image of the ideal seminar constructed, a *socius* implied, repeated, or displaced, invented, transformed, threatened, or destroyed. An institution is not merely a few walls or some outer structures surrounding, protecting, guaranteeing, or restricting the freedom of our work; it is also and already the structure of our interpretation.[26]

Here Derrida points to the fact that institutions are not simply things that are embodied externally in the form of buildings and paperwork. Institutions are also modes of interpretation that are embodied materially, discursively, and subjectively, modes offering visions of community and communal engagement. Commenting on the interpretative and textual aspects of institutions, Derrida goes on to say that

[the] interpretation of a theorem, poem, or philosopheme, or theologeme is only produced by simultaneously proposing an institutional model, either by consolidating an existing one that enables the interpretation, or by constituting a new one in accordance with this interpretation. Declared or clandestine, this proposal calls for the politics of a community of interpreters gathered around this text, and at the same time of a global society, a civil society with or without a State, a veritable regime enabling the inscription of that community.[27]

Derrida's argument about the simultaneity of institution-building and hermeneutical practices accurately suggests the place of interpretation and textuality in institutional struggle. Institutions are the outcome and locations of imagined communities, with interpretative modes representing the brick and mortar of those imaginations.

The ethnic and women's movements moved to the heart of this relationship between institutionality and textuality. Indeed, the admission of women and people of color into predominantly white universities and colleges forced new modes of interpretation and new institutional visions within the American academy. At the same time, the student movements and student demands had to negotiate with and appeal to prevailing institutional structures. The student movements of the sixties and seventies constituted and inspired interpretative communities that would propose institutional models that were both disruptive *and* recuperative of existing institutions. In sum, the relationship between institutionality and textuality accounted for a constitutive contradiction within the student movements—their simultaneous estrangement from and appeals to institutional power.

We can actually situate *Self-Portrait 2000* within this critical genealogy. *Self-Portrait 2000* tries to delineate the overlapping institutional models that have come to characterize the post–civil rights moment. The collage asks us to rethink the presumption that the major institutions of civil society—the academy, the state, and capital—have fostered institutional concepts that protect and shelter minoritized differences and cultures. It asks us to consider how those differences and cultures have been archived in power's newest arrangement and how they have attempted to close critical universes established in the name of new formations around race, gender, and sexuality.

As a piece that worries over the relationship between the institutional and the interpretative and how it bears on minoritized lives, *Self-Portrait 2000* actually bears the properties of minority cultural forms and practices in general. As the genealogical issue of those contradictions that inhered within the student movements, minoritized cultural forms and practices represent both an aspiration to and estrangement from processes of archivization, institutionalization, and professionalization. Indeed, this book attempts to provide a theorization of minority cultural forms and practices as expressions of complex relationships between institutionality and textuality in the post–civil rights moment.

We need a critical itinerary that can outline and interrogate the constitutive contradictions of minoritized formations in the years after the sixties social movements, contradictions that have to do with the simultaneous identifications with and antagonisms to the institutional embodiments of power, a deconstructive meditation that can assess power's calculus as one that both estranges and entices. We also need analytic models that will help us imagine ways to maneuver taken-for-granted contradictions so that their economies are not constantly tilted toward identification but move in the direction of disidentification and on to more sustained embodiments of oppositionality.

We need to retain and elaborate an awareness of the contradictory nature of modes of difference as a way to simultaneously appreciate and evaluate our radical vulnerability and as a means of imagining strategies of intervention. Oppositional critiques of difference run the risk of a totalizing depiction of power's relationship to difference. Such a risk demands that we theorize the institutionalization of minority difference away from what philosopher Jacques Rancière calls "the space of consensus" within various schools of critical thought. Defining this "space of consensus," he writes: "there is a whole school of so-called critical thought and art that, despite its oppositional rhetoric, is entirely integrated within the space of consensus. I'm thinking of all those works that pretend to reveal to us the omnipotence of market flows, the reign of the spectacle, the pornography of power."[28] Accordingly, consensus assumes a policing quality once it abolishes "dissensus," that "political process that resists juridical litigation and creates a fissure in the sensible order by confronting the established framework of perception, thought, and action with the 'inadmissible.'"[29] Noting the ways in which critical formations are vulnerable to becoming disciplinary apparatuses, he argues that "[by] abolishing dissensus and placing a ban on political subjectivization, consensus reduces politics to the police."[30]

Critiques of the university that presume the derivative nature of the academy from the economy implicitly and unconsciously place a ban on modes of difference as sites of political subjectivization. They become spaces of consensus as they dismiss minority culture and minority difference as formations completely overwhelmed and determined by commodity culture, whether within or outside the academy. Such stances disqualify minority difference and minority culture as potential sites of dissensus with the potential to create fissures and to make room for the inadmissible.

Given the flexibility of minority difference, ours must be an ongoing experimentation with the ruptural possibilities of modes of difference. *The Reorder of Things* is, therefore, a provocation to not only evaluate the vulnerabilities of sixties social movements and the interdisciplinary formations that they inspired but also "develop modes of analyses which . . . are capable of discerning, in good faith, the finite but significant openness of many actual initiatives and contributions."[31] Such an investigation requires that we find ways to slip away from the archival maneuvers of power/knowledge, recognizing that power's archival advance is ever encroaching. The context of power/knowledge might be the occasion for interdisciplinarity's revival rather than its demise. The possibility for a generative inquiry into institutionality lies in the interrogation of those relationships between textuality and institutionality and what they reveal about the co-constitutive anatomies of institutional belonging and minoritized subject formations. As a letter frames a plane crash, so the academic frames our social predicament. In doing so, the collage suggests the means by which minority difference is brought into regimes of representation and fundamentally reconstitutes them. This examination is the business of a critical interdisciplinarity.

So, this is what inspires me to tell you not to forsake this image and the lessons that it bears. Some will see this picture and become like that Watcher who "turns his eyes away in resignation" as his dreams are mocked to death by power and institutions, his cynicism validated by his experience of the facts. Others—not beholden to any breed of positivism—will take its cautions to mind and heart, crafting deeds and working up visions that are in the institution but not of it, knowing that the dream is still the truth.

The Birth of the Interdisciplines

IF WE THINK OF THE ARCHIVE not simply as an institution but as a social formation, we might say that the United States is the archival nation par excellence. In *Archive Fever: A Freudian Impression,* Derrida argues that the word *archive* is derived from the Greek *arkheion,* which was understood to be the residence of "those who commanded."[1] The archive was the house where official documents—no matter their heterogeneity—were filed and entrusted to speak and impose the law.[2] As archives provided homes for those documents, they placed them under certain jurisdictions, not only consigning them to prescribed areas but also gathering them under certain sets of meanings. Thus, in the archive a diverse assemblage of documents were coordinated so that they might articulate an ideal unity. Whatever diversity those documents possessed, whatever secrets they might contain would have to be managed so that the ideal of the archive would be preserved rather than ruined;[3] archives represented the places to put those documents and the regimes that would discipline them.

As an archival entity, the United States is simultaneously the fabled home that promises to put different peoples in their rightful places and the infamous regime that disciplines in the name of freedom. As such, it embodies the quintessential properties of all archives. Indeed, the motto "e pluribus unum" (one out of many) expresses, as literary scholar W. C. Harris observes, both the identity and the experiment of the U.S. nation-state, an experiment that harks back to Greek philosophical thought, one that attempts to resolve the imperative of unity with the reality of heterogeneity. For Harris, this experiment finds unprecedented momentum in the social, cultural, and political contexts of the nineteenth-century United States, a momentum that gains footing and speed in those documents that first made "the problem of unity and multiplicity" into the American preoccupation—the Declaration of Independence, the Articles of Confederation, the Constitution, and the *Federalist Papers*.[4]

The motto and imperative "e pluribus unum" represents a logic that sits at the core of American government. In the national debates of the time, race provided the overwhelming conditions by which the principle was tested and adjusted. Indeed, the American Civil War symbolized a violent struggle over how to resolve a nation heterogeneous in terms of race, region, and ideology. In the context of the nineteenth-century United States, the motto captures the fact that the American ethos was not simply defined in terms of the abolition and expulsion of difference through slavery, genocidal wars, lynching, and rape. The American spirit was also secured in the question of how best to represent social differences and the communities and people that presumably symbolized those differences. As a motto and an edict, "e pluribus unum" connoted a national struggle with difference in general and racial difference in particular.

As Harris goes on to say, nineteenth-century literature was the cultural form that addressed that motto directly and the racial conditions that contradicted it. It was the job of nineteenth-century literature—and the work of writers like Edgar Allan Poe, Walt Whitman, Herman Melville, Mark Twain, and Henry James—to "reconcile the opposing interests of the one and the many."[5] Put simply, American literature was supposed to finish writing the American nation-state by helping it resolve the paradox of the many and the one. In doing so, literature attempted to identify the nation-state as a "writerly" formation, that is, one whose aim is to inscribe "the many" into the national body. As such, literature worked to promote the archival functions of the American nation-state. In this regard, American culture would help to turn American social institutions into archival economies.

The nation's reputation as a domain of resolution would only grow internationally. As Eqbal Ahmad argues in "Political Culture and Foreign Policy," the idea of the United States as a former colony that threw off the yoke of its oppressors was so powerful in the Third World that "America served as an inspiration and an example."[6] The image as a place that resolved ideological and social differences persisted for national liberation movements in Africa and Asia despite "more than a century of counterrevolutionary American interventions in the Third World."[7] The significance of the United States' reputation for settling conflicts over social and ideo-logical diversity would promote the emergence of neocolonial power rela-tions in the post–World War II moment and the rise of a mode of power built around minority recognition and legitimacy. To this end, we may think of the 1950s and afterwards as historic moments in which power began to assume a new archival significance. This was a period in which revolu-tions and liberation struggles throughout the world would test power's archival flexibility. As peoples in North America, Latin America, Africa, Asia, and the Caribbean were trying to secure a place, power would work to place them.

We get a glimpse at the archival tactics of power in Kwame Nkrumah's description of the rise of neocolonial formations. In *Neo-colonialism: The Last Stage of Imperialism,* he writes, "Faced with the militant peoples of the ex-colonial territories in Asia, Africa, the Caribbean, and Latin Amer-ica, imperialism simply switches tactics."[8] As Nkrumah argues, the colonial apparatus would dispense with its paraphernalia and its representatives, ostensibly "'giving' independence to its former subjects, to be followed by 'aid' for their development" (ibid.). But with flags and officials gone, the colonial apparatus would begin to "[devise] innumerable ways to accom-plish objectives formerly achieved by naked colonialism" (ibid.). Hence, neocolonialism—or, as he puts it, the very "modern [attempt] to perpetu-ate colonialism while at the same time talking about 'freedom'"—was born (ibid.).

As former colonial modes of power transitioned into neocolonial ones, they achieved archival heights, admitting recently held colonies into the domain of independence. The former colonies were thus like documents gathered together into the library of modern nations. As such, these newly minted nations were *consigned* to the location of sovereignty and coordi-nated according to the ideal of freedom. Yet archiving those former colonies was also a kind of house arrest in which freedom signified genres of sub-jugation and domiciliation.

One of the ways in which this archontic power began to domesticate demands for independence was through invitation rather than wholesale rejection. In the context of neocolonialism, such invitations and acts of inclusion represented the mutation rather than the annihilation of prior forms of power. As Nkrumah argues, "The essence of neo-colonialism is that the State which is subject to it is, in theory, independent and has all the outward trappings of international sovereignty. In reality its economic system and thus its political policy is directed from outside" (ix). Neocolonialism would persuade by presumably conceding to the efforts of self-determination by minoritized nations and peoples, by placing them within a presumably horizontal and modern terrain. Hence, neocolonialism was the moment in which the manifold strategies of conquest, management, and regulation would take place within and through the outward appearance of anticolonial independence and freedom. This was a form of power that had cultivated a solicitous rather than a primarily dismissive manner. As the legendary nation that would admit new people under the banner of independence while subjecting them to a new law whose borders would increase with every admittance, the United States would become—in Nkrumah's words—"foremost among the neo-colonialists" (239). The history and theorization of neocolonialism is important inasmuch as it is one segment in a larger transformation of power—that is, power's ability to incorporate formerly marginalized and excluded subjects and societies, an ability signified through the extension of recognition and sovereignty for people who spent much of their histories under colonial yokes. The specific circumstances of neocolonialism are thus only a piece of a more general mode of power that was developing in the days of independence. This mode would derive its international character from its ability to select from insurgent practices what it needed to carry out its own hegemonic authority. A mode of power was forming that would ingest various revolutionary formations and, in fact, build its strategies around their dissection.

The Management of Difference and the Management of the International

A form of power that would engage insurgency rather than run from it could only come from a context with a history like that of the United States. In addition to being the legendary land of resolution, the United States for much of the world was the emblem of anticolonial triumph. As Ahmad notes, "Americans had waged the first successful struggle against colonialism," a fact that granted the United States an "inexhaustible reservoir of goodwill" from colonized people.[9] This image of the United States as a site of recognition for national liberation struggles was part of the country's archival economy and its promise to absorb marginalized constituencies.

As a nation-state, the United States proved adept at distributing recognition and legitimacy. As historian Greg Grandin argues, Franklin Delano Roosevelt's Good Neighbor Policy of the 1930s and 1940s seemingly represented the United States' recognition of the sovereign integrity of nations in Latin America,[10] and during the 1960s the United States fashioned itself as the "anti-colonial power in condemnation of British imperialism."[11]

The United States' status as the protector of national liberation and freedom was very much at play during the Cold War era as well. As Mary Dudziak has famously shown, the federal government's support of civil rights struggles within the country was part of its attempts to secure ideological and material status as a global superpower.[12] Through its support of civil rights, American democracy came to represent a respect for and recognition of the international sovereignty of formerly subjugated nations and the civil rights of domestic minorities. In its putative recognition of national liberation and civil rights, the United States has had a very long history of representing anticolonial rights of sovereignty, a fact that made it fertile ground for the rise of a mode of power organized around the absorption of heterogeneity.

That mode of power gained much of its inspiration and identity from the founding documents of the U.S. nation-state. As Michael Hardt and Antonio Negri argue, the genealogy of what we know and experience as contemporary globalization derives, in part, from the principles of American federal government, namely, from the U.S. Constitution. According to them, the Constitution is imperial because of the ways in which it designates social terrains as infinitely open and changeable, as items that can be forever reinvented and rearticulated as parts of the American promise. Because of the imperial imperative of the U.S. Constitution, "The contemporary idea of Empire is born through the global expansion of the internal U.S. constitutional project."[13]

Inasmuch as the U.S. constitutional project presumes and "[rearticulates] open spaces and [reinvents] incessantly diverse and singular relations,"[14] it incorporates a variety of social, national, and transnational formations. As such, the constitutional project helped to give birth to neocolonial formations *and* provided the juridical conditions for struggles around race and gender in the nineteenth and twentieth centuries. In their discussion of the Fourteenth Amendment, for example, Hardt and Negri argue that in addition to "[inaugurating] more than a century of judicial struggles over civil rights and African American equality," the amendment and the debate that occasioned it "[redefined] the space of the nation," tying the debate over slavery to the debates over new territories. As a clause that officially granted citizenship to former male slaves, the Fourteenth Amendment represented one of the first constitutional attempts to admit a marginalized constituency into the legal and ideological fabric of the nation, enrolling subjects differentiated by citizenship status, corporeality, history, and language into a national body whose compatibility was dubious at best. Out of the Fourteenth Amendment came a new ethical project for the American nation-state, one that would try to administer difference for the expansion of national power and territory. In their words, "The new nation could not but be the product of the political and cultural management of hybrid identities."[15] In sum, the U.S. constitutional project would give birth to twins—the modern idea of empire and the modern idea of difference; under that ideological formation, the management of the international would coextend with the management of diversity.

As George Lipsitz has observed, a vast range of social struggles has relied on the "social warrant" of the Fourteenth Amendment. Through it, immigrants and their children would find "inclusion and religious liberty"; because of it, Asian Americans and Latinos would end "racist barriers against immigration," and with it, "women, workers, gays and lesbians, and people with disabilities" would challenge discrimination.[16] Hence, many people credit the social movements around race and gender with finally ushering in the social warrants of the Fourteenth Amendment. Indeed, we may understand Michael Omi and Howard Winant's classic observations in *Racial Formations in the United States* within the context of the Fourteenth Amendment. They write: "The upsurge of racially based movements which began in the 1950s was a contest over the social meaning of *race* . . . The racial minority movements were the first to expand the concerns of politics to the social, to the terrain of everyday life."[17] Like Lipsitz, Omi and Winant also note the communicable nature of certain political struggles: "New social movement politics would also prove 'contagious,' leading to the mobilization of other racial minorities, as well as other groups whose concerns were principally social. As playwright David Edgar has noted, most of the new social movements of the 1960s—student, feminist, and gay—drew upon the black struggle 'as a central organizational fact or as a defining political metaphor and inspiration.'"[18]

The Fourteenth Amendment would set the terms for participation within the nation as well as the ideological and discursive parameters for struggles over equality. The amendment is one of the historical texts that authorized subjects differentiated by race, gender, sexuality, disability, class, and ethnicity to contest their minoritized status. As an archival mechanism that worked to incorporate various political subjects, the amendment helped to situate U.S. jurisprudence as one of the genealogical landmarks for oppositional politics within American society. Put simply, the Fourteenth Amendment inscribed itself on oppositional maneuvers, threatening them with a domiciliation that could enlist them in power's archive.

If the Fourteenth Amendment encouraged the expansion and management of the national community and if that amendment became the grammar for future social struggles, then our contemporary notions and practices of social justice and inclusion partly arise out of and may often unwittingly foster that expansion and management. If power within the United States has historically been based on the simultaneous management of the international and the socially heterogeneous, then it means that minority politics within the United States have had to negotiate these various levels of management as well. The triumph of national liberation and civil rights and the emergence of neocolonial social formations signified more than the ascendancy of the U.S. nation-state. National liberation, civil rights, and neocolonialism should be understood as part of a larger social context that proclaimed the command of a new mode of power, a mode that was composed of power's new techniques of management, especially around internationalism and minority difference, as well as its insinuation into political agency.

The Archivization of the Social Movements and the Rearticulation of Political Economy

In addition to being archivable elements for a transforming U.S. nation-state, social movements in the post–World War II era were also crucial "documents" for that archiving apparatus known as contemporary global capitalism. In his classic essay "The Local and the Global," Stuart Hall locates the social movements that Omi, Winant, and Edgar discuss within the emergence of a new trajectory for global capitalism. Specifically, Hall points to the ways in which the emergence of various social movements around race and feminism were part of the same historic moment in which global capital set its sights on local difference. Global capital's turn toward local difference was simultaneous with an epistemic turn toward vernacular cultures as well. According to Hall, the emergence of contemporary globalization was simultaneous with the emergence of anticolonial, black liberation, and feminist movements, the time when "the unspoken discovered that they had a history that they could speak, that they had languages other than the languages of the master."[19] For Hall, liberatory movements were both political *and* epistemological formations that attempted to simultaneously disinter and reconstruct subjugated histories around race, gender, and nation. Unearthing and reinventing those histories was also not unrelated or coincidental to global capital's interest in local cultures and differences. As the grip of the nation-state began to weaken because of the capitalist crisis and the internationalization of the economy, the Western nation-state also suffered—as Hall implies—because of the social and epistemic crises brought about by movements led to a large degree by students. Ironically, though, as those social movements advanced and reconceptualized local culture and difference, bringing national culture to crisis, capital turned toward local culture and difference in the very moments that national identity was being revised. Contemporary globalization attempted to feed on those local histories and languages, producing flexible regimes of accumulation "founded on segmented markets, on lifestyle and identity."[20] Hence, one of the ways in which capital mediated its split from a now weakened and damaged nation-state was to work with and through the very local, vernacular, and subjugated histories and differences that helped to bring the nation-state to crisis in the first place. The beginnings of contemporary global capital represented the simultaneous management of difference and the international as well.

In the context of the United States and the relative collapse of a national culture that portrayed itself as homogeneous, we can also see the ways in which the American nation-state used local differences to mediate the upheavals brought about by the student movements. For instance, in Michael Omi and Howard Winant's *Racial Formations in the United States,* the authors define the racial state in the moments after the various antiracist movements in terms of the state's institutionalization of certain parts of those movements, arguing that the "The racial state, in its turn, has been historically constructed by racial movements; it consists of agencies and programs which are the *institutionalized* responses to racial movements of the past."[21] The racial state for Omi and Winant is not simply the entity on which political demands are made. It is also that political formation that receives its identity and contours from having archived the social movements.

Building on the idea that the racial state is the conglomerate of institutionalized responses to the sixties and seventies social movements, Omi and Winant go on to argue that state institutions within the United States responded to political pressures of antiracist movements by, in part, adopting policies of absorption.[22] About absorption, they state: "Absorption reflects the realization that many demands are greater threats to the racial order before they are accepted than after they have been adopted in suitably moderate form."[23] What Omi and Winant refer to as "absorption" we might understand as the gestures and routines of archival power. Indeed, in its absorptive capacities, the state becomes a subarchive that "documents" past struggles and thus achieves power through control of that broad assemblage of "documents" known as "the student movements."

To speak through and with local culture and difference and to absorb them, state and capital needed the assistance of the academy. In point of fact, the academy was positioned prominently in this moment because of its historic task of representing national culture. In the moment of the sixties—because of the student movements around race and gender—the U.S. academy would take on the imperative of American literature. Put plainly, it would attempt to resolve the contradictions that govern and constitute the U.S. nation-state. In the moment of the multinational firm's emergence and capital's explicit engagement in local culture and difference, the academy would become the handbook on the absorption and representation of those differences, the manual for state and capital's unprecedented deliberation. As such, the U.S. academy would become the model of archontic power—using and assimilating texts to engage the problematic of "e pluribus unum." In doing so, U.S. higher education would become the capitol of archival power, training state and economy in its methods of representation and regulation. Rather than the academy losing importance because of the attack on national culture, the American academy and things academic would become the place where enfeebled institutions might make sense of difference, its fortunes, and its disruptions.[24] Things academic would provide a new opportunity for power, one that would allow power to foster an entirely new relation between academy, capital, and state. This new relation would revolve around the very question promoted by the U.S. student movements, the question of minority difference—how to understand it, how to negotiate it, how to promote it, and how to regulate it. This question would inspire power to run a new archival errand.

Put differently, we might say that the link between the epistemological pressures brought about by social movements of the sixties and seventies and the rise of global capital's interest in local differences lies in the academy. The entrance of local cultures and differences into epistemological representation would also inspire and inform their entrance into law and commodification—into state and capital's arenas of representation. While this was the moment in which state and capital suffered a devastating rupture, this was also the period in which those entities began to enjoy a new form of communicability with the academy. Through a reinvented discourse of difference, power would inspire a new form of relationality between state, capital, and academy. The academy—transformed by insurgent modes of differences—would begin to educate state and capital into a new type of awareness.

The U.S. student movements would inspire power to focus its maneuvers around the keywords of revolutionary upheavals—"minority autonomy," "self-determination," and "freedom." In doing so, power would attempt to find ways to make the articulation of difference consistent with power's guidance rather than antagonistic to it. In their discussion of the minority movements of the sixties, Omi and Winant argue: "In response to political pressure, state institutions adopt policies of absorption and insulation. Absorption reflects the realization that many demands are greater threats to the racial order before they are accepted than after they have been adopted in suitably moderate form."[25] We might read their theorization of the minority movements of the sixties as an example of the "economistic resource of an archive which capitalizes everything, even that which ruins it or radically contests its power."[26] In the sixties and thereafter, the archival propensities of power reached out to new horizons, attempting to archive the presumably unarchivable components of antiracism, feminism, and so on. In doing so, power would attempt to invest the radical aims of antiracist and feminist movements of the sixties and seventies with another logic, capitalizing those movements and their ensigns, cataloging them in the very institutions that those movements were contesting. In sum, relations of power would try to make those movements and their demands into its reason for being.

What came after the challenges of the ethnic and women's movements was not the end of power but its new beginning. In terms of national ideology, what came after those great confrontations was not the downfall of a cultural center per se but its reconfiguration. Indeed, the cultural center was recalibrated in terms of diversification rather than standardization, no longer a center organized around a homogeneous national identity but now a center structured according to the capacities for and the principles of heterogeneous absorption.[27] This is the historic period that tried to perfect the motto "e pluribus unum" as a technique of power, as a strategic situation for the U.S. nation-state, for American capital, and for the American academy. This perfection, in a moment of movements and agitations, would inaugurate a new dramatic turn for modern institutions in the United States, a shift that entailed a manifest rather than latent engagement with marginalized differences and cultures, an engagement that helped to constitute new modes of regulation and exclusion, modes that simultaneously engaged modern difference and modern transnationalism. This is how we might interpret the history of power in response to the radical movements of the fifties, sixties, seventies, and beyond. It is also how we might decipher the contemporary history of state, capital, and academy in the late twentieth century and afterwards.

Man and the Order of the Human Sciences: The Prehistory of the Interdisciplines

It should be clear by now that I am not simply engaging the student movements of the sixties and seventies as conventional or discrete historical markers but as pivots in the history of power's relationship to difference. The student movements around race and gender inspired a shift in power's networks. Given the enormous diversity between social movements of the fifties, sixties, and seventies, they were all joined by a critique and displacement of Western man and by the great reclamation of tongues and histories besides those of the master. Such a narrative of the student movements permits us to ask what networks of power were authorized in our late-modern age, how those networks worked through marginalized subjects and social formations, and how those networks were modeled after the networks built by the human sciences, that assemblage of fields that the ethnic and women's studies movements worked to challenge.

We can locate the genesis of those networks that predominated before the rise of the student movements within the founding of the discursive figure known as Man. In *The Order of Things,* for instance, Foucault writes that the human sciences were called into being because of the figure of man, an epistemological object that did not exist until the end of the eighteenth century.[28] According to Foucault, the human sciences rose to prominence at the very moment when "man constituted himself in Western culture as both that which must be conceived of and that which is to be known."[29] Rather than man existing as an a priori item from preceding epistemic traditions, "[Man was] an event in the order of knowledge," both the creation of and impetus for the human sciences.[30]

Foucault turns his attention to the ways in which the human sciences conceived man as a living, laboring, and linguistic being, one that is put together by a variety of fields. Each field situates man socially: as a living being he is "[interlaced] through and through with the rest of the living world." As a laborer, he exchanges, and organizes according to the things that he has produced, a fact that fuses his life with that of others. As a linguistic animal, man "can constitute a whole symbolic universe for himself, within which he has a relation to his past, to things, to other men, and on the basis of which he is able equally to build something like a body of knowledge."[31] The human sciences represent the heterogeneous modes by which man was analyzed and produced as a diversity of elements available for critical scrutiny. Theorizing the human sciences and man as such, Foucault interrupted those interpretations that presented man as a single and homogeneous unit. Instead, Foucault analyzed man as a conglomeration of biological, linguistic, and economic aspects that require distinct and specialized knowledges for their assessment. Those distinct and specialized knowledges designed for the production and evaluation of man are what we popularly know as the disciplines. The common denominator that unites the disciplines is, for Foucault, their interest in a particular type of historical errand oriented around the figure of man.

In *Discipline and Punish,* Foucault parlayed his observations about the production of man under the human sciences to theorizations about the simultaneous enhancement *and* subjection of the individual, reading this enhancement and subjection as the foundation for the emergence of modern power. To begin with, Foucault addressed the classical age as the occasion of a new—disciplinary—type of power, one invested in, rather than repressive of, individuality. In the seventeenth century, Foucault argued, the "chief function of disciplinary power" was to "'train,' rather than to select and to levy; or, no doubt, to train in order to levy and select all the more."[32] For Foucault, disciplinary power was not about producing homogeneity but "binding [forces] together in such a way as to multiply and use them. Instead of bending all its subjects into a single uniform mass, it separates, analyzes, differentiates, carries its procedures of decomposition to the point of necessary and sufficient single units."[33] In his analysis and theorization of disciplinary power, the individual would be the object and instrument of power in ways that were analogous to man being the project and tool of the human sciences.

In Foucault's description of discipline, power diversifies its techniques not for individual degradation but for personal edification and invigoration. Disciplinary power, in short, produces new forms of agency through individuation and multiplication. As such, man and the individual's discursive statuses as the products of and grounds for knowledge help to seal the contract between epistemology and power relations. *The Order of Things, Discipline and Punish,* and *The History of Sexuality: Volume 1* represent efforts to address how knowledge and power extend themselves not necessarily through the subject's repression but through its affirmation. Despite his demotion by the social movements in the post–World War II era, Western man would persist as the archetypal figure for attaching agency to regulation. As such, Western man would lay the groundwork for disciplining minority difference—making its activation concomitant with its regulation. This aspect of discipline—that side of power that edified and assured the debased and omitted—would find its most sublime consummation in and around the U.S. ethnic and women's movements and, in doing so, inaugurate a transformation with which we have hardly reckoned.

The Biopolitics of Institutionalization

The U.S. ethnic and women's movements represent powerful confrontations with and evaluations of the figure of Western man as well as attempts to replace him with other characters, characters that represented the real existence and viability of other idioms and histories. A new pantheon arose with figures like the Black, the Woman, the Asian American, the Chicano, the American Indian, the Gay, and the Lesbian, each one auguring the end of Man and all that he represented. Discussing that transformation in relation to the ethnic studies and people of color, as Asian American activist Mike Murase argued in the context of Asian American studies, the development of ethnic studies

> marks the first organized effort within the context of the formal educational system to reinterpret the history of Third World Peoples in this country to accurately reflect our perspectives: as an ideal it represents an honest attempt . . . to disseminate the life stories of millions of non-white people in America.[34]

The history that Murase describes is precisely the one that Hall addresses as the "moment when the unspoken discovered that they had a history that they could speak."[35] That reinterpretation can only be seen as part of a critical endeavor to expose the faux universality of Western man, a universality that posited him as the basis of *all* life, labor, and language.

The development of the interdisciplinary fields—African American studies, Asian American studies, Chicano studies, American Indian studies, Women's studies, and so on—put specific pressures on the human sciences and the disciplines. In particular, they helped to formally introduce differences of race, gender, and sexuality into how we understood and narrated systems of work and language. Displacing man as the basis of positivities meant not only questioning and jettisoning the universal and abstract foundations of labor and language; it also meant determining the ways in which labor and language were differentiated and specified by race, gender, sexuality, and ethnicity. Indeed, we might say that the various histories of ethnic and women's studies denote the moments in which minority difference entered historical narration.

Fully apprehending that historical entrance means that we must also consider the ways in which interdisciplinary engagements with forms of minority difference and culture occasioned a shift in the personality of power. The classical age erected institutions that would promote the itinerary of the human sciences—that is, knowledge of and the meanings attributed to and produced by men, individuals, and populations. The classical age was, for Foucault, also the period that worried over how best to disseminate and administer that knowledge and those meanings. Those disciplines included "universities, secondary schools, barracks, [and] workshops."[36] In fields such as political science and economics, there was the "emergence . . . of the problems of birthrate, longevity, public health, housing, and migration."[37] The classical period designated the rise of a form of power/ knowledge embodied in intellectual practice and sustained by institutional structures, a transformation that led to and emanated from an "explosion of numerous and diverse techniques for achieving the subjugation of bodies and the control of populations, marking the beginning of an era of bio-power."[38]

If the classical age was about the multiplication of formal inquiries organized around the figure of Man, then a new mode of power came into being in the context of that figure's interdisciplinary subversion. The rise of the student movements and the ensuing ascent of the interdisciplines was not some wild revolt against classical Man and his claim to universality and abstraction. It was a thorough transformation of the character of institutions and a radical assertion of the importance of minority culture. Indeed, during the post–civil rights period, there was a rapid development of various interdisciplines. Here, we might not only include the literal programs and departments of ethnic and women's studies, but also take into account new admissions policies, "campus cultural centers, [and] minority faculty recruitment and hiring."[39] In fact, from 1968 to 1969 alone, close to seven hundred institutions of higher learning "instituted ethnic studies courses, programs, or departments."[40] There was the Equal Pay Act of 1963 and the Civil Rights Act of 1964. In 1965, Executive Order 11246 mandated affirmative-action requirements for government contractors and subcontractors. In 1973 there was the Rehab Act barring federal contractors and subcontractors from discrimination on the basis of disability.

The period of the ethnic and women's movements and the rise of women's and ethnic studies represent a new era of biopower, occasioning a change in power/knowledge. In this moment, new disciplines rose to study previously excluded subjects. New populations differentiated and marginalized by race, gender, sexuality, ability, and so on began to assert their existence in ways that were unprecedented. This mode of biopower was thus the outcome of power's attempts to archive previously excluded subjects and epistemes. This biopower prompted by the emergence of the interdisciplines would be different from the one that Foucault wrote about in *The History of Sexuality*. It would not be occasioned by the human sciences and their advancement of Western man as a living, biological species who would have to learn what it meant to have a body, or as an economic being who produces, consumes, and exchanges; or a linguistic subject who constitutes symbolic universes and bodies of knowledge that express his own sociality and historicity.

The interdisciplines would not jettison a concern for the positivities long associated with man. Instead, the agencies and processes of life, labor, and language would be subjected to an unprecedented scrutiny that sought to determine their constitution through historical particularities rather than transhistorical universalities. This new biopower would take as its representative the subject constituted through difference, the one who had to learn what it meant to have a particularized history, the one who would have to access how the probabilities for life have everything to do with those particularities; this is the subject who has to confront publicly or privately how those particularities and differences have historically shaped the quality and meanings of life, and whether to maneuver these historic legacies for conservative or disruptive ends.

Put differently, modern subjects in the United States of the sixties and seventies would begin to learn to think of themselves in terms of their constitutive and historic differences of race, class, and gender and how those differences and histories accounted for present-day privileges and disfranchisements. In ways that were unprecedented, racial, gender, and sexual existence could be reflected in and exposed simultaneously through political and epistemological existence. This new interdisciplinary biopower placed social differences in the realm of calculation and recalibrated power/knowledge as an agent of social life. For the American academy, the American state, and an Americanized capital in the sixties and seventies, the question would then become one of incorporating difference for the good rather than disruption of hegemony.

The rise of the interdisciplines would grant new possibilities for the analysis and articulation of minority culture and difference as well as provide new relays for hegemonic power. Getting at the enabling and troubling aspects of interdisciplinary transformation, the black literary critic and scholar Barbara Christian would reflect in 1989 on the emergence of black women's literature as a field of interest in her essay "But What Do We Think We're Doing Anyway." Starting its observations in 1974, Christian's essay interestingly begins in a moment before a minoritized community—

black women—had been fully absorbed into the academy's structures of representation. The essay ends in a moment—the 1990s—when that community had been incorporated into those structures, through curricula, faculty lines, and graduate recruitment. Touching on this end time of incorporation and its implications for practices that started partly outside the formal institutional realms of the academy, Christian wrote: "Canon formation has become one of the thorny dilemmas for the black feminist critic."[41] She went on to say that even while minoritized subjects—"white women, blacks, people of color"—worked to expand the boundaries of American literature, many black feminists found themselves "confronted with the realization that we may be imitating the very structure that shut our literatures out in the first place."[42] For Christian, this possible imitation might in fact determine the worth of black literature not in terms of its "quality" but in terms of how well it fits within the points of view, genres, and forms sanctioned by academics. For Christian, the incorporation of black literature within the academy possibly activates and inspires evaluative structures that might "stifle" the very literatures that black literary scholars were promoting. As Christian suggests, in the moment in which subjects minoritized by race, ethnicity, and gender become both the subjects and objects of representation, canon formation emerges as the ironic repetition of disciplinarity, but a repetition within interdisciplinary contexts. As she worries over the restrictions produced by incorporation, she gestures toward the need to produce analyses of the limits of institutionalizing and archiving minority difference and culture *even as we promote them as levers for institutional change.*

In 1996, Lisa Lowe also pondered the limits of institutionalization:

> institutionalizing such fields as Ethnic Studies still contains an inevitable paradox: institutionalization provides a material base within the university for a transformative critique of traditional disciplines and their traditional separations, and yet the institutionalization of any field or curriculum that establishes orthodox objects and methods submits in part to the demands of the university and its educative function of socializing subjects into the state.[43]

The historical development of interdisciplinary fields like ethnic studies and women's studies placed real material pressures on disciplines to transform themselves and reengage questions of minority difference and culture. Some of those pressures involved ensuring the presence of those subjects within the academy as students and faculty. At the same time, the development of that discursive and material incorporation of new subjects and knowledges must also be understood within the context of an institutionalizing and archiving power that, as Lowe puts it, subjects it to university demands and "its educative function."

In his 1992 article "Cultural Studies and Its Theoretical Legacies," Stuart Hall similarly points to institutionalization as a necessary horizon for critical analysis. Observing "the enormous explosion of cultural studies in the United States [and] its rapid professionalization and institutionalization," he argues that while such an institutionalization is not a phenomenon that one can regret "in any simple way," it is "a moment of profound danger."[44] Interestingly, Hall points to the curiously American character of cultural studies' institutionalization. Part of that Americanness seems to reside in the affirmative ethos that characterizes institutionalization within the States. As Hall counters that ethos with a decidedly British suspicion about the nature of institutionalization, he begs the American reader to denaturalize the innocence and exultation that so often attend institutionalization within this national context. In doing so, we might imagine that he calls to account that subject who believes that institutionalization is the proper mode for the consummation of noncanonical and oppositional interventions. Indeed, we might say that Hall gestures toward the institutionalizing ethos of the United States as an "imperial tendency" that threatens to envelop even oppositional formations.

Interdisciplinary critiques of minority difference thus become the critique and the maneuvers of hegemony. As both agent and effect of institutionalization, interdisciplinarity represents not only an obstacle for and a challenge to dominance but the expansion and multiplication of power's relays. Interdisciplinarity becomes much more than a matter contained within the academy. It becomes the episteme that organizes the regimes of representation for academy, state, and capital. Isn't this the implication of Omi and Winant's arguments that the ethnic movements changed the meaning of race within the United States and reorganized the protocols and identity of the state according to that changed meaning? And if the student movements inspired changes within how the state understood difference and its own identity, isn't it reasonable to say that political economies were changed as well? Hence, the institutionalization of difference becomes a question much larger than any single institution but becomes a logic of practice that establishes a network between all institutions in the United States. As interdisciplinarity constitutes difference as a site of contradiction, it also designates the institutions that are rearticulated in terms of minoritized differences as active locations for contradictions.

In addition to fostering new conditions for the expansion and multiplication of power, interdisciplinarity also provides new circumstances for the potential critique of that expansion and multiplication.[45] The critique of institutionalization, therefore, provides a new condition for, rather than the termination of, critical deployments of race, gender, sexuality, and so on. Instead of representing the confirmation of power's totalizing character, interdisciplinarity connotes a site of contradiction, an instance in which minoritized differences negotiate and maneuver agreements with and estrangements from insitutionalization. The extent to which interdisciplinary sites work up a critical suspicion of institutionalization is also the measure by which they alienate the American ethos that surrounds institutionalization.

A theorization of contradiction also means developing a critical awareness of the potential vulnerabilities that accompany all deployments of difference. One such vulnerability arises from the historic deployment of difference for the purpose of social recognition. The roots of this deployment lie in revolutionary and cultural nationalism. Indeed, several thinkers have pointed to this aspect of minority nationalisms. In her essay "Black Nationalism and Black Common Sense," for instance, cultural critic Wahneema Lubiano addresses this particular feature within black nationalist movements. As "Black nationalism [resisted] racialized domination for all classes of the group," she argues, "it has also historically appealed to the white bourgeois state" as protector and liberator of black communities. Moreover, while black nationalism has rebelled against state imperatives, it has also "[reinscribed] the state in particular places within its own narratives."[46] In the context of anticolonial movements, Lisa Lowe and David Lloyd capture this feature by arguing that "the ends of anticolonial nationalism are defined by the goal of the capture of the state, and its ideology is in large part structured in terms of liberal discourses and for liberal state institutions."[47] As such, anticolonial nationalism "speaks of rights and the citizen, of equality, fraternity and liberty, makes its claims to self-determination on the basis of enlightenment universality, and asserts the cultural if not

economic and military equivalence of its nation-people to that of the imperial power."[48] In the racialized contexts of the U.S. women's movement,
Norma Alarcón captures this contradiction between an insurgent articulation, on the one hand, and its recognition through dominant ideologies,
on the other: "[The] most popular subject of Anglo-American feminism is
an autonomous, self-making, self-determining subject who first proceeds
according to the logic of identification with regard to the subject of consciousness, a notion usually viewed as the purview of man, but now claimed
for women."[49]

All of these writers identify various modes by which minoritized cultures and differences are put in the service of recognition and legitimacy:
for Lubiano, the state is ironically lifted as the representative and recog-
nizer of minoritized subjects; for Lowe and Lloyd, minoritized cultures
and differences exhibit elements that are consistent with rather than
antagonistic to liberal state institutions and the developmental discourses
of modernity; for Alarcón, minoritized subjects begin to identify with and
reinscribe themselves as rational subjects and thus invoke and endorse those
properties archetypically associated with Western man. Lubiano, Lowe,
Lloyd, and Alarcón point to a hard fact that characterizes nationalist formations: they are fundamentally grounded in systems of recognition and
desire. They are formations that constantly strive to make themselves legible to power, even as they contest power. This feature, probably more
than any other, made cultural- and revolutionary-nationalist formations
vulnerable to institutional solicitation. In a moment in which modern U.S.
institutions were turning to the recognition of difference as part of a new
archival economy, minority nationalisms' desire for recognition would make
for a golden weakness.

One way of framing the internal contradictions of the student movements would be to say that those contradictions evolved out of a constitutive negotiation between the writerly and the readerly elements of those
movements. Distinguishing between the writerly and the readerly texts,
Roland Barthes argues that texts with "writerly" values stipulate that "the
goal of literary work (of literature as work) is to make the reader no longer
a consumer, but a producer of the text."[50] As the student movements and
interdisciplinary uprisings called for a different social and epistemological
order within the academy and within society, they identified academy and
society as writerly texts that could be revised and rewritten. In doing so,

they were confronting the readerly histories of the American academy—that is, the long tradition that would establish the academy as above revision and transformation, that is, as a protected text. But as interdisciplinary formations reproduced and reinscribed the logics of the state and canon, they gave way to "readerly" aspects, which Barthes describes as the "countervalue" of the writerly text—that is, "its negative, reactive value: what can be read, but not written: the readerly. We call any readerly text a classic text."[51] In the context of a changing archival economy, the writerly features were threatened with the possibility of being absorbed into the readerly, cultivated into the realm of canons and orthodoxies. Taking the most readerly elements among those radical and writerly formations—that is, the invocation of logics of identification, the investments in liberal discourses of state and ethical development, the assertions of normativity—power would use them for its own affirmations and to tie a different knot.

This simultaneous alienation from and solicitation of dominant institutions would begin to underwrite not only the contradictions internal to the student movements but also the social contradictions external to them. As those movements were integrated into academy, state, and capital, it also meant that the contradictions that characterized them—the simultaneity of the recuperative and the disruptive, the writerly and the readerly—would be dispersed onto social formations outside the American academy. Another way of stating this is to say that the concurrent oppositional and concordant nature of nationalism would become hegemonic for minoritized subject and social formations. For instance, if cultural and revolutionary nationalism became a "common sense," to paraphrase Lubiana, the production of that common sense meant the insertion of this defining contradictory element within personal and institutional projects of integration, upward mobility, inclusion, and participation. Not that the simultaneity of oppositional stances and interpellative states was unprecedented, but it would achieve a new span in the years after civil rights. More pointedly, networks of power would take contradictions that inhered in those movements and cast them wide, making those contradictions the terms of minoritized social life, acceptance, representation, and participation. Being a minority would no longer mean a simple geopolitical exclusion. It would become an economy organized to produce bargains between the oppositional and the concordant. The minority would represent a new institutional being that would be the stimulus for unforeseen positivities in the midst of newly evolving regulations and exclusions.

A mode of power was forming in the post–World War II moment whose DNA was based on a nation-state's dictum, the management of the international, the supervision of difference, and the contradictions of interdisciplinary enhancement and subjection. A new mode of biopower—one that affirmed minority difference and culture—would emerge and work with necropolitical social formations to simultaneously activate and disfranchise minoritized subjects and communities, forming and re-forming institutions according to the advancement and regulation of minority difference. If truth be told, institutionalization—for radical social and intellectual movements—was never a simple and innocent cause for celebration. What we find in the history of interdisciplinarity is that incorporation has always been a reason for meditation, scrutiny, and awareness.

TWO
TOW
OTW
OWT

The Proliferation of Minority Difference

YOU HAVE HEARD THAT IN THE FIRST DAYS Zeus and Mnemosyne, the goddess of memory, had nine daughters, each one a muse for a different talent. But in fact there was a tenth muse, an even more outside child whose province would be those bastard inspirations of minoritized communities. Anyway, there would come a time when this nameless girl would inspire minor and major alike. She would be history's latest motivation, and her charms would yield arts for not only poets but for merchants, bureaucrats, and statesmen, too.

This chapter looks at how minority difference was being constituted as an affirmation for revolutionary forces within the United States as well as for capital, state, and academy. If the preceding chapter theorized the ways in which U.S. imperial and constitutional projects helped to install a mode of power that hegemonically affirms minority difference and culture, this chapter looks at a specific instance of that affirmation. More specifically, the chapter analyzes how the U.S. nation-state and American capital in the 1960s used U.S. revolutionary movements to bolster the global standing of U.S. political economy.

To look at the overlap between political economy, minority difference, and revolution, I focus on the Lumumba-Zapata movement at the University of California at San Diego, a movement that took place from 1969 to 1972 and that worked to establish a progressive college that would educate blacks, Chicanos, and poor whites. I investigate the Lumumba-Zapata movement alongside changes in state and capital to demonstrate how affirming minority difference revolutionized American institutions, creating a political economy that was uniquely American, one that provided power with unprecedented opportunities for hegemony and simultaneously mobilized important critiques of hegemonic authority. From this chapter, we will see that what that muse had to offer would change the institutional landscape of the United States, introducing a new and powerful contradiction into society, a contradiction that arose as hegemony versed itself in minority affirmation.

Difference and the Political Economy of Power/Knowledge

As the introduction and preceding chapter argue, in order for a political economy around minority affirmation to develop, there had to be an assault on Western knowledge and the ways in which it underwrote the institutional foundations of the West. Assaulting the metaphysical presumptions of the West meant inevitably assessing how Western knowledge excluded difference as a mode of social formation. That assessment also entailed outlining how difference presented certain alternatives to abstract notions of being and knowing. This turn to difference shaped social movements all across the globe in the 1960s. In Europe, for instance, it was absolutely constitutive of the rebellions of May '68. As artist and critic Liam Gillick notes in his article "The Difference Engine," the progressives of 1968 "demanded that *difference*—the specificity of histories, identities, and desires— be acknowledged at all times. They believed that difference could and should be the primary marker of a creative and democratic society, to which end they claimed solidarity with others and developed new forms of meta-identification."[1] Discussing the role that difference played in the events leading up to May '68, political scientist Anne Sa'adah comments on student protests against living conditions at and state control of the University of Nanterre: "In the lead-up to the May events, protests at Nanterre crystallized around two issues: One was sex; the other was Vietnam."[2] When the French educational system went coed in the sixties, it caused "a sea-change in gender relations."[3] For students in French universities, sexual freedom and pleasure thus became modes of difference antithetical to the repressive order of the French educational system. The repressive order of French society engendered as well mass organizing against the Vietnam War.

In the 1960s United States, difference galvanized minorities like never before. The black power movement would rearticulate the meaning of blackness and black culture. In 1967, the Black Panther Party would publish the first issue of its newspaper, the *Black Panther*. In 1968, young, militant

Native Americans founded the American Indian Movement, espousing Red Power as a means of contesting federal control of Native lands and rearticulating the meaning of American Indian culture.[4] In April 1969, organizers in Santa Barbara, California, would meet to found the Chicano studies movement.[5] And, as in Europe, U.S. social movements would tie local articulations of difference to global circumstances.

One place where local and global engagements with difference came together was at the University of California at San Diego, particularly over what became known as the Lumumba-Zapata movement. If minority difference was a rallying cry for students at schools like San Francisco State, Berkeley, Cornell, Northwestern, and City College, it was no less so for African American and Chicano students at UCSD. At this campus that sat way up on a hill were competing ideals of minority difference among students of color. There were black and Chicano nationalists, for instance, who only wanted to work with members of their own ethnic groups. Then there was a group of Chicano and black internationalists who, as one student leader put it, "'held the view that the best way to get anything through . . . was to work together.'"[6] So, in 1969, those coalitionally and internationally minded students proposed to the university administration that the new "third" college should be named Lumumba-Zapata College after the "assassinated Congolese revolutionary leader Patrice Lumumba and the Mexican revolutionary Emiliano Zapata."[7] They proposed this Lumumba-Zapata College as "a place where [their] peoples could acquire the knowledge and skills [they] needed in order to more effectively wage [their] liberation struggles."[8]

The Lumumba-Zapata experiment, like so many of the other minority student movements of the day, represented an attempt to maneuver difference for oppositional purposes. We can see the Lumumba-Zapata movement's interest in difference and its relationship to other articulations of difference outside the United States in the 1996 film *Herbert's Hippopotamus*. Made by former UCSD film student Paul Alexander Juutilainen in 1996, *Herbert's Hippopotamus* uses late-sixties student movements in Europe and the student struggles at UCSD to document the influence of Herbert Marcuse's influence on those struggles. But in doing so, the film suggests how difference was becoming a local and global element of social organizing.

Shortly into the film, we see a frame that reads "Part 1: Philosophy in May," a frame that depicts a scene from the filmmaker's contemporary philosophy textbook. In that scene Marcuse is holding forth at what appears to be either a panel or a press conference. A tape recorder hovers to the side of his face, being held by an anonymous interviewer. In the film's next frame, we see a C-SPAN clip of a famous black woman and scholar-activist speaking at Harvard's Kennedy School of Government. She, Angela Y. Davis, a student of Marcuse, discusses how he taught her "that it was possible to be an academic and an activist, a scholar and a revolutionary."[9] Then the scene moves to archival footage of that same student twenty years earlier, speaking at a UCSD campus rally. Juutilainen's voice interrupts the silence of that archival scene and frames it this way: "Looking at this student of Marcuse at age twenty-four brought me back to 1968, about ten years after the emergence of the civil rights movement and several years into the U.S. military involvement in Vietnam. Angela Davis is known as a defender of civil rights, a Black Panther, and radical college professor." Beginning with the figure of an African American female radical to introduce the philosophical underpinnings of the May events, the film begins to play havoc with the identity of Western philosophy, invoking a minoritized subject as *the* subject of philosophy and thereby disrupting the presumably abstract and universal identity of Western knowledge. Through Davis, the film invokes and departs from the stock figure of the May uprising—a white male *soixante-huitard* decrying the shibboleths of Western history. In doing so, the film begins to point to the forms of difference that constituted May '68 but are left out of the hegemonic rendering of those events.

In an attempt to identify the significance of various forms of difference, the film then moves to former *soixante-huitard* Marcuse student and San Diego State professor Andrew Feenberg. About Marcuse's book *One-Dimensional Man*, Feenberg observes: "*One-Dimensional Man* provided the theoretical basis for not relying on the working class but instead looking to marginal groups for leadership in the struggle,"[10] yet it's debatable whether or not we can attribute *One-Dimensional Man* with this sole distinction. Feenberg is correct in suggesting that *One-Dimensional Man* was observing a signal but underappreciated feature of the May '68 events— the different constituencies that constituted them. Indeed, Kristin Ross in *May '68 and Its Afterlives* turns our attention to how '68 compelled people to engage and foster different forms of community and sociality, turning '68 into a historical moment "that took students outside of the university" and into the countryside and "brought farmers and workers together," making difference the overarching theme for "a new kind of mass organizing."[11]

The student movements on both sides of the Atlantic deployed difference as a means to challenge the existing order of being and knowing, compelling a search for new orders. Social movements in the United States would intersect with ones in Europe as they all attempted in various contexts to formulate critical ventures founded on "the pleasure of discovering a new humanity, a deep joy in [themselves] and around [them], of realizing that elements of expression, imagination, and life can exist together."[12] But even while there were important connections between U.S. student movements and their European counterparts over the claim to difference, there were also important distinctions that made American and European engagements with difference not so identical after all.

May '68 and the European Critique of Difference

To appreciate the distinctions between the European deployment of difference and the American articulation, we might begin with the powerful and contradictory role that the West has played in European intellectual thought and social practice. As discussed in chapter 1, man—according to Foucault—became the standard by which a "culture experiences the propinquity of things, how it establishes the *tabula* of their relationships and the order by which they must be considered."[13] Later, Foucault "replaced" his deliberation on man with that of the (Western) subject. In *The Archaeology of Knowledge,* Foucault theorized that subject as the figure that presumably linked all forms of Western knowledge, the *tabula* that established the relationships between those forms. That subject would be the sign of a continuous history, one that guaranteed "that everything that has eluded him may be restored to him."[14] This subject would ensure that all those things that difference keeps at bay would one day be brought back under that subject's influence.[15]

As Foucault suggests, the Western subject is a mode of appropriation that will arrogate to itself all knowledge and jurisdiction, the formation that presumes and contrives continuous narratives of history, narratives that propose that all forms of knowledge will continue the sovereignty of the Western subject. As such, the subject both enables and embodies continuous history. As Foucault states, "Making historical analysis the discourse of the continuous and making human consciousness the original subject of all historical development and all actions are two sides of the same system of thought."[16] The subject is that entity that will ostensibly continue along history's route and guarantee that the way to history is one based on continuity.

Foucault's description of man and the subject intersects with what Stuart Hall has called the "internalist story" of European development. That story

> has been the dominant narrative of modernity for some time—an "internalist" story, with capitalism growing from the womb of feudalism and Europe's self-generating capacity to produce, like a silk-worm, the circumstances of her own evolution from within her body.[17]

The narrative of European development becomes a way of tabulating a progressive and continuous relationship between feudalism and capitalism, revealing that narrative's debt to the discourse of Western man as a mode of organization and to the notion of the subject as a discourse of historical continuity. Put simply, we might say that what Foucault describes in *The Order of Things* and *The Archaeology of Knowledge* are internalist narratives of European development organized around the figures of Western man and the subject.

But Foucault himself reproduces that internalist narrative in *The Order of Things* and *The Archaeology of Knowledge,* precisely through the ways in which he approaches the issue of difference. In *The Order of Things,* for instance, Foucault initially invokes ethnology's interest in other cultures and societies, defining it as a human science organized around differences concerning "the normalization of the broad biological functions, the rules . . . of exchange, production, and consumption, and the systems that are organized around or on the model of linguistic structures."[18] But Foucault then moves from this interest in the expansive workings of different cultures to defining ethnology in terms of its relationship to this exceptional and singular figure called man. For instance, he writes, "Ethnology, like psychoanalysis, questions not man himself, as he appears in the human sciences, but the region that makes possible knowledge about man in general."[19] The broad interests that characterize ethnology in the first passage are then narrowed and focused on the complexity of a single figure in the second. Indeed, Foucault describes man's relationship to difference in ways similar to how he would later describe the "subject's" relationship to difference in *The Archaeology of Knowledge*. Using language that would show up later on in *The Archaeology of Knowledge*, he says, in *The Order of Things*, that ethnology and psychoanalysis could be called "sciences of the unconscious" because "they are directed towards that which, outside man, makes it possible to know, with a positive knowledge, that which is *given to or eludes his consciousness*."[20] For Foucault, those elements that are "outside man" are understood as *internal* to man inasmuch as they are observations of his consciousness or his unconscious. Pointing to the ways in which Foucault's definition of ethnology takes for granted man's—and by extension Europe's—status as the explanation of all cultural difference, Robert J. C. Young observes, "In producing a general model of how cultures organize and define themselves, ethnology for Foucault is therefore not about the particular differences of other cultures, but about how such differences conform to an underlying theoretical pattern formulated according to the protocols of European thought."[21] For Foucault, the proper use of ethnology might indeed have been to produce a "critical ethnography of the west,"[22] but it was a conception of ethnology that retained a notion of cultural differences as ultimately serving to explain the West.

But we shouldn't think of Foucault's ironic fixation on Europe as the isolated incident of one thinker. Indeed, that fixation would characterize other white European intellectuals who, like Foucault, saw themselves as displacing the hegemony of the West. For instance, in an interview with Sylvère Lotringer, Antonio Negri said that the May movement in France and Italy was about "the pleasure of discovering a new humanity, a deep joy in ourselves and around us, or realizing that elements of expression, imagination, and life can exist together." For him, "The only comparison possible with '68 would be the revolution of 1848 . . . [At] that time, Europe was the world."[23] In his remarks, Negri turns an intellectual event of no doubt global significance into an internal narrative about European development. But, as we will see, May '68 was not simply a moment in which "Europe was the world." In fact, there were comparable and contemporaneous struggles and revolutions, struggles and revolutions that illuminated the heterogeneity of that revolutionary moment.

With an eye toward that heterogeneity, Ross writes against a "consensus view of '68" that narrates it as "a mellow, sympathetic, poetic 'youth revolt' and lifestyle reform," believing that such a view excludes not only the largest general strike that France had ever seen but also "May's prehistory," which dated back to "the ending of the Algerian War in the early 1960s."[24] For Ross, turning May simply into a story about the subjective transformations of European youth occludes, for example, the massacre that took place as French police set upon thirty to forty thousand Algerians in Paris, people who were peacefully demonstrating against curfews imposed against their communities during the Algerian War. On October 17, 1961, at least a hundred Algerian men, women, and children were pursued and beaten by the police and then thrown into the Seine because of this act of civil disobedience. Those who did not meet their end in the river were either taken to the courtyard of the police prefecture or to several sports arenas where they were bludgeoned or killed. No newspapers would cover the murders, and a consensus narrative would arise only to eclipse the slaughter, permitting the West to reassert itself in state violence and in the narration of May '68. In doing so, May's encounters with epic struggles around race and empire would be threatened with oblivion. Summing up this danger and what it has meant for our understanding of May '68, Ross states:

> a whole fifteen- to twenty-year period of radical political culture is occulted from view, a political culture whose traces were manifest in the growth of a small but significant opposition to the Algerian War and in the embrace by many French of a "third-worldist" north/south analysis of global politics in the wake of the enormous successes of the colonial revolutions.[25]

An internalist narrative would arise that would help to banish October 17 from the telling of May and excise racial formations from the critiques that paralleled or inspired it.

But the costs of that internalist story would stretch even beyond the question of race and empire's significance for European intellectual and political histories. This internalist story would disqualify Europe from participating in an epic adventure to which power was increasingly drawn, a venture that could only have taken place in the United States perhaps. There, difference would not be another way to retell the story of man, or resuscitate the fiction of national homogeneity, or theorize the superimportance of the Western episteme. Difference, on that side of the Atlantic, would be a rallying cry for various types of minoritized embodiments, vernaculars, and histories to rise. There, in the United States, minority difference and culture would be thoroughly articulated into social practice and swell the sails of many a revolutionary—instead of being lost or drowned in the deep.

The Institutional Possibilities of Minority Difference: An American Political Economy

While difference in the French context often meant the suppression of the worker and the colonial militant as revolutionary figures,[26] difference in the U.S. setting meant calling for the presence of those subjects deemed to be outside the American academy and its systems of representation. Difference during the sixties United States would become the moment in which minoritized subjects of all types would brim with versions of that question that Angela Davis asked herself upon arriving on the UCSD campus: "Where are my people?"[27]

The conditions that allowed for various responses to that question could be found in the institutional, demographic, and political transformations taking place in the United States generally, and on U.S. campuses in particular. After World War II, the American university would expand both in terms of resources and in terms of students. Federal funding of university research would begin to outdistance the funding provided by private foundations. As historians Wilson Smith and Thomas Bender write, "In 1947–1948, the Veterans Affairs Administration paid for almost half of the male college students in the United States, and by 1962 higher education had received $5.5 billion from that source on behalf of veterans of World War II and the Korean War."[28] In fact, the post–World War II American university owed much of its expansion to militarization. For example, the GI Bill accounted for the largesse that many universities would enjoy, as did the National Defense Education Act, which extended loans to students in "defense"-related fields as well as English, history, and geography. As Smith and Bender note, "By 1968 the country had spent $3 billion on fifteen thousand NDEA [National Defense Education Act] graduate fellowships and on loans to 1.5 million undergraduates." A historic contradiction would thus emerge from specifically academic circumstances, one in which the itineraries of war would—along with civil rights gains— help to produce the conditions for expanding student-body populations. In such a context, the realities and benefits of war and state expansion would run up against the histories and circumstances of the disfranchised, creating the conditions in which subjects minoritized by differences of race, gender, and class would come face-to-face with hegemony.

Indeed, as an institution that was being transformed by minority difference, the American academy was quickly becoming the arena for "the people's" entrance into all spheres of representation. Before World War II, American universities were primarily regional entities, but after the war, government support and social protest helped to nationalize university policies by making the federal government the enforcer of public policies around race and gender as well as the primary benefactor of research funding and student aid. At the moment that the American university nationalized, "underrepresented" students would also become the newest constituency of that quickly transforming institution, bypassing regional specificities and instead taking on national and—as we'll see—international distinctiveness.

That international distinctiveness was achieved for many by elaborating what became known as the internal colonial model of racial formations, a theory that posited that there "were 'domestic' or 'internal' forms of colonialism operant within nation-states."[29] Internal colonialism first emerged as a model of racial formations when Latin American intellectuals began theorizing underdevelopment in Latin American countries; those theorizations quickly caught the eye of African American and Chicano intellectuals and activists, many of them, like the students from Lumumba-Zapata, searching for ways to link various struggles and address local exclusions. As Ramón Gutiérrez notes, internal colonialism encouraged young activists of color to "[reason] that their oppression was not only personal, but structural, not only individual, but institutional."[30] The internal colonial model was, therefore, a way of imagining institutions not only as sites for addressing racial exclusions but as locations for illuminating formations from multiple geopolitical terrains.

In the context of the Lumumba-Zapata movement and the radical organizing of the 1960s, "internationalism" was a way of imagining the political economy of empire and the ways in which it was shaping social practice within the United States. During that time, the U.S. nation-state was engaging in an imperial war, one that would narrow the distance between the United States and Asia. For sixties and seventies activists in the United States, internationalism was a means of imagining coalition across national boundaries and conjoining internationalism to a radical deployment of minority difference.

Addressing the internationalism produced out of the Vietnam War, *Herbert's Hippopotamus* turns to a bit of archival footage from the period. In one of the film's scenes, the missile cruiser known as the USS *Jouett* taxies into the San Diego Bay. A crowd made up of women and children stand on a dock enthusiastically greeting its arrival. The brass section of a military band is there to welcome the cruiser to town. The USS *Jouett* was the cruiser that made voyages from the Pacific Ocean into East Asia. It was commissioned December 3, 1966, and deployed early on for the Vietnam War. With the figure of the cruiser, the film connects the conservative and predominantly white town of San Diego to communities and peoples in East Asia, especially Vietnam. The film situates the hegemonic internationalism of the U.S. government against the internationalism of the student activists, an internationalism that attempted to challenge emerging imperial ventures. In doing so, the film dramatizes how competing internationalisms were struggling against one another.

Part of that struggle over internationalism entailed an effort on the part of relations of power to seize the opportunities for coalition building and maneuver them for hegemonic purposes. As Carlos Blanco—a UCSD literature professor and adviser to the Lumumba-Zapata students—stated, "Lumumba-Zapata was not conceived as a 'coalition' to train Black and Chicano aspirants to their own bourgeoisies."[31] Hence, Blanco recognized how the erection of a college could potentially become a vehicle for the production of bourgeois classes among black and brown students. As Mariscal notes, gaining middle-class privileges was indeed the goal for some of the more sectarian nationalist students of color. But Blanco and the Lumumba-Zapata students in fact held to an alternative conception of institutionality, one that would make internationalism into something other than an alibi for the diversification of the status quo. For them, this new institution on the hill would be designed to diversify and multiply critical ruptures.

For many student militants throughout the United States, and for Lumumba-Zapata certainly, the question of minority difference and representation was never simply about increasing the numbers of minoritized bodies. Instead, the question of minority difference was an attempt to make sure that demographic growth would *contract* with epistemological and institutional transformations. Articulating minority difference into U.S. social life entailed designating institutional and epistemic practices as simultaneous sites that could be reorganized in favor of minoritized communities. From this context, minority difference would not be a simple matter of identity; it would become an emergent lexicon for social practice throughout the country.

Movements like Lumumba-Zapata tried to establish that lexicon by deepening and broadening minority difference's relationship to political and institutional practice. Indeed, the students' proposal for Lumumba-Zapata College exemplifies that attempt. In an effort to create a college "expressly devoted to the needs of students from oppressed social groups,"[32] the Lumumba-Zapata members wrote:

> We demand that the Third College be devoted to relevant education for minority youth and to the study of the contemporary social problems of all people. To do this authentically, this college must radically depart from the usual role as the ideological backbone of the social system, and must instead subject every part of the system to ruthless criticism. To reflect these aims of the college, it will be called Lumumba-Zapata College.[33]

Like similar efforts throughout the country, Lumumba-Zapata College was meant to reconceptualize the very possibility of institutional life and practice. As the proposal states, "Despite the Chicano rebellions in the Southwest and the Black revolts in the cities, the University of California, San Diego, which is part of the oppressive system, has not changed its institutional role."[34] With an eye toward the relationship between minority insurgencies and institutional life, the proposal understood social protests to be provocations to change the institutional practices that made up American colleges and universities. As the proposal suggests, minoritized rebellions were ways of designating institutional realities as contingent rather than necessary formations. In doing so, proposals like the Lumumba-Zapata one advanced minority difference as a social category with profound institutional and social implications.

The institutional pressures that minority difference presumed required epistemic transformations as well, transformations that meant imagining new forms of community and new ways of producing and disseminating knowledge. Like their counterparts at City College, institutional transformation, for the Lumumba-Zapata students, meant demanding epistemic reorganization. So, to reflect their desire for epistemic and institutional transformation, the students at UC San Diego, like the ones at City College, put together a curriculum that would symbolize the interests of their movement. Noting the simultaneity of institutional and epistemic change, they stated in their proposal, "So far, what education the few minority students have received has been from a colonial perspective. We now seek to learn about ourselves from a minority perspective."[35]

For the Lumumba-Zapata militants, achieving a "minority perspective" was not a simple matter of reading authors that reflected black and Chicano life in any straightforward way. In truth, their curriculum called for a heterogeneous list of authors that included not only Malcolm X, Kwame Nkrumah, Frantz Fanon, George Padmore, Che Guevara, and Mariano Auzela but Marx and Lenin as well. In doing so, the Lumumba-Zapata movement attempted to integrate Western as well as non-Western critical formations and traditions. Advising the students on the curriculum, Blanco proposed that they adopt "a course of study that was 'humanistic' and designed to 'offer the possibility for minority students to apply the critical and analytical tools of modern learning to the problems they face in their environment and to provide for White students an understanding of the problems involved in present-day society.'"[36]

The resulting curriculum proposed "a general outline of areas to be studied at Lumumba-Zapata College." Those areas were "Revolutions," "Analysis of Economic System [sic]," "Science and Technology," "Health Sciences and Public Health," "Urban and Rural Development," "Communication Arts," "Foreign Languages," "Cultural Heritage," and "White Studies." Each area presumed powerful challenges to the canonical orders of academic knowledge. For instance, the section titled "Analysis of Economic System" states: "The understanding of the economic exploitation of minority peoples in the United States will entail in depth analysis of the historical and contemporary development of capitalism in the Western world, including the crucial roles played by colonialism, imperialism, slavery, and genocide."[37] This curricular demand challenges (Western) man's self-representation as the universal basis of life, labor, and language. Indeed, the various units of the curriculum point to investigations of how Western man achieved a terrible specificity through the violent suppression of racialized and economically disfranchised communities. At the heart of the curriculum is also a rebuttal to the presumptions of the Western rational subject and the discourse of continuous history, presumptions that would claim that minoritized differences and histories could be neatly enfolded into the normative consciousness of the Western subject and comfortably located within the capacious chambers of Western history. Indeed, the Lumumba-Zapata curriculum marks Western consciousness and history as modes that have excluded the histories and knowledges of minoritized cultures, announcing the fact that those histories and knowledges required other types of epistemic and institutional accommodations and arrangements, particularly in the moment of unprecedented growth for American higher education.

In this time of internationalism, minority difference would become the scene for a "sudden vicinity of things that have [presumably] no relation to each other.[38] San Diego would live next to Europe. The United States would visit with Latin America; blacks and Chicanos would talk and fight together; West Coast would adjoin Asia while democracy abutted empire. Minority difference would become the occasion for new systems of simultaneity to arise, systems characterized by dramatic communications between peoples, institutions, and knowledge formations. Yes, minority difference would signal the era of a new mix of things, one in which new species of communicability would assemble questionable juxtapositions and put them to critical and conservative ends. And just as old man Blanco worried, modes of power would begin to communicate with minority difference so that they could update their range of mastery.

The Hegemonic Affirmation of Minority Difference

Updating power's range of mastery would involve a politician from California. In 1968, then presidential candidate Richard Nixon would try to respond to black unrest in urban areas, the lure of communism, and desires to increase membership in the Republican Party by developing a concept that would be inspired by—of all things—the black power movement. Nixon would give that concept a name that would presumably resonate with the identitarian ideals of that movement and the aims of the U.S. nation-state. So, with the advice of friends and supporters, one of whom was the basketball great Wilt Chamberlain, Nixon used the campaign trail to promote the idea of "black capitalism." And in doing so, he would attempt to make state, capital, and minority difference sit down and chat with one another.

With an eye cast toward Nixon's scheme, the Lumumba-Zapata students wrote in their proposal:

> In the case of minority students, it is miseducation which has caused us to unconsciously sever ourselves from our communal and cultural roots, if not to be seduced into the system which exploits our community. Black capitalism, especially as formulated by the Nixon administration, divides the minority people into exploiters and exploited, the exploiting class being the college-trained bourgeoisie. Each new Chicano or Black businessman has already been enlisted into the war army of exploiters.[39]

In this passage, the students point to black capitalism's ability to reroute minority affirmation away from the critique of institutional seductions and toward the hegemonic appeals of liberal capitalism. In doing so, the proposal points to an emergent and strategic situation, one in which power was beginning to reconfigure minority affirmation. But while the students believed that black capitalism was part of a process that would "sever" minorities from their communal and cultural roots, a mode of power was arising that would articulate itself as the embodiment of those roots. Far from being a moment signifying state and capital's alienation from minority culture, "black capitalism" emanated from a broad and emergent courtship between hegemonic institutions and minority difference.

Again, this courtship can be framed partly within the nationalization of the American university system. Smith and Bender note, for instance, "After the war . . . a broad recognition of the importance of knowledge for national security and the high costs of the relevant research brought the government and universities into tight partnership, indispensable to each — both in respect to funding research and support of students."[40] During the postwar years, the state eyed the American university with unprecedented interest. As the state looked on, it observed opportunities as well as obstacles that it needed to overcome. In the midst of student agitation over social exclusions and militarization, for example, the government would have to find ways to reconcile its need for knowledge with the fact of student rebellion. The Nixon administration attempted to do just that with its concept of "black capitalism."

In their article about Nixon's development and deployment of black capitalism, historian Robert E. Weems Jr. and political scientist Lewis A.

Randolph situate that concept within national divisions over the "evolving Vietnam War and domestic race relations," the assassination of Dr. Martin Luther King Jr., and the direction of the civil rights movement.[41] As they argue, Nixon devised the notion as a way to capitalize on the ideological uncertainty that characterized 1968. With the concept of black capitalism, Nixon believed that he could quell antigovernment protests and therefore forestall the appeal of communism for young black militants and at the same time recruit African Americans into the Republican Party (51–52). With this concept, Nixon did not attempt to manage the black power movement by denying the allure of minority difference. Instead, he evolved a mode of regulation based on affirming and redirecting nationalist ideals of self-determination, redirecting them toward state and capital's interests, rerouting those ideals by presenting state and capital as the very entities that could offer self-determination to minoritized subjects. In doing so, he helped to inaugurate a new strategic situation for power, one in which the very institutions that dismembered the people would be responsible for sewing them back together again.

We can get a glimpse of a shift toward this new strategic situation even in the 1950s, during the time Nixon was vice president under Eisenhower. In fact, Nixon's interest in minority difference went back to his years as chair of the Committee on Government Contracts (CGC), a committee with no enforcement powers but with the mission to "receive complaints of alleged violations of nondiscrimination provisions in government contracts and forward them to the appropriate contracting agencies" (50). With the CGC, Nixon would begin to use minority difference as a means to boost the Unites States' standing internationally, attempting "[to create] better relations between free nations" and eliminate the problem of communist propaganda and recruitment (51). In addition to chairing the CGC, Nixon stayed in close contact with civil rights leaders during his vice presidency. In 1957, for instance, he accompanied Dr. King to Kwame Nkrumah's presidential inauguration in Ghana, signaling the U.S. government's support for independence struggles and outcomes in colonized regions.

As Nixon's interest in quelling the appeal of communism suggests, his articulation of black capitalism was filled with Cold War imperatives. Indeed, placating black radicals by "offering blacks a substantial 'piece' of the proverbial American 'pie' through government and private-sector programs" (57) was indelibly tied to Cold War strategies. As Weems and

Randolph note, "Just as Nixon and Kissinger linked concessions associated with 'détente' to Soviet and Chinese behavior modification, 'Black Capitalism' offered U.S. black militants a monetary incentive to move away from notions of 'Burn Baby Burn'" (ibid.).

Through Nixon, "black capitalism" became a management strategy for affirming minority self-determination and preventing insurgency. Hence, in the presidential campaign of 1968 Nixon would promote strategies that "combined repression with reform."[42] While calling for expanded police forces and broadened police powers in order to obtain confessions, Nixon "proposed tax incentives to corporations investing in depressed neighborhoods, expansion of tutorial assistance and job training, and more government loans to fledgling minority entrepreneurs and homeowners."[43] His efforts to affirm minority difference culminated in the signing of Executive Order 11458 on March 5, 1969, a move that founded the Office of Minority Business Enterprise (OMBE) within the Commerce Department. With the OMBE, the Nixon administration hoped to win political favor among an emergent African American middle class by "[increasing] minority business holdings, minority home ownership," and minority jobs.[44] Indeed, as historian Dean Kotlowski notes, "Between 1969 and 1991, federal grants and loans to minority-owned firms jumped from $200 million to $7 billion while government purchases from such firms grew from $83 million to $17 billion."[45] With these maneuvers, black capitalism revealed itself to be a category that was simultaneously fetishistic of and phobic about black racial difference.

In a similar vein, Nixon would also work to curry the favor of American Indians, attempting to do so while luring American Indian sentiment away from the militancy of the American Indian Movement. Nixon would attempt to woo American Indians by reversing the "termination" policies passed by the House of Representatives in 1953, policies that severed the treaty rights that the federal government established with tribal nations. With termination, tribal lands could be sold to non-Indian buyers, and Indians could be subjected to the same laws as whites. Operating under the slogan "Self-determination without termination," the Nixon administration "repudiated the policy of termination, protected tribal rights, and encouraged reservation Indians to run many federal programs for themselves."[46]

With the government's overtures to minority communities and its promotion of nationalist ideals like "self-determination," the state began to refashion itself into a structure that would partially and selectively affirm minority difference, evolving ways in which institutions could use rather than absolutely dismiss the demands of minority activists. In such a context, minority activism would be for power both a potential antagonist and a collaborator, inspiring critical transformations and new funding technologies at the same time.

In order to refashion minority difference as an opportunity for power, the state would also construct racism as an increasingly illegible phenomenon in U.S. society, the unfortunate past that was gradually receding. Indeed, in 1969 President Nixon argued, "a grave injustice has been worked out against [Indians] for a century and a half and the nation at large will appreciate our having a more active policy of concern for their plight."[47] To render racism illegible, the U.S. government would manage and incorporate the relative illegibility of minority difference and culture through administrative and financial machineries that would turn minority difference and culture into categories intelligible to the nation-state and its protocols for managing consent and elaborating systems of inequality.

In the 1960s, a new hegemonic logic of minority affirmation began to arise, one that sprung from the U.S. nation-state's efforts to deal with militants but that quickly became a mode of discipline for all minoritized subjects. Contrary to the presumption that the emergence of the student movements meant that issues of minority difference would be arrogated to minorities themselves, what we see, in fact, is the production of an assortment of subjects who would enunciate minority difference—activists, students, lawyers, artists, intellectuals, entrepreneurs, and politicians. In this time of transformation, minority difference would arise as a formation that could occupy more than one position at the same time—at one moment inhabiting academy and activism, and in that same moment residing in politics, bureaucracy, and business, all the while signaling its potential for constant use, invention, and interchange. As minority difference and culture were reconjugated into affirmative agencies, new speakers would be produced, old positions would be reinvented, and institutions would be remade. Indeed, the affirmation of minority difference and culture within the United States established a new set of relations between a vast number of distinct, odd, and often internecine elements—all of which would come together over this single but multisided issue.

As both hegemonic and radical formations conjugated minority difference into an affirmative agency, new institutional contexts would arise to accommodate minority culture and identity. As the state's interest in minority business implies, minority difference would not only transform state and academy but American capital as well. Far from being a moment of separatism, this proliferation of minority difference and culture across a variety of formations began a period in which cats and dogs would anxiously reside on the same bit of land.

The Political Economy of Minority Difference in the Revolution of Global Capital

U.S. capital's turn toward minority difference and culture partook of two historic formations taking place in the 1960s—the emergence of the student movements and the reconsideration of Taylorism and Fordism's emphases on hierarchy and conformity. Discussing the ideologies that constituted Taylorism and Fordism, Grace Hong writes, "Taylor's 'Scientific Management' and Henry Ford's assembly line aimed to produce an undifferentiated, homogenous worker whose embodied, human differences and particularities [were] foreclosed in the workplace."[48] Reconsidering Taylorism and Fordism was an essential turning point for power's affirmation of minority difference and culture, a turning point achieved within the corridors of capital itself.

In *The Conquest of Cool: Business Culture, Counterculture, and the Rise of Hip Consumerism,* for instance, business and cultural historian Thomas Frank argues that, contrary to the popular and academic assumption that American business in the sixties recoiled from the attacks of emerging countercultural movements, many in the corporate world saw those movements as an affirmation of their own frustrations about corporate culture. Frank states that the counterculture was, for many in American corporations, a "hopeful sign, a symbolic ally in their own struggles against the mountains of dead-weight procedure and hierarchy that had accumulated over the years."[49] To rebel against procedure and hierarchy, the American corporate world became interested in the youth revolution not as a means to topple capital but as "a comrade in [corporate] struggles to revitalize American business and the consumer order generally."[50] Describing the shift from

Taylorism to counterculture, Frank states: "If American capitalism can be said to have spent the 1950s dealing in conformity and consumer fakery, during the decade that followed, it would offer the public authenticity, individuality, difference, and rebellion."[51]

Capital's rendezvous with "authenticity, individuality, difference, and rebellion" lies partly in the epistemic pressures that took place within capital itself, pressures brought about by American business's own "organic intellectuals." For example, in 1960, management professor and former president of Antioch College Douglas McGregor published *The Human Side of Enterprise*. McGregor's book had an enormous impact on business management and attempted to inaugurate a management practice that would be an absolute rejection of Taylorist models. The book represented Taylorism as "Theory X," which held that the best way to motivate workers was through coercion and supervision by an immediate hierarchical power. As an alternative to Theory X's insistence on standardization, regulation, and hierarchy, McGregor proposed "Theory Y," which suggested that the most ideal way to achieve productivity was by affirming and recognizing worker ingenuity and uniqueness. McGregor's thesis was so popular that it was taken up in numerous sectors of the corporate world and became the urtext for later publications about business management and leadership.

One such publication was *Up the Organization*. Inspired in part by McGregor's *The Human Side of Enterprise,* Avis Rent-a-Car executive Robert Townsend would write "the characteristic business text of 1970,"[52] *Up the Organization: How to Stop the Corporation from Stifling People and Strangling Profits*. In that text, Townsend crusaded for Theory Y and blasted Theory X exemplar Alfred Sloan who, in his 1963 book *My Years with General Motors*, boasted of GM's participation in various U.S. wars and summed up GM's role in national defense by saying, "General Motors will no doubt continue to play a prominent role in the national defense program. Should we be called upon, we stand ready to be of service to national defense to the maximum."[53] By critiquing Sloan, Townsend not only pointed to capital's investment in the war machinery of the twentieth century, he also identified and elaborated capital's emergent capacity to critique its own hegemonic practices. Identifying and elaborating this capacity meant that Townsend's book would seek inspiration from the anticolonial and national liberation movements of the day. Indeed, *Up the Organization* is both business text and homage to those radical times.

As a symbol of the book's investment in capital's immanent critique and national liberation movements, Townsend wrote the introduction of the book as a memorandum but reworked that memorandum form, turning it into an antibureaucratic document. Making the subject of the "memorandum" "How to Use *Up the Organization*," he wrote, "Two solutions confront each of us: Solution One is the cop out: you can decide that what is must be inevitable; grab your share of the cash and fringes; and comfort yourself with the distractions called leisure. Solution Two is *nonviolent guerilla warfare.*"[54] By this, Townsend recommended, "start dismantling our organizations where we're serving them, leaving only the parts where they're serving us. It will take millions of such *subversives* to make much difference."[55] For him, *Up the Organization* was "about Solution Two," and the book was "for those who have the courage, the humor, and the energy to make a non-monster company, or a non-monster piece of a monster company, operate as if people were human."[56]

Recalling the nonviolent social movements of Gandhi and King as well as the guerrilla tactics of the Vietcong, Townsend addresses American capital as an entity constituted by histories of imperial exploitation and racial domination *and* as a formation that can potentially assess and reject the legacies of those histories. As a book that attempted an immanent critique of capital, *Up the Organization* helped to set the conditions for how capital would absorb revolutionary movements.

Absorbing those movements meant that capital would use them to reorganize its most fundamental assumptions. For instance, in a chapter titled "People," Townsend argues on behalf of the affective results of Theory Y for corporations: "The only excuse for organization is to maximize the chance that each one, working with others, will get for growth in his job... You can create a climate in which most of your people will motivate themselves to help the company reach its objectives."[57] Framing Theory Y within movements for revolutionary change and liberation, Townsend invokes Ho Chi Minh as a symbol against the repression of Theory X proponents: "Theory Y is the explanation for Ho Chi Minh's unbelievable twenty-five-year survival against the mighty blasts of the Theory X monsters of three nations."[58] Townsend thus casts the United States, France, and Japan as Theory X juggernauts in kinship with Taylorism and Fordism. As an alternative capitalist formation, Theory Y, for Townsend, was part of a new and revolutionary brotherhood that included national liberation movements.

Like *The Human Side of Enterprise, Up the Organization* was attempting to initiate a capitalist revolution organized around the de-alienation of managerial labor, seeing this project as part of the efforts of people in the Third World to throw off the yoke of colonial disfranchisement.

In the conventional narrative of the sixties, capital was a space of a numbing homogeneity and stasis, the very antithesis of the diversity and dynamism of youth culture. Noting this assumption, Frank writes: "[Whether] the narrators of the sixties story are conservatives or radicals, they tend to assume that business represented a static, unchanging body of faiths, goals, and practices, a background of muted, uniform gray against which the counterculture went through its colorful chapters."[59] This narrative informs us that state and capital are monolithic and unmoving entities that are geared primarily toward the repression of minority difference and the communities that it produces. This conventional account of radicalisms that transgress and hegemonies that recoil mobilizes the sixties to produce a repressive hypothesis that locates hegemonic power only within the work of repression. But capital's investment in social movements compels us to rebut this repressive hypothesis because it cannot help us appreciate the role that minority difference played in the transformation of power. Indeed, in the following section, we will see how the advertising industry in the United States engaged minority difference to establish new global marketing campaigns and in doing so demonstrated minority difference's potential for animating global enterprises.

Advertising Minority Difference across the Globe: McCann-Erickson

In "The Local and the Global," Stuart Hall argues that a "new globalization" characterized by a direct engagement with local differences was dominated by mass advertising, television, and entertainment. To appreciate this new globalization and its engagement with local difference, we can turn to the history of the world-renowned McCann-Erickson advertising agency. Even as advertising agencies were caricatured as "slow-moving, WASPy, and serious,"[60] McCann-Erickson would become a symbol of hipness and difference by the late 1960s. Formed in 1902, McCann-Erickson became the leading agency in global advertising, opening markets in Europe in the late 1920s, in Latin America in the 1930s, and in Asia and the Pacific by the 1950s.[61] McCann-Erickson would in many ways pioneer contemporary globalization's interest in the "new exotica"[62] and make minority difference a hallmark of post–World War II capital.

In fact, in the second half of the forties, McCann-Erickson would begin to coordinate multinational accounts, signaling the emergence of global advertising. By the sixties, "[multicountry] marketing and advertising [would become] more deliberated and controlled" at McCann-Erickson, a maneuver that involved "geographic expansion," "global account strategy," and creativity," properties that were to be embodied in the international ad man.[63] The ad man's job was to integrate McCann-Erickson's "approaches and formats for global advertising" with the international interests of clients such as Gillette, Nestlé, Goodyear Tire and Rubber, and Coca-Cola, interests that covered countries throughout Europe, Latin America, and Asia. Through this figure, McCann-Erickson would achieve global advertising formats by pondering possible relationships between local cultures and global representations. To do so, the ad man would ask himself, "How do you achieve a family look for a company's world-wide advertising and still fulfill local needs?"[64] Ad men answered that question by coming up with themes and concepts that would resonate universally *and* locally. For Goodyear, that theme was "safety." For Coca-Cola, the theme was "Things Go Better with Coke," followed by the 1969 launch of "It's the Real Thing." In other words, the international ad man was responsible for producing themes and images that would, in Stuart Hall's words, "[speak] across languages" in very immediate ways.[65]

Speaking across linguistic frontiers was not only achieved visually but aurally as well, an achievement captured in the notion of "One sight, one sound." Discussing this notion, its use of music, and its relationship to Coca-Cola in particular, a McCann-Erickson company newsletter stated:

> "One Sight" indicates that wherever an advertisement for Coca-Cola appears, it will bear a strong "family" resemblance to every other advertisement for Coca-Cola. Each varies as the requirements of a particular medium dictate; but all are related by certain basic and universally repeated elements . . . The "One Sound" concept assures that advertising for Coca-Cola will have a familiar ring no matter where it meets the ear. The music for the new jingle was composed with two objectives in mind. First it had to give appropriate musical support to the

words themselves. Secondly, the music had to achieve an individuality of its own which would enable it to carry a refreshing message reminiscent of Coca-Cola even when it was heard without words.[66]

With "One Sight, One Sound," ad men could balance global circulation with local resonance. Through the concept, advertising agencies were surpassing the conventional strictures of homogeneity and instead achieving standardization and diversity at the same time. "One Sight, One Sound" became a calculus for deriving a company's identity from an advertisement that was designed to capture the particular tastes, interests, and comprehension of a local setting. As a notion designed to tap into local systems of intelligibility, "One Sight, One Sound" mediated the emerging imperatives of global capital and the cultural particularities of local terrains.

But "One Sight, One Sound" would achieve a new scope as international ad men applied it to the student movements and inadvertently helped to affirm minority difference as an emergent system of hegemonic possibility. It all happened when international ad man Bill Backer was sent on a business trip to London in 1971. Backer was in charge of the Coca-Cola account and responsible for "It's the Real Thing," the international jingle and advertising campaign for Coca-Cola in 1969. On this trip to London, Backer was supposed to meet up with former Four Tops member and record executive turned McCann-Erickson ad man Billy Davis. Backer and Davis planned to write radio commercials for Coca-Cola. But because of dense fog in London, Backer's plane had to be redirected to Shannon, Ireland. There, Backer saw formerly bickering passengers soften to one another over bottles of Coke. Remembering the experience, Backer observes:

> In that moment, [I] began to see a bottle of Coca-Cola as more than a drink . . . [I] began to see the familiar words, "Let's have a Coke," as a subtle way of saying, "Let's keep each other company for a while." And [I] knew they were said all over the world as [I] sat there in Ireland. So that was the basic idea: to see Coke not as it was originally designed to be—a liquid refresher—but as a tiny bit of commonality between all peoples, a *universally liked formula* that would help to keep them company for a few minutes.[67]

About the international significance of the moment, Backer said, "I could see and hear a song that treated the whole world as if it were a person—

a person the singer would like to help and get to know. I'm not sure how the lyric should start, but I know the last line." As the tale goes, he took out a napkin and scribbled these words: "I'd like to buy the world a Coke and keep it company."[68]

When Backer arrived in London, he told Davis and the British song-writer Roger Cook, who was also part of the Coca-Cola radio assignment, about his idea "to buy the world a Coke and keep it company." But Davis was not keen on the idea, particularly the bit about what the world needed was a soft drink: "Well, if I could do something for everybody in the world," he said, "it would not be to buy them a Coke . . . I'd buy everyone a home first and share with them in peace and love."[69] To that Backer responded in the affirmative, "Okay, that sounds good. Let's write that, and I'll show you how Coke *fits right into the concept.*"[70]

The song they created came only after fits and starts, but it would even-tually evolve into one of the most famous commercials in advertising his-tory, becoming so influential that the Library of Congress enshrines it by saying, "through the enduring popularity of this ad . . . Coke has borne out something of Backer's ambitious claims for it, becoming a common connection among people."[71] The commercial begins with a close-up of a young white woman who starts the first line of the song: "I'd like to buy the world a home and furnish it with love." After that, the camera reveals a crowd of other young people differentiated by race, gender, and nation-ality. Following the white girl, they sing:

> Grow apple trees and honey bees, and snow white turtle doves.
> I'd like to teach the world to sing in perfect harmony,
> I'd like to buy the world a Coke and keep it company.
> It's the real thing, what the world wants today.

As the camera pans the multicultural crowd of young people standing on this hillside in Italy, it is apparent that what they share in common—across racial, cultural, and national differences—is Coca-Cola. The young peo-ple—dubbed the "First United Chorus of the World"[72]—hold the bottles of Coke as if they were the flags of some international federation. The com-mercial ends with an aerial view of the young people gathered on a hilltop, seeming to signify the Coca-Cola Company's expanded horizon and global jurisdiction. In one fell swoop the commercial manages to represent the various feminist, peace, antiracist, and anticolonial movements, bringing them together through the universalizing potential of a commodity.

The ad represents a convergence of advertising's global transformation with the emergent and international legibility of student activism. Moreover, the Hilltop ad crystallizes a global mass culture that, in the words of Stuart Hall, "wants to recognize and absorb those differences within the larger, overarching framework of what is essentially an American conception of the world," becoming part of a strategic situation organized around the management of difference and heterogeneity.[73] As the commercial and its history suggest, power was attempting to achieve a new strategic situation in which student activism and the broad assertions of minority difference could be mobilized for the extension rather than the curtailment of hegemony. The commercial would therefore become part of a developing lineage of hegemonic affirmation, a bloodline that could boast of such ancestors as the American academy's engagement with minority difference, the Nixon administration's flirtation with black power, and American advertising's courtship with counterculture.

As it was brought into the public sphere, minority difference would achieve new forms of positivity in this historic moment, forms of positivity inspired by the social movements themselves. Discussing how the "song culture" of the civil rights movement, for instance, helped to bring minority culture to the attention of the United States and the world, historian and former Student Nonviolent Coordinating Committee (SNCC) freedom singer Bernice Johnson Reagon states: "All the established academic categories in which I had been educated fell apart during this period, revealing culture to be not luxury, not leisure, not entertainment but the lifeblood of a community."[74] Here Reagon invokes the civil rights movement as the context in which minority culture would become a relay for all sorts of social formations during the 1960s. In this context, the Beat generation would engage African American vernacular to challenge mass culture while singers and songwriters would use indigenous American folk traditions to stand against commercialism.[75]

But the movements did not simply make culture available to people like Jack Kerouac, Allen Ginsberg, and Peter, Paul, and Mary; what students, artists, and everyday folk did would be of interest to hegemony as well. While minority culture was—in movement terms—the "lifeblood of a community," it was the lifeblood of an emergent form of capital coming of age through social agitation. As the counterculture impacted McCann-Erickson and other advertising agencies, a new strategic use of minority culture would provide the conditions for the emergence and success of an industry-defining enterprise like Motown Records. As Motown historian Suzanne E. Smith argues, "[The] civil rights movement created the environment in which broader cultural integration—as typified by Motown's wide appeal—could occur."[76]

The antiracist and feminist movements of the sixties and seventies created the conditions for changes in television programming as well. Kirsten Marthe Lentz, for instance, argues that *The Mary Tyler Moore Show, Rhoda, Phyllis,* and *The Betty White Show* demonstrate that "1970s television, far from distancing itself from feminism, adopted a position of proximity to it, using feminist logics to improve [television's] own modes of self-representation."[77] Other shows would come along and make plain the broad influence of the student movements as well. Indeed, *All in the Family, Good Times, The Jeffersons,* and *Sanford and Son* would translate student movement demands for greater societal representation of gender and racial minorities into programming that would simultaneously boost ratings and boast of a "new sense of responsibility to the public."[78] The changes in television programming further illustrate just how broad power's new strategic situation really was, enlisting government, business, and media.

While Lumumba-Zapata and numerous other student groups had articulated an oppositional relationship to academy, state, and capital, a new strategic situation was developing that would attempt to turn the critiques of the student movements into the hegemonic maneuvers of American institutions. Indeed, the history of the student movements reveals that it was not only protest and agitation that developed the social capacities of minority culture. Beginning in the sixties, state and capital would help shape those capacities as well. In that moment a new situation for power was emerging in which minority difference and our consciousness of it would be part of political economy's historical development, a moment in which oppositional forces and hegemonic institutions would take minority difference and disperse it in all directions, providing the conditions for an epoch struggle over the meanings and uses of things once too minor to care about.

The American '68 and the Rearticulation of Value

If the official European '68 represented the triumph of a narrative that obscured histories of antiracist struggle, then the American '68 seemed to represent both the oppositional *and* hegemonic assertion of racial difference and minority culture. In his 2008 installation "Unbranded: Reflections in Black by Corporate America from 1968 to 2008," visual artist Hank Willis Thomas reflects on the hegemonic affirmations of the American '68. The installation was part of the High Museum of Art's 2008 exhibition in Atlanta, an exhibition titled "After 1968: Contemporary Artists and the Civil Rights Legacy." About "Unbranded" Thomas states: "For this series I have appropriated ads from popular periodicals of the past forty years, choosing two examples from each year and digitally removing all of the advertising text, revealing what Roland Barthes calls 'what-goes-without-saying.'"[79] Referencing Barthes, "Unbranded" asks the viewer to confront how '68 was a moment in which blackness went through not only a powerful politicization but a depoliticization as well. Indeed, Barthes discusses this depoliticization as part of mythmaking, as a process in which things are not denied but talked about to the point of simplification and purification. Elaborating on his theorization of mythmaking, Barthes argues that myth "abolishes the complexity of human acts, [giving] them the simplicity of essences, [doing] away with all dialectics, with any going back beyond what is immediately visible, [organizing] a world which is without contradictions because it is without depth, a world wide open and wallowing in the evident."[80] "Unbranded" suggests that what was previously inadmissible in corporate and advertising culture of the Fordist era became the increasingly desirable object of American capital in the moments of '68. Moreover, the installation points to how a form of racial difference was depoliticized, becoming the footman for capital rather than its adversary.

We can situate "Unbranded," partly, within pop art traditions of the late 1960s. In 1956, for example, Allison and Peter Smithson, architects and members of the Independent Group (IG), published "But Today We Collect Ads." The Independent Group was a coterie of sculptors, painters, writers, critics, and architects in Britain who introduced mass culture into discussions of art and architecture. The Smithsons' essay expressed IG ideals by arguing that pop art was achieving a status equal to fine art. They wrote, for instance, that "ads are packed with information—data of a way of life and a standard of living which they are simultaneously inventing and documenting."[81] For the Smithsons, ads were discursive units that not only registered the social world but developed it as well. They underlined this sentiment and its relationship to mass culture: "Mass-production advertising is establishing our whole pattern of life—principles, morals, aims, aspirations, and standard of living."[82]

"Unbranded" develops the claims of the Smithsons' essay by assembling ads that feature black people, styles, and vernaculars, collecting them to illustrate how mass culture was turning to minority difference in the 1960s, turning to it as a way to establish a standard of living ordered around an explicit engagement with minority culture. "Unbranded" also recalls 1960s pop art as a medium that—in Kobena Mercer's words—responded "to the cycle of modernisation that introduced mass consumerism, youth culture, and anti-establishment attitudes into the mainstream of western capitalist democracies."[83] As "[pop] encouraged audiences to look again at everyday images that were mostly overlooked on account of their 'ordinariness,'"[84] "Unbranded" mobilizes pop imagery to inspire investigations of how capital in the sixties and onwards was so roused by marginal cultures and anti-establishment movements that it would resolve to make black minority difference one of the principles of mass culture.

In addition to having roots in pop art, "Unbranded" is also part of what art critic Hal Foster calls the "archival impulse" in contemporary art. Describing such work, Foster says, "the work is archival since it not only draws on informal archives but produces them as well. Further it often arranges these materials according to a quasi-archival logic, a matrix of citation and juxtaposition, and presents them in a quasi-archival architecture, a complex of texts and objects."[85] As an archival project, "Unbranded" points the viewer to how contemporary capital has produced an archive of black cultural and racial difference. Moreover, "Unbranded" asks the viewer to reflect on capital's archival practice by illuminating the matrix of capital's own interest in black culture. "Unbranded," therefore, compels the viewer to confront the fact that we recognize black cultural difference as part of corporate culture even when the visible markers of that affiliation have been removed. Hence, it goes without saying that these photographs of black culture are advertisements as well. Demonstrating the links between the direction of advertising and interest in black culture, "Unbranded" attempts to mobilize the viewer's awareness of capital's affirmation of black culture as a means to question capital's integration with minority difference.

As a pop and archival installation, the series cites advertisements for hair and skin-care products, shoes, slacks, stockings, underwear, movies, automobiles, cigarettes, airlines, McDonald's, jeans, gasoline, food, liquor, breath mints, and more. Rather than concentrate on a single advertisement, "Unbranded" observes dozens of ads as a way to underline capital's rolling attention to all things black. In doing so, the series suggests that capital did not retreat from marginality and heterogeneity at all; instead, capital was investing in those very formations.

Discussing the ways in which corporate capital absorbed the critiques of the European '68, Tim Griffin argues that contributors for the special issue of *Art Forum* "repeatedly underline the ways in which the very creative models and concepts that propelled '68—from the flexible, structuralist thought underlying institutional critique . . . to the pedagogical endeavors presenting viable alternatives to social bureaucratization . . . ; from principles of individual autonomy steeped in aestheticism . . . to applied ideas of difference . . . are now threads in the vast fabric of commerce and industry."[86] Similarly, Thomas's "Unbranded" also critiques the ways in which American capital absorbed the creative models and concepts emerging from the U.S. social movements. But "Unbranded" underlines a crucial element that was relatively neglected in the European context but thoroughly poked and probed in the American setting—minority culture.

For example, there is an ad in "Unbranded" from 1968 that captures the simultaneous interest in U.S. social movements and black culture. The ad features a group of young black men and women wearing jeans ranging from deep denim to pastel blues and pinks and wildly patterned shirts that are just as colorful.

Despite their very hip attire, the young African Americans are congregated on a sidewalk littered with trash and crates that some of them use for stools. What goes without saying is that this is an advertisement for jeans that mobilizes the images of the peace movement and the familiar image of black urbanism. While the image in the series is unmarked, Willis's Web site attributes the ad to Levi's and notes that the advertisement is aptly titled "The Oft-Forgotten Black Flower Children of Harlem."[87] The ad implies that Levi's—and, by extension, capital—will reveal and celebrate those

Hank Willis Thomas, "The Oft-Forgotten Black Flower Children of Harlem,"
1969/2006. Digital C-print, 34 x 27.5 inches. HWT06.016. Courtesy of the artist
and Jack Shainman Gallery, New York.

hybrid elements of African American culture, detailing how that culture
intersects with other countercultural formations.

As "The Oft-Forgotten Black Flower Children of Harlem" and the other
images in "Unbranded" suggest, American capital was studiously relaxing
its dependence on a conventional mode of abstraction responsible for capitalist exchange, circulation, and valorization, a mode that would abstract

particularity and difference. Indeed, "Unbranded" points to how minority difference was beginning to revolutionize the very nature of exchange value. According to Marx, exchange value suggests an illusory quality that presumably inheres within the commodity itself. He says that the exchange value of the commodity is what accounts for the "mystical character of the commodity," how it "transcends sensuousness, . . . [evolving] out of its brain grotesque ideas far more wonderful than if it were to begin dancing of its own free will."[88] As the commodity transcends sensuousness, it attempts to hide its "real" and "objective nature" from the consumer, that real and objective nature known as the history of abstract labor.[89] Pointing further to the constitutive nature of labor for the commodity's value, Marx states, "The determination of the magnitude of value by labour-time is therefore a secret hidden under the apparent movements in the relative values of commodities."[90]

But if we take Thomas's "Unbranded" to be a history of commodities, we are confronted with the curious exchange values of black hair-care products that promise to make your hairdo right, hip new jeans that shine in funky colors, and ground beef sold in the language of the street. These products and their values turn us to the history of the very social movements that rearticulated minority difference in the first place rather than to the presumably abstract history of labor. As an archive of capital's rearticulation of black culture, the ads redirect us to a new strategic situation, an emerging mode of power that was trying to use the social movements of the sixties and seventies to reimagine minority difference and put it to ample use. If rearticulation was, as Omi and Winant suggest, the "labor" of those social movements, then the products of that "labor"—the evolving meanings of race and gender—would become capital's new domain of articulation.

In terms of capital, the sixties encounter with minority culture was nothing less than the period in which new secrets were injected into the commodity form, secrets that reveal not only the history and time of labor but the history and time of student protests as well. During that time, companies would recalibrate exchange value so that the value of the commodity would be gauged in terms of its potential equivalence not only to other commodities but also to principles asserted by student-led social movements. American capital would begin to use the revolutions of the sixties and seventies to suggest to consumers that they were buying ideals such as safety, hipness, and difference when they bought products, and therefore participating in revolutions that did not antagonize capital but presumed it. Another way of observing this phenomenon would be to say that if—as Hong puts it—"the fetishization of difference" came to characterize capital in the post-Fordist era, then the genealogy for that fetishization lies in capital's employment of social movement aims and principles.

In such a context, state and capital's campaign for a new legibility would not be based only on the suppression of minority difference but also on its selective activation. This campaign was quite different from other conquests of illegibility in that it did not seek to impose the same universal standard that everyone had become so familiar with. Capital and state's operation did not presume that anthropologization that Foucault talks about in *The Archaeology of Knowledge,* an anthropologization that took man as history's lead character and sovereign consciousness, the character who would time and again look down on difference. It was also not the development of a false consciousness about the meanings of minority cultures and histories. If "false consciousness" assumes a contrast between the real meaning of minority difference and how that difference is put into practice, then what we have in this moment is a period in which the various ideas about minority difference and culture would put a variety of practices into play.[91] Sometimes minority difference would be hegemonic; at other times it would be oppositional; many times it would be both. Each profile would be available for articulation, and neither one would be "false."

Europe may have regarded minority difference as an element external to its borders and history, as that which its subjects were told to ignore, dismiss, and extinguish. But in the United States, power would not instruct spectators to look away from minority difference and its contradictions. There, power would say to viewers far and wide, "This is what minority difference is. Come quick and see." As the commercials, advertisements, television shows, billboard hits, and political strategies of that moment suggest, power was maturing a simultaneously affirmative and regulatory agenda, a plan that was not a wholesale turn away from difference but a *discriminating* turn toward it. This strategic situation was not the typical disciplinary ordeal that most had become used to; it was an *interdisciplinary* experience that took minorities as crucial cast members of a "hegemonic" saga, a saga over whether subjects would give their consent to the institutions of state, academy, and capital.

Minority difference, as a mode of reorganization, would permeate all spheres of activity within the United States. It would be a mode that yielded contradictory articulations. Formations like Lumumba-Zapata would rearticulate minority difference as a way to achieve new forms of access, critique, and community while a new strategic situation would rearticulate forms of difference as a means to expand what institutions could claim as their own. The college was approved as Third College rather than the name that the students intended, but, as Mariscal notes, "between 1970 to 1972 . . . [it] was a bold experiment in multiracial organizing and the democratic reform of higher education."[92] The College's black and Chicano alumni would remember that coalition as a grand agreement to begin to trust one another; the first dean of the college would talk about it as "the creation of a learning community that [was] concerned with the process of continual growth—where there is an effort to probe and to search for better ways of living for all human beings, particularly those formerly left out altogether."[93]

But the UCSD administration would ensure that this multiracial experiment—at least as the students intended it—would come to an end. As Mariscal notes, the university attempted to drive a wedge in the coalition between blacks and Chicanos by appointing administrators who would use black nationalist rhetoric to speak out against antiblack racism without addressing the administrative exclusion of Chicanos in recruitment and hiring. In addition, the university began a campaign to cut back the recruitment of underrepresented students and the development of a racially diverse faculty, a campaign that would ensure that Third College would be 60 percent white by 1976.[94] Angela Davis reflects on that moment:

> We had put up a fierce struggle. Large numbers of UCSD students had experienced the radicalization that was occurring on campuses throughout the country. The university hierarchy decided, apparently, that it was best to make the concessions we were demanding, rather than risk a prolonged disruption of campus activities. To tell the truth, we had not really expected them to agree so readily to our notion of the third college. And when they did, those of us leading the movement knew that despite our victory—of which all of us were proud—Lumumba-Zapata College would never become the revolutionary institution we had originally projected.[95]

The local circumstances of UCSD illustrate a larger mode of power that was trying to determine how best to manage insurgent articulations of minority difference, without absolute suppression but through selective revision and deployment. What happened at that university just above the sea is a microcosm of the chronicles of minority difference, a chronicle of how minority difference was deployed against institutional hegemony and a report of how it was claimed by and managed within the province of institutions and thereby alienated from its originary mission.

To be sure, the repression of minoritized communities was concerted and systematic, yielding programs and institutional formations designed to quell even the possibility of revolutionary fervor. For instance, in 1968 the FBI instituted its counterintelligence program (COINTELPRO) to "neutralize militant Black nationalists."[96] Around that time, the FBI also worked to infiltrate the American Indian Movement.[97] State repression of minority communities was expressed through rapid prison expansion. As Ruth Wilson Gilmore argues, after the assassination of Martin Luther King Jr., federal and state governments responded to the rioting taking place in U.S. cities by investing monies into what would eventually become the U.S. prison-industrial complex.[98] Without question, there was a new policing of minority difference by federal, state, and local governments. But alongside that repression was a veritable explosion in the affirmation of minority difference in both grassroots and official venues. Affirmation and regulation would become bound up with one another like never before, producing minority difference as the site of a new contradiction that straddled valorization and devaluation, change and status quo, a contradiction that would become more elaborate in the years to come.

Yes, Zeus and Mnemosyne bore a tenth muse, an illegitimate child blotted out but now raised to prominence, a left-out daughter who would become a figure of contingency in the sixties and thereafter, representing the capacity of minority difference to move in the way of ruptures and hegemonies. In the next chapter we will see how new hierarchies and regulations were established through the seductions of excellence.

The Racial Genealogy of Excellence

NOT UNTIL THE YEARS AFTER WORLD WAR II would "yes" become a word attached to minority difference. Prior to that minorities would be most familiar with "no" and its many lacerations. In the decade of the sixties, however, new technologies would arise for saying "yes." One of the earliest installments in this dubious repertoire of affirmations was the category "Excellence." Somewhere amid the struggle over rights and inclusion, excellence emerged as a discourse that would try to reconcile the disqualifications of liberal democracy with the pressures of antiracism. Yet a long history of suspicion has existed in certain quarters—vernacular and erudite—of the politics of affirmations. Indeed, African American folklore tells us that another affirmation—the phrase "uh hunh"—was a term the devil made up. Given this, it should come as no surprise that the category "excellence" would incur many people's distrust as well. In this critical suspicion of excellence and the strategic formations that it presumed, the open admissions movement at City College would gain momentum.

One October morning in 1969, two hundred or so African American and Puerto Rican students would lock the South Campus gates of City College and threaten to keep them so unless the college admitted more minority students. The gates stayed closed for two weeks before the administration agreed to the students' demands, a move that would permit thousands of blacks, Puerto Ricans, and poor whites to enroll as undergraduates. The students would have a list of five demands—to build a "[separate] school of Black and Puerto Rican Studies"; to establish "a separate orientation program for Black and Puerto Rican freshman [sic]," one that would help them address "conflicting pressures arising from college and their communities"; to give disadvantaged students "a decision-making role in faculty selection, promotion, and firing"; to install new admissions practices that would mandate that student diversity reflect the diversity within Harlem; and to require "Black and Puerto Rican history and the Spanish language for all education majors."[1]

For those two weeks, a kind of critical utopia was created—Puerto Rican parents would bring "pots of rice and beans and pork and *pasteles*" and hold the gates so that the police would not come in. The students held a free breakfast program and day care for the children in the neighborhood, and political education classes would be held while the official curriculum was shut down.[2]

The board of education would respond by agreeing to establish an open admissions policy that would guarantee that every high-school graduate in New York who wished to matriculate could do so in one of the CUNY colleges. The college would be transformed from a predominantly white institution to one made up of a majority of black and brown students. Twenty years after the open admissions movement at City College, the City University of New York would graduate the largest number of black and Latino students with master's degrees, far outshining its larger sibling institution, the State University of New York. For some, open admissions would be a corruption of academic standards, and for others it would represent the democratization of higher education.

In 1967 the open admissions movement came to a young professor's attention. She had been asked to fill in and teach Freshmen Comp for a friend who needed some time to write. So, the day after her friend's request and long before she would become a renowned activist and writer, June Jordan would become a faculty member at City College. Her colleagues—Toni Cade Bambara, Barbara Christian, Addison Gayle Jr., David Henderson, Audre Lorde, Adrienne Rich, and Mina Shaughnessy—would go on to become luminaries in their own right. There at City College she would join these same colleagues and many of the young people of that institution in a struggle to make the college open to all who wished to enter. Teacher and student alike would move into history, hoping that there would be an end to days that were drylongso.

By way of history, City College was founded in 1847 as the Free Academy. Its former name was both odd and appropriate in that it gave thousands of working-class native-born and immigrant whites access to a college education, making sure that they—at least—would not be held back from freedom. This whitewashed freedom congealed so that by the 1960s, more than a hundred years after its founding, City College and its sister campuses remained predominantly white,[3] a history that would inspire African American and Puerto Rican students to shut down seventeen buildings and demand that the student body reflect the black and brown makeup of Harlem.

Its biographical details notwithstanding, the open admissions movement is significant for what it says about an emergent form of power and the critical formations that were mobilizing against it. In fact, a 1969 essay that Jordan wrote about the open admissions struggle helps to elaborate this book's account of the forms of power that arose in the moment of the social movements. Turning her attention to the historic racial formations that set the stage for the birth of the American academy and U.S. society, Jordan's essay "Black Studies: Bringing Back the Person" is an artifact that begs us to interrogate the histories of racial domination that make up the underside of excellence. Pointing to how those seemingly abstract discourses of "standards" and "excellence" were part of the racialized genealogies of colonialism, slavery, and neocolonialism, she demonstrates the ways in which the open admissions struggle marked and contested the administrative maneuvers and discourses that simultaneously solicited and excluded people of color.

Moreover, as "Black Studies: Bringing Back the Person" disinters this genealogy of necropolitics and its evolutions around power/knowledge, the essay ascribes the academy with a historical significance that—contrary to certain versions of postmarxism—cannot be reduced to universalizing narratives about capitalist economic formations. At odds with the ways in which those narratives invalidate cultural interventions, the essay and the open admissions struggle demonstrate how the intersections of race and bureaucracy are illuminated and critiqued through minority cultural production.

More pointedly, that movement's cultural production is part of an undertheorized archive, one that has much to teach us about how hegemonic power responded to minority demands and used the category "excellence" to reshape institutional engagements with minoritized subjects and knowledges. As a cultural and archival artifact, Jordan's essay illuminates the deep genealogical layers within the category "excellence," layers that go much further back than recent theorizations of the category suggest, strata accumulated by histories of racial conflict, sediments grounded in the very definition of the human. Through Jordan's essay we can see how the academy becomes a historical icon that projects a complex array of discourses around race, class, gender, ability, and sexuality. In doing so, the essay challenges the Western academy's history of disavowing colonialism and slavery as part of its institutional biography.

Inasmuch as the essay is part of an undertheorized archive, it suggests how we have yet to grapple with the implications of a mode of power that intertwines race and bureaucracy and how that mode reaches into conservative and progressive realms alike. The absence of this archive in the analysis of the contemporary university and the forms of power that occasion it beg us to consider whether we too often proceed as if we can critique institutional formations while neglecting cultural and archival ones, not realizing that they may provide the very links we need to understand how modes of difference shape institutional life and practice. A metacritical analysis of this sort demands that all of these observations be deployed at once. In the context of the open admissions struggle, for instance, "excellence" became the rubric for producing overlapping discourses about African Americans and Puerto Ricans, making City College the site whereby subjects differentiated by diverse histories of migration and racialization would engage one another. Such historic encounters—there and elsewhere—would make the American academy the place for contending with diversities produced out of the racialized contradictions of American liberal democracy and U.S. imperialism.

The Deracination of "Excellence"

Given contemporary conversations about the category "excellence"—ones that "tie the University to a . . . net of bureaucratic institutions" in the 1990s—"Black Studies: Bringing Back the Person" is a curious artifact indeed.[4] Written during the open admissions takeover, the essay situates the discourse of excellence much earlier than the end of the twentieth century, reading that discourse as part of a racial formation composed of a student movement, a university bureaucracy, and histories of racial domination. In her discussion of faculty and "Third World students who wanted to inaugurate an Open Admissions policy," for instance, Jordan argues that those opposed to open admissions believed that the policy "would catapult the university into a trough of mediocrity"[5] and "preclude *excellence*:

excellence of standards and of achievement."[6] If a concept like excellence was powerful enough to mobilize an opposition, why have contemporary discussions occluded that essay, the open admissions movement, and this story of excellence?

Part of the answer to that question lies in the framework that has been established for talking about the category. To begin with, Bill Readings's *The University in Ruins* has—more than any other book—shaped how we conceptualize discourses of excellence in and outside the contemporary Western university. Published in 1996, the book argues that excellence is the "watchword of the University" and has become its "unifying principle."[7] Readings maintains that "excellence" has become the academy's keyword because of the ways in which multinational corporations disseminate "excellence" as a standard for all practices within the university—from the management of parking services to the significance of scholarship. "As an integrating principle," he states, "excellence has the singular advantage of being entirely meaningless, or to put it more precisely, nonreferential" (22). For Readings, "excellence" can thus be applied anywhere and to anything. Its power comes not from the content that it bears but from the wide application that its lack of content affords. Excellence, he says, "functions to allow the University to understand itself solely in terms of the structure of corporate administration" (29). Hence, "excellence" is not only an ideal shared by the contemporary university and present-day corporate capital; it is the principle that defines their relation to one another.

As a principle of relation, though, Readings's use of *excellence* presumes that the academy is the simple reflection of capitalist economic formations: "[the university] is not just *like* a corporation. It *is* a corporation" (22). He states later that "Excellence serves nothing other than itself, another corporation in a world of transnationally exchanged capital" (43). As the reflection of capital, the university assumes the role that art suffered in base–superstructure arguments. Discussing that role, Raymond Williams argues in *Marxism and Literature,* "The usual consequence of the base–superstructure formula, with its specialized and limited interpretations of productive forces and the process of determination, is a description—even at times a theory—of art and thought as 'reflection.'"[8]

While "the metaphor of reflection has a long history in the analysis of art and ideas,"[9] it was dismantled years later by one poststructuralist and postmarxist critique after the other. Curiously enough, reflection attains a new viability and elaboration through Readings, not through a discussion of art but through the image of that institution where artistic and intellectual practices are so often produced—the university. The metaphor of reflection enables marxism to commit itself once again to forms of universality and abstraction that ultimately marginalize the autonomy and significance of minority difference and culture. As the category "excellence" promotes the idea that the university is the unrefuted picture of capital, this formulation fosters the notion that modes of difference that arise from interdisciplinary studies around race, gender, sexuality, and disability are simple mirages compared to the real phenomena of capitalist economic formations.

We can in fact see this notion at work in Readings's arguments about racism. He states that "racism is no longer primarily a matter of *representation;* it is a complex *economic* issue as well as a straightforward *political* one."[10] Suggesting that struggles against and analyses of racial exclusion were, once upon a time, unadulterated "matters of representation," Readings goes on to imply that—in the moment of global capital's looming significance—racism has revealed itself to be primarily the stuff of economics and politics. In such an understanding of "excellence," culture and difference become once again the symptoms of political and economic processes.

Indeed, by arguing that the university and the cultural representations thereof reflect capitalist economic formations, Readings resuscitates the reductive shortcomings of marxism. Again addressing this shortcoming through the figure of art, Williams argued that understanding material processes as simple matters of reflection only worked to suppress the "social and material character of artistic activity."[11] Similarly, by arguing that the university is simply the corporation's reflection, Readings suppresses the social and material character of cultural formations, and by relegating cultural difference to a position of insignificance and obsolescence, he underestimates the possibilities that minority culture holds both for the consolidation and for the disruption of political economy. If the academy and things academic are indeed like art, then they are not only imprinted by society; they cast their silhouettes on the social world as well. More important, if the conversation around excellence is shaped by a theorization that regards minority difference and culture as marginal, then there is little wonder that the racial itinerary of excellence and its critique in the open admissions movement would be consigned to the dustbin of history.

The Multiplicities of the American University

As an archival element, "Black Studies: Bringing Back the Person" suggests that the discourse of excellence actually arose in the racially turbulent period of the 1960s, during the postwar expansion of American higher education, the diversification of American student-body populations, and the student agitation that propelled it. Indeed, John W. Gardner's 1961 text *Excellence* was the book that popularized that category as a standard not only for education but for U.S. social practice as well. Gardner was an academic who at various points was on the faculty at Mount Holyoke, Connecticut College, and Stanford. He was also a public servant, having served on President John F. Kennedy's task force on education and as President Lyndon Johnson's secretary of health, education, and welfare.

In 1961, after serving on Kennedy's task force, he published the book *Exellence*. In it, he argued: "Our society cannot achieve greatness unless individuals at many levels of ability accept the need for high standards of performance and strive to achieve those standards within the limits possible for them."[12] With that book, Gardner was attempting to establish excellence—in Foucault's terms—as a mode of governmentality, one in which those who wished to "govern the state well must first learn to govern [themselves]."[13] As Gardner argued, "We want the highest conceivable excellence, of course, in the activities crucial to our effectiveness and creativity as a society; but that isn't enough." Emphasizing the need for a pervasive distribution of that standard, he went on to state, "We must foster a conception of excellence that may be applied to every degree of ability and to every socially acceptable activity . . . The tone and fiber of our society depend upon a pervasive, almost universal striving for good performance."[14]

For Gardner, excellence would be a mode of agency for every individual, but one calibrated according to the particular abilities of that individual. Understood as such, excellence presumed not just a diversity of abilities but an *inequality* among abilities, a presumption that arose in the context of social agitation. Gardner, as communication studies scholar Laurie Ouellette notes, "was the first to concede that those who actually achieve excellence will be few at best." Discussing his belief in the hierarchy of abilities and his insistence on equality of opportunity, Ouellette goes on to say, "[The] meritocracy he envisioned was a competitive business . . . [The] Great Society would still be a pyramid with a limited number of spaces at the top."[15] And as Wilson Smith and Thomas Bender note about Gardner's text, "The major theme of educational excellence in the post-*Sputnik* years was increasingly posited in a sometimes tense relation to egalitarian social pressures of the 1960s."[16] Within the discourse of excellence, deliberating on ability was a way of promoting national distinction while anxiously negotiating with increasingly visible and insurgent minority populations.

As the category that emerged within the context of powerful social pressures to diversify student-body populations, excellence would also become a principle for engaging the demands of minoritized constituencies. In the civil rights era, the question of minority difference and American democracy was posed in every sphere of American society and presented as a problem that might inhibit distinction and greatness. In fact, Gardner's text led official responses to that question, becoming "the most widely read delineation of this cultural problem in the American democracy."[17] Indeed, Gardner saw the principle of excellence as the medium between two extremes. "People calling most noisily for quality in education" characterized one extreme, and "fanatics who believe that the chief goal for higher education should be to get as many youngsters as possible—regardless of ability into college classrooms" represented the other.[18] Gardner theorized excellence as the principle that would mediate this contention between racialized understandings of "quality education" and what in the language of City College was called "open admissions." In sum, excellence arose out of the interface between academy and federal government, an interface that was motivated by minority difference, and Gardner's book would launch excellence as a standard for state and civil society, promoting it as a principle that would help to determine the character of social and subject formations alike, fostering it as a technology of power that would target both institutional and personal horizons.

Another text arose out of the historic intersection between academy and federal government and within the "egalitarian social pressures of the 1960s." Shortly after the publication of *Excellence,* the former chancellor of UC Berkeley and former president of the University of California Clark Kerr published his 1963 text *The Uses of the University.* Similar to Gardner, Kerr would write, "'How to preserve a margin of excellence' in an increasingly egalitarian society has become a most intense issue."[19] At the same time, Kerr argued that the American university was attaining unprecedented significance because "[we] are just now perceiving that the university's invisible *product,* knowledge, may be the most powerful single element in our culture, affecting the rise and fall of professions and even of social classes, of regions and even of nations" (xiv; emphasis added).

For Kerr, the intensity of the issue lay in the fact that the university's status as the manufacturer of this "invisible product" was not entirely synchronized with its position as the incubator of social change and minority liberation. The state's new racial project was occasioned by what Kerr dubbed the "two great new forces of the 1960's," that is, "the federal government and protesting students" (99). During that period, the federal government became the main granting agency of American research universities. Moreover, its financial technologies became the strategies for a new and more affirmative racial project and mode of power. As Kerr states, "The federal government emphasized science and research, equality of opportunity, impartiality of treatment among the races, and the innovative role of the federal agency" (ibid.). The state, because of student protests, was both changing its racial character and evolving a new relationship with American research universities, one that was attempting to make the goals of research standards and excellence consistent with demands for a more integrated society. Said another way, federal grants would become the first genre of funding technologies used to reconcile the commodification of knowledge with the assertions of diversity. That reconciliation would call for both research innovation and "equality of opportunity." The American university would, therefore, help to innovate a new horizon of interpellation, one that would socialize the state's financial resources according to a new racial project around equality and antidiscrimination, making the law and funding the dominant purview of antiracist resolution. With the publications of *Excellence* and *The Uses of the University,* the American academy was fast becoming the hub of a knowledge-based economy, the center of discussions around minority difference and democracy, and the laboratory that might integrate those two institutional identities.

This was not the first time in which the state used the American academy to foster the state's racial project. Indeed, we can see the academy functioning as a facilitator of the state's racial vision in the nineteenth century. For instance, with the emergence of the land-grant movement in the 1840s, the American academy was used to uplift poor and working-class whites for the good of an industrializing agricultural economy. About the land-grant movement and the eventual passage of the Land Grant College Act, formerly known as the Morrill Act of 1862, Kerr wrote: "The land grant movement brought schools of agriculture and engineering . . . , of home economics and business administration" (12). As it widened the academic horizon to the professions, the land-grant movement opened professional terrains to "the children of [white] farmers and workers, as well as of the middle and upper classes" (ibid.). The land-grant movement also "introduced agricultural experiment stations and service bureaus" (ibid.). The historian Allen Nevins voiced what has become the established sentiment about the Morrill Act of 1862: "The law annexed wide neglected areas to the domain of instruction. Widening the gates of opportunity, it made democracy freer, more adaptable and more kinetic" (ibid.). Yet freedom, adaptability, and kinesis would be arrogated to whites and withheld from blacks and Native Americans, demonstrating the racialized foundations of academy's partnership with state and economy. More pointedly, the land-grant movement elaborated the state's racialized contradictions between freedom for some and unfreedom for others and assisted in the development of a white professional class necessary for a changing economy.

Architects of the Morrill Act of 1862 designated the professions as the disciplinary curriculum appropriate for industrialization and its potential benefit for the social and economic advancement of white working-class youth and families. The professional (i.e., white subject) who would become the academic ideal of that act would thus be the fully industrialized alternative to the unlettered slave who hailed from a plantation-based economy. In contrast to the disgraceful diversity produced by slavery, the land-grant movement would usher in a more respectable class diversity organized around the professional expansion of white working-class families and households. As Christopher Newfield notes, the Morrill Act "gave a new and lasting momentum to the idea of college education for a growing middle class," occasioning the founding of the University of Illinois (1867), the University of California (1868), and Cornell University (1865).[20] The development of the professions was thus part of a larger racial project designed to uplift white working-class families as the new symbols of professional endowment for a new industrializing democracy.

It was obvious that the Morrill Act of 1862 would not cover all the costs of building new institutions. It was also apparent that Southern states were not going to cooperate with the federal government's efforts to establish land-grant institutions for African Americans under the Morrill Act of 1862. So, in 1890, Congress passed a second Morrill Act as a way to coerce Southern states into either admitting African Americans to predominantly white institutions or building separate institutions for African Americans altogether. Congress did so by stipulating that the use of federal funds would have these conditions tied to them. Out of the Morrill Act of 1890, sixteen African American institutions were established throughout the South.[21] We might think of the second Morrill Act as an attempt to resolve the tension between racial hierarchy and democracy in ways that were consistent with the state's new racial project—segregation. The act helped to produce a "separate but equal" doctrine at the level of higher education, making college campuses simultaneously the incubators for racial and class cleavages.

In many ways the rise of the land-grant institutions and the institutionalization of teaching, research, and professional training are the beginning of the American academy's project of "excellence." As such, the Morrill Acts sought to professionalize white and minoritized subjects so that they conformed to the ideal of professional, scientific, and humanistic service to the nation and so that they embodied national principles of uplift and respectability. The academy would become the place to model and inspire uplift within a larger context of social disfranchisement. The Morrill Acts, particularly the 1890 one, would help designate the American university as the location to resolve national contradictions over the inclusion and exclusion of minoritized subjects. A discourse of excellence, whether implicit, as in the periods of the Civil War or Reconstruction periods, or explicit, as in the days of civil rights, has always been a means of producing a partnership between state, capital, and academy, a partnership that took as a principal task that of negotiating the racial diversity within the United States. As a way of engaging diversity, excellence would ingratiate minorities by making ability not only a standard of incorporation but a mode of surveillance, exclusion, and measurement, one that Jordan would decry—along with other ideals such as "efficiency" and "competence"—as a "deadly, neutral" word.

Excellence and the Alienation of the People

One of the ways Jordan summarized the "deadly" and "neutral" aspect of excellence was by demonstrating how it rendered black and Puerto Rican students as the antithesis of standards and achievement. In doing so, she pointed to the constant tension between a discourse of excellence and the figure of the people, a tension that persisted even as excellence was erected to reconcile the goal of state distinction with the demands of minority communities. We can locate the history of this tension again within *The Conflict of the Faculties*.

In that text, Kant touched on the function of the people in the discourses of state and academy. Claiming the academy as a site for best articulating how to represent the people and provide for its welfare, he wrote: "Now the faculties engage in public conflict in order to influence the people, and each can acquire this influence only by convincing the people that it knows best how to promote their welfare."[22] The lower and higher faculties, according to Kant, cannot promote the people's welfare without regulating them. The people do not understand their welfare in terms of freedom "but as [the realization] of their natural ends and so as these three things: being *happy* after death, having their *possessions* guaranteed by public laws during their life in society, and finally, looking forward to the physical enjoyment of *life* itself (that is, health and a long life)" (49). The lower faculty can help the people realize these goals only through the mutually constitutive principles of freedom, reason, and self-regulation or, as he put it, "[living] righteously, committing no injustice, and by being moderate in [their] pleasures and patient in [their] illnesses" (ibid.).

But, according to Kant, the people are not naturally inclined toward this kind of freedom and "self-exertion" (ibid.). They are more apt to follow the less demanding requirements of the higher faculties:

> For the people naturally adhere most to doctrines which demand the least self-exertion and the least use of their own reason, and which can best accommodate their duties to their inclinations—in theology, for example, the doctrine that they can be saved merely by an implicit faith, without having to examine (or even really know) what they are supposed to believe, or that their performance of certain prescribed rites will itself wash away their transgressions; or in law, the doctrine that compliance with the letter of the law exempts them from examining the legislator's intentions. (51)

For Kant, the people were naturally given to superficial, rote, and egocentric practices that leave them only mildly desirous of introspection and collective aspirations. Inasmuch as theology, medicine, and law recommend certain prescribed rites without requiring reflection, the higher faculty encourages the people away from reason. The higher faculty, therefore, can never be the basis of state law. Instead of basing its practices on the higher faculties, Kant argued that the government must legislate according to the ideals of the lower faculty, which were also the principles of regulation—rationality and freedom—principles that would provide the best ways to manage a people held in suspicion.

Through Kant's theorizations, the Western academy became the site that theorized the university as representative government's counsel about matters of rationality and the people's propensity for it. Under his theory, the people represented the pivot on which the lower faculty was distinguished from the higher faculty. While insulated from the vulgarities of the people, that portion of the academy most intimate with government—the lower faculty—was integral to the maneuvers of state regulation. The people thus helped to constitute the collaboration between state and lower faculty—as the population to be managed by the state, as the constituency to be constructed as irrational and egoistic. In this way, the people become the biopolitical lever on which the philosophy faculty could declare its identity in relation to the state as well as clarify the state's relationship to the people. In effect, Kant said to the king, "the state should give the philosophy faculty power because they can best alienate the people from their inclinations and desires, and upon this alienation the state can better represent them."

In the moment of the student struggles, the American academy would assume the role of the philosophy faculty and help government reconsider both the state's and the university's relationship to the people. As the embodiment of the lower faculty, the American academy would thus assist in rearticulating the people's capacity for rationality and freedom. In the moment of minority inclusion, the academy would become the laboratory within which those ideals might be extended to the people historically figured as their antitheses. Contradictorily, the academy would also become the place for refining the reasons for regulation and exclusion. As Kant made alienation and regulation the condition for representing the people, Jordan's essay points to how the entrance of people of color into the academy—as the possible subjects of excellence—would be based on disciplining the historical and cultural differences that constituted the people's lives.

The American University and the Histories of Race

While the student protests of the 1960s and the essay itself shed light on the racial and class exclusivity of the category "excellence," "Black Studies: Bringing Back the Person" also interrogated excellence as an ideal of resolution and absorption, an ideal that held out the certainty of both discipline and exclusion. As such, the essay wonders out loud about the standards for inviting minoritized subjects into hegemonic domains and practices. More pointedly, it indicates the various strategies by which the American nation-state and the American academy have attempted to absorb and archive populations minoritized by the United States' racial and imperial projects. In doing so, Jordan implies that the presumably benevolent integration of minoritized subjects is dialectically connected to the violent absorption and extermination of nonwhite populations. In contrast to Readings, Jordan periodizes excellence within a moment of national and international conflict around the subject of race, and unlike Gardner, she does not construct excellence as the benign resolution to minority difference and agitation. For her, "excellence" fundamentally antagonizes democratic understandings of "the people," constructing them as the antithesis of that category's principles. In terms of the open admissions movement and the people of Harlem, that antagonism would be directed toward African Americans and Puerto Ricans.

As a contradictory formation—one not only built around exclusion—excellence also promises to resolve minority assertions of autonomy and advancement, resolving them toward the needs of state, business, and canonical knowledge. Pointing to such a resolution, Floyd McKissick argued in a 1968 essay titled "Black Business Development with Social Commitment to Black Communities": "It is my belief that the development of Black Economic Power offers White America its last chance to save the Republic. If we are to exist together, it will be as equals. Equality depends on black control of its own institutions."[23] As McKissick indicates, the discourse of excellence—seen here in the thesis about "Black Economic Power"—was steadily becoming the language of political, educational, and economic integration, a language that would bring the institutions of American society into a new relation over the management of minority difference. For McKissick, that management would depend on white capital and black labor, a dependence that he argues would somehow yield black self-determination: "Much

of the capital for our undertakings will be forthcoming from white financial institutions and business corporations. The success of our endeavors
is dependent, however, on the effort and toil of Black People."[24]

Hence, we might read Jordan's essay for the ways in which it traces not
only the exclusion but also the incorporation of new forms of minority
difference. For instance, Jordan elaborates her understanding of excellence
by identifying how that discourse is rooted not only in academic parlance
but also in the genealogies of slavery and colonialism and within the discourse of the liberal individual, that supreme figure of integration and incorporation into democratic and capitalist societies:

> We know the individuality that isolates the man from other men, the
> either/or, the lonely-one that leads the flesh to clothing, jewelry, and
> land, the solitude of sight that separates the people from the people,
> flesh from flesh, that jams material between the spirit and the spirit. We
> have suffered witness to these pitiful, and murdering, masquerade exten-
> sions of the self.[25]

In this passage, Jordan presents a picture of African Americans and Puerto
Ricans as witnesses to the horrors and deformations of Western progress.
As she figures those terrors through the emergence of the liberal self, she
frustrates the assumption that the Western individual is the benevolent horizon of achievement and agency. Through the emergence of the liberal individual, she counters, foreign lands and subjects were incorporated into the
Western nation-state—as possessions, as bounties, and as colonial and en-
slaved laborers. Making possessions, taking bounty, and stealing land would
become the liberal individual's blueprint for adventure, an adventure that
would take on new itineraries as excellence solicited minority difference,
inserting the elements of individualism into minoritized subjectivities. In a
time of economic expansion, civil rights gains, and national independence,
the intermingling of individualism and minority difference would yield
unprecedented possibilities for mobility and institutional advancement.
For Jordan, this intermingling—even with the chance for uplift—is part of
excellence's disfiguring imperative.

At the heart of the aforementioned passage is a tale about modernity's
systems of calculation, systems that are responsible for the enfranchisement of the Western individual and the dehumanization of all else. As Jordan says, "There seldom has been a more efficient system for profiteering,

through human debasement, than the plantations, of a while ago."[26] Here she turns our attention to how the slave trade was a key moment in reconciling progress with degradation. In *Saltwater Slavery: A Middle Passage from Africa to American Diaspora,* Stephanie Smallwood discusses the ways the slave trade provided not only a new economic moment for modern Western nation-states but a new regime of calculation by which to measure and utilize human life. Discussing slavery as a revolution in market systems of classification, she argues: "[The] economic exchange had to transform independent beings into human commodities whose most 'socially relevant feature' was their 'exchangeability.'"[27] Locating the beginnings of that revolution on the shores of the Gold Coast of West Africa, she goes on to say, "The shore was the stage for a range of activities and practices designed to promote the pretense that human beings could convincingly play the part of their antithesis—bodies animated only by others' calculated investment in their physical capacities."[28]

As slavery was the context for measuring human capacity, slavery became an early component of capital's "scientific" innovations. Because of its innovative role, we might also situate slavery alongside the human sciences, which, in the language of Foucault, placed man at the foundation of all knowledge about life, labor, and language. In similar fashion, Smallwood points to how slavery placed Africans at the center of calculations about how far a life could be stretched and tried for the necessities of capitalist economic formations. As a result, life would become a factor in capital's equations, and the marketing of Africans into commodities would unleash a profound epistemic revolution in which slavery's computations would be the prototype to Marx's free laborer.

In the post–World War II moment, student movements and notions of excellence that were friendly to diversity promised to end all of that. As the shore was the stage on which capital could calculate human life for the debasing rigors of the market, the campus yard became the setting on which those historic calculations could be contested and then restaged. On this terrain, minoritized subjects would be evaluated in terms of their fitness for standards of excellence and merit, and the American campus would be the site for a range of activities and practices assembled to advance the idea that minorities would no longer have to play the part of their antithesis, that they would go from being history's humiliations to becoming its most renowned and uplifted achievements. No longer would they be "bodies animated only by others' calculated investment in their physical capacities." They would become minds energized by institutional measurements of their intellectual attributes. With the emergence of excellence, minoritized life would be subjected to presumably more affirming judgments, assessments that might allow that life to break free from its days of debasement. "Excellence" signaled that long-awaited morning about which liberals and radicals dreamed—when the past could finally be sloughed off and the day would totally begin anew.

Yet, while "excellence" may have promised to install a new tomorrow, that ideal could not help but betray its kinship to prior and emerging regimes of calculation and alienation. As Jordan indicates, one of the ways in which the category did so was through its "endorsement" of that moment's devastations. In an apparent reference to the Vietnam War, she notes, "Today, the whole world sits, as quietly scared as it can sit, afraid that, tomorrow, America may direct its efficiency and competence toward another forest for defoliation, or clean-cut laser-beam extermination."[29]

Efficiency, competence, and excellence were very much the aspirations of the Vietnam era. The political theorist Eqbal Ahmad turns our attention, for example, to how those aspirations played a part in the United States' counterinsurgency strategies in the Vietnam War. While the conventional counterinsurgent strategy favored by senior military officers was characterized by "aerial bombardment," "invasion of enemy sanctuaries," and baiting "the enemy [into] a concentrated attack," the "chief exponents" and "most sophisticated programmers" of conventional counterinsurgent maneuvers were the liberal reformers, theorists of "impeccable credentials," typically from the United States and France, professionals who couched their counterinsurgent doctrines in terms of "[freedom], progress, development, democracy, reforms, participation, and self-determination."[30] The democratic tone of counterinsurgency belied the fact that its goals were oftentimes achieved in the most punitive ways. For instance, on May 16, 1968, American soldiers entered the My Lai village on a "search-and-destroy" mission and slaughtered "three hundred unarmed civilians—including women, children, and old people."[31] Shortly thereafter, General William Westmoreland would congratulate the servicemen for their efficiency and competence, because the soldiers had not only met but exceeded their body count of 129.[32]

As a matter of violent incorporation, the Vietnam War "reflected the general desire to incorporate the extractive economies of Asia into the [United States'] industrial core" and provided "the means for the U.S. to perform its technological modernity and military force in relation to the Asiatic world."[33] The war in Vietnam suggested that individual excellence was needed not only in academy and government but in military operations as well. Such was the wide and universal application of this ideal, which helped to constellate the diverse arrangements of academy, state, and capital over the simultaneous legal enfranchisement and affirmation of U.S. minorities. This was the arrangement presumed in Jordan's use of that taken-for-granted, presumably insular, supposedly abstract institution known as the American university. Through Jordan we see the ways in which the American academy was a heteroglot institution, bearing the traces of various historical formations. Imprinted by these histories, the category "excellence"—like "black capitalism" in the preceding chapter—is haunted by the unacknowledged and matted itineraries of race and administration, a haunting that would bring the shores of West Africa and the villages of Vietnam to the halls of academe.

Excellence and the Othering of African Americans and Puerto Ricans

In addition to being branded by transatlantic slavery and the Vietnam War, the category excellence also, for Jordan, presumes national and international migrations and the discourses that helped to constitute them. In the context of City College and the open admissions movement, the regulation of African Americans and Puerto Ricans by state and academy was yet another prehistory to the drama of excellence. Indeed, the background for the open admissions movement and the discursive context for African Americans and Puerto Ricans in New York was the pathologization of those groups by government, sociology, and the media, a pathologization that involved manipulating constitutive discourses of race, gender, class, and sexuality. Both African Americans and Puerto Ricans were figured as non-heteronormative constituencies during and after their periods of migration. In the case of African Americans, conservative, liberal, and radical authorities constructed them as tangled up in matriarchal pathologies that led to crime, poverty, emasculation, homosexuality, and unwed births. Puerto Ricans were pathologized in similar ways as people characterized by loose morals, prostitution, and excessive reproduction.

While Jordan specifically focused on the circumstances of black studies and African American students, it was part of a larger rebuttal to the social construction of both African American and Puerto Rican communities. For example, during the 1960s, Puerto Rican artists and activists were also challenging the pathologization of Puerto Rican communities. Groups such as the International Ladies Garment Workers, the Young Lords Party, the Young Lords' Women's Caucus, the Welfare Rights Organization, and the Nuyorican Poets argued that Puerto Rican disfranchisement could not be explained in terms of a dysfunctional sexual and familial culture but was the outcome of international labor exploitation.[34] These pathologizing discourses would inspire the contradictory articulations of excellence—as an edict against diversity and as a developmental resolution to minority dysfunctions.

As Laura Briggs argues in *Reproducing Empire: Race, Sex, Science, and U.S. Imperialism in Puerto Rico,* in the immediate post–World War II environment, Puerto Rican migration, along with its African American counterpart from the South, "was thoroughly rendered a problem." In similar fashion to African American migration, Puerto Rican migration became a specific sociological problem with wide policy implications. Indeed, 1947 saw a media explosion around Puerto Rican migration to the mainland, with stories of "children abandoned in the airport, disease, substandard housing, rising crime levels" and overreproduction. Pundits believed that this presumed dysfunction would lead to a future of poverty and crime in Puerto Rican communities.

Oftentimes, accounts of Puerto Rican cultural pathologies contradicted other reports of Puerto Rican investment in respectability and hard work. Despite the contradictions to Puerto Rican sexual, familial, and social degeneracy, political and academic authorities pursued this thesis as if it had no inconsistencies. Hence, media accounts about Puerto Ricans created hysteria on the mainland and in Puerto Rico. So, in 1947, the governor of Puerto Rico commissioned Columbia University sociologists to study the Puerto Rican migration problem. As Laura Briggs observes, "the uproar in the newspapers died down, and a cottage industry for social scientists in and around New York was born" (168).

It was not until the 1960s, however, that Puerto Ricans became a fully developed social-scientific problem. Sociologists, in particular, rooted "the problem" in a culture-of-poverty framework that emphasized overpopulation in Puerto Rico and the threat that it posed for the mainland United States. Narratives about the "deviant sexuality of poor, usually non-white women" were a key component in that discourse and its effects in public policy and public hysteria (170). As Briggs notes, "The story that 'backwardness' and 'poverty' were caused by women's sexuality and reproduction followed Puerto Rican migrants to the mainland, producing a literature about the 'chaotic families' of Puerto Ricans in New York" (ibid.). Here Briggs underlines the specific role that gender and sexuality played in the racialization of Puerto Rican migration as socially pathological. Similar to the pathologization of African Americans, the social-scientific construction of Puerto Ricans as pathological helped to produce the relevance of social science beyond the academy. For instance, in a discussion of anthropologist Oscar Lewis's deployment of the culture-of-poverty thesis in his 1965 text *La Vida,* Briggs writes: "The work of Lewis in *La Vida* marked Puerto Rican Families as considerably worse than those portrayed in his earlier work in Mexico, and it joined with the sociology of African Americans' disorganized families to produce a particularly powerful synthesis" (ibid.). Similar to Kant's philosophy faculty, American social science was outlining the specifics of the irrationality of "the people" — in this case, the gender and sexual irrationality of African Americans and Puerto Ricans. This discourse of irrationality would help shape public policy.

This discursive context is key to understanding the opposition to open admissions and the function of excellence. When Jordan wrote, for instance, "Those opposed to Open Admissions argued, in effect, that the people, as in a democratic state, preclude excellence: excellence of standards and of achievement,"[35] she was in fact obliquely referencing the social construction of African Americans and Puerto Ricans as culturally pathological subjects unfit for civic participation and educational advancement, a construction assisted by members of the academy, government, and media. Such a construction — with its talk of wild reproduction, sexual degeneracy, and social disorganization — made it next to impossible to imagine Puerto Ricans and African Americans as part of an institution built around rationality, excellence, and standards. The open admissions struggle, like its peer student movements across the country, represented a hegemonic fight over the dominant meanings of minoritized communities and the exclusionary parameters of excellence.

In the following passage, Jordan interrogates the antinomy between university curricula as a measurement of excellence and the communities of color that sat outside the gates of City College:

> Black Studies. White Studies: Revised. What is the curriculum, what are the standards that only human life threatens to defile and "lower"? Is the curriculum kin to the monstrous metaphor of justice, seated, under blindfold, in an attitude and substance of absolute stone? Life appealing to live, and to be, and to know a community that will protect the living simply because we are alive: This is the menace to university curriculum and standards. This is the possibility of survival we must all embrace: the possibility of life, as has been said, by whatever means necessary.[36]

Jordan rejects both the notion of an abstract law and the idea of an abstract university curriculum, particularly eschewing how abstract articulations of law and curricula tend to turn away from the material differences of race and class that constitute the lives of African Americans and Puerto Ricans. Her use of "life" is thus a rebuttal to that abstraction and tries to capture the salient differences of Puerto Rican and African American communities.

Noting the material contexts for open admissions, Jordan poses a series of questions:

> Will the City College of New York resort to importation of students from Iowa and Maine? The children of the city are Black and Puerto Rican; they are the children of suffering and impotence; they are the children coerced into lower grade education that alienates upward of 65 percent of them so that the majority of this majority disappears into varieties of ruin.[37]

For her, the viability of City College — as a potential site of transformative learning and social change — depends on its imaginative engagement with African American and Puerto Rican communities. Inasmuch as excellence excluded these communities, it enabled the varieties of racialized ruin that troubled their already precarious circumstances. For Jordan, universities are accountable to the minoritized young that constitute the neighborhoods, towns, and cities in which those institutions reside, accountable in such a way that critical agents within universities have to develop strategie⌐ imagine those young people as constitutive parts of the academy, not as objects of exclusion or investigation but as vital components of their intellectual functions.

In this way, the question of admissions becomes not only a demographic matter relating to a university population but an epistemological proceeding necessitating the reorganization of knowledge. The simultaneity of that demographic and epistemological intervention is captured in the fourth demand. About it, Jordan writes:

> Black and Puerto Rican students at the City College, nevertheless, insist upon the fourth demand; they insist upon community. Serving the positive implications of Black Studies (Life Studies), students everywhere must insist on new college admissions policies that will guide and accelerate necessary, radical change at all levels of education.[38]

Jordan's use of *community* addresses blacks and Puerto Ricans as part of a dynamic and edifying material base that makes up Harlem and New York. As such, her use of *community* works against the university's claims to abstraction in matters of admission and curriculum. In this way, Jordan deploys *community* for the purposes of negation, to define the university in terms of the very elements and possibilities that it repels.[39] She suggests that the fourth demand attempted to make "community" part of a critical and negative philosophical tradition—one that used African American and Puerto Rican communities to not only mark what the administration and disciplinarity were excluding but to provoke new possibilities for university life and practice. Under such a reading, minority communities become epistemological catalysts for creative alternatives to positivist notions of university life, notions that said the way things are defines the only way that they can be.

Iconographic Rebuttals

To fully appreciate the interventions that Jordan's essay was attempting to make, we must locate the essay within a wider array of cultural production from the open admissions movement that would—like the essay—address the racial projects taking place at City College and, in the name of "excellence," projects made up of racial discourses about black and Puerto Rican cultural pathology. By looking at the flyers and posters produced—sometimes ad hoc—we can see how the artistic work of that movement pondered the material conditions of City College itself. For instance, a flyer for a protest titled "STRIKE!" illustrates how the movement theorized the materiality of local discourses about race and bureaucracy.

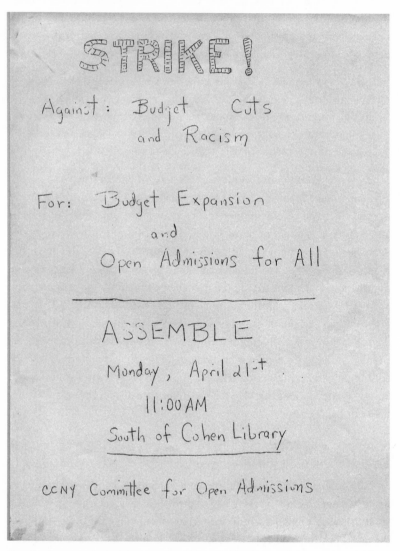

Flyer for the open admissions student strike at City College.

We might think of the flyer's use of imagery and text as an example of what cultural theorist W. J. T. Mitchell argues is the core of representation: "[The] interaction of pictures and texts is constitutive of representation as such: all media are mixed media, and all representations are heterogeneous."[40] We can see the interaction of the visual and the textual in the flyer. Visually and textually minimalist, the word *STRIKE!* is in all capital letters with an exclamation point. The sparseness of the rhetoric and the imagery—oversized but thin letters—suggests that the reason and nature of the strike are simple and straightforward. Particularly compelling is the way in which the flyer links budget cuts to racism. In doing so, it points to the fact that university bureaucracies are not the abstract and universal formations often presumed in social theory but entities constituted out of particularities found in their immediate locales. In the specific case of City College, the flyer suggests that the particularities of Puerto Rican and African American racializations frame university practice. The iconology of the flyer suggests the obviousness of links between bureaucracy and race, for instance, because of the racial subjects who exist at the conceptual heart of the open admissions struggle—African American and Puerto Rican students. Race's relationship to bureaucracy, the flyer suggests, is foundational rather than auxiliary to the university.

Emphasizing the situation of black and Puerto Rican students, the iconography also points to the multiple historical and social formations at work in the open admissions struggle and in Harlem. For instance, in a poster titled "UNITE!," we can see how the image gets at the heterogeneous makeup of the College and of Harlem by evoking symbols that would resonate with African Americans and Puerto Ricans.

The image is of two men—one Puerto Rican and one African American, both looking at each other with their fists extended outward. In their opposite hands, each figure holds a book. The fists are drawn as if they are rocks or boulders, the arms as if they are long and extensive columns. Both of these suggest that the constituencies that the men are supposed to represent are powerful and endowed, repeating a convention of much of the writing and visual art of the student movements, framing power and endowment in masculinist terms. At the same time, the image provides a compelling rebuttal to claims that the student struggles were extraneous to the administrative and institutional maneuvers of the American academy.

Poster calling for student coalitions between blacks and Puerto Ricans around the open admissions struggle.

Indeed, positioning the books to the side and rear of the fists suggests that whatever force the fists represent is in fact to make way for the life of the mind against university forces that threaten that life.

The figures also lean in toward each other as if they are in conversation; they are drawn as if they are two triangles that at times unite as a single power. Here the image again suggests that African Americans and Puerto Ricans are powerful formations that, when united, can challenge an institutional structure as formidable as the American academy. The likely union of the two forces is both demanded and predicted through the word UNITE!, the letters of which are drawn as monoliths themselves. The figures are framed by two rectangles. For the Puerto Rican figure, the rectangle is shaded black with a swipe of white. For the black figure, the rectangle is shaded white with a swipe of black. One way in which we might read that is, of course, that the Puerto Rican is placed in the black rectangle to indicate Puerto Rican immersion in a predominantly and identifiably African American Harlem. The African American is placed in a "white" rectangle to indicate African American immersion in a Harlem that is also Puerto Rican. The "white" might also refer to the racialization of Puerto Ricans as nonwhite but as officially "white" according to the U.S. census. The white and black blotches are there to frustrate the notion that Harlem is monocultural or homogeneous, reminding the Puerto Rican community of Harlem's African American elements, and prompting the African Americans to acknowledge the Nuyoricans.

Although the flyers may seem like minor texts compared to theoretical monographs, they contest the notion that the student protests were not interested in interrogating the administrative and institutional maneuvers of the academy. Indeed, the diverse array of cultural forms deployed by the student movements question the presumption that there are major and minor forms when it comes to hegemonic struggle. The iconography serves as a counterarchive to theorizations of minority difference as insignificant to the theorization of the academy. The iconography recalls the ways in which the open admissions movement was identifying the intersections of race and bureaucracy and using cultural forms such as flyers and posters to illuminate that intersection. Culture, contrary to Readings, was not an example of representation's alienation from considerations of political economy but an example of culture's concern over the material practices of bureaucracy. In a discussion about why he chooses not to focus on the movements over race, gender, and sexuality in *The University in Ruins*, Readings argues that "the lesbian and gay, African American and feminist movements are different in that neither their genesis nor their goals are essentially linked to the University."[41] For Readings, understanding the contemporary university means producing a historiographic narrative about how subjugated modes of difference are inappropriate frameworks from which to understand post–civil rights academic, political, and economic formations. The ephemera and iconography of the open admissions movement rebut this argument and point to how political, economic, and administrative matters were part of the campus's racial project and the student movement's critique, emphasizing what political scientist and ethnic studies scholar Pedro Cabán refers to as an awareness of the university as a "repository of political and academic power,"[42] an awareness that was constitutive of the activism that led to black, Chicano, and Puerto Rican studies.

The Contradictions of the Five Demands

Yet we cannot simply understand the open admissions movement as a rebellion against institutional forces; we have to engage it as a desire for institutionality as well. We can see both elements at work in the Five Demands. For instance, the first demand for a separate school of black and Puerto Rican studies represented the activists' interest in curricular stability. As the authors put it, "We prefer a school because we think that it is best that a program in Black and Puerto Rican studies have the greatest degree of autonomy and the most lattitude [sic] with which to experiment." Touching on the possibilities for autonomy and latitude, the first demand reads, "We believe that vigorous innovation in a school, able to confer degrees and to gargain [sic] for its budget, would rub off on the other schools of the college and the total educational ambiance enhanced."[43] The first demand thus represented—to a large degree—a faith in the idea that the school as an institutional form was the horizon of innovation and self-governance, a faith not altogether different from the Morrill Act's presumption that establishing schools would move American education toward unprecedented breakthroughs.

While separate, the school would not be separatist. Indeed, contrary to popular belief about the inherently separatist nature of various student struggles, the advocates for open admissions actually did not press for the school to be a separatist venue only for African American and Puerto Rican students. Clarifying this point, they wrote, "We are opposed to a segregated school; the school we envision would be open to students with an interest in . . . the subject. We would expect such a school to be controlled by its faculty and students." The authors concluded this demand by arguing that forms such as a program or department would be "confined . . . even harassed . . . by its lack of autonomy that its activities will be diluted, its potential denied."[44] The school as an institutional form was thus meant to be both an acknowledgment of administrative vulnerability when it came to minoritized students and knowledges and an investment in administrative accomplishment and fortification on behalf of minoritized students and epistemes.

As a form that suggested self-determination, we can locate the first demand's stipulation of a school for black and Puerto Rican studies within the larger anticolonial movements of the time. We might read the demand as analogous to the efforts of national liberal struggles to capture not only state offices but the state form itself. In such a context the takeover of administration buildings and the erection of schools and departments were modeled on the grand adventures of state capture by national liberation movements. In such a context, identifying with dominant institutional forms and attempting to maneuver them would become the modus operandi for many minoritized subjects.

As a phenomenon inspired by national liberation struggles, the open admissions movement—like its counterparts in other parts of the country—would inherit the contradictions of those struggles. Indeed, the five demands symbolize contradictions at the heart of many of the U.S. student movements. For example, while the fourth demand emphasized the dynamism of minority communities and the critical pressures that minority admittees could put on institutions, that emphasis could only exist in tension with an investment in administration as a horizon of dynamism and experimentation. While administration has proved itself to be capable of experimentation, institutionalization in the form of schools and departments, historically, has not helped to rearrange knowledge but to reconsolidate it. Discussing the anatomy of this reconsolidation, the sociological theorist Zygmunt Bauman has rightly argued that discursive practices achieve institutional identity by setting boundaries on the meaning and analysis of their objects, boundaries that stipulate which language may be mobilized to interpret an object and who has the right to deploy it.[45] Whether in the form of a school, a department, a text, or a curriculum, institutionalization eventually means conferring the right to speak about a given object and determining the contours for speaking about that object.

In addition to establishing the community of speakers and the laws of enunciation, institutionalization tries to construct its discursive object as factual and objective. Discourses often map boundaries as a way to attribute coherence and legibility to their objects.[46] Institutionalizing a discourse—even a critical one—in the form of departments, programs, and schools runs its errand in the name of coherence and legibility, putting the reorganizing energies suggested by the admission of minoritized subjects at odds with the institutional imperatives for stability and transparency implied by bureaucracy. Hence, the open admissions movement—like many other students movements—was founded on a contradiction: the dynamism of minority communities, on the one hand, and the desire for institutional forms that would ultimately restrict and arrest that dynamism, on the other. This contradiction would begin a new point of departure for minoritized life in the late twentieth century.

Factoring Race

As a matter of fact, the post–civil rights years represent moments in which bureaucratic institutionalizations would be handed out to people worn out from waiting. In the moment of exclusions and student struggles, mechanisms of power would expand the borders of excellence and take some of the people in. In 1961, President Kennedy would issue Executive Order 10925, establishing the Committee on Equal Employment Opportunity, charging that committee "to realize national policy of nondiscrimination in the executive branch of government" and mandating government contractors to "take affirmative action" by employing and managing "without regard to their [applicants' or employees'] race, creed, color or national origin."[47] In 1965, Lyndon Johnson would issue another executive order—numbered 11246—which required government contractors to comply with nondiscriminatory policies in hiring and promotion or be subject to sanctions. Affirmative-action measures would be a way for campuses across the country to reconcile the ideal of excellence with the demands of democratic change.

In the context of the American academy, one way of practicing affirmative action and reconciling excellence with democratic change was by making race "a factor" among others, such as test scores, grade point averages, recommendation letters, and so on. Yet, turning race into a factor would not circumvent power so much as confirm it. In truth, turning race into a fixed and stable entity would strip the category of the very dynamism that the student movements helped to reveal. Discussing the idea of race as a "factor" in affirmative-action considerations, Judith Butler concludes: "Even if we understand such categories to be one among many that enter into the constitution of a student's profile, the language of the factor still presumes that minority status might be contained and represented in a quantifiable form."[48] Although affirmative action and excellence signaled new times and new possibilities for minority participation, they would at the same time be moments that ensured minority representation and regulation. Butler notes that even as the language of "one factor among many" suggests an appreciation for the partial significance of a student's racial background, that "language nevertheless performs a totalization of the status, suggesting its containment and representability as a statistical unit or discrete attribute."[49] By "factoring" race, what the antiracist movements demonstrated as the protean and dynamic character of racial meaning would be turned into the fixed and discrete unit of academic calculation. In other words, what was publicly shown to be a category of considerable innovation and experimentation was turned into a stable and totalizing factor in the name of integration.

As quantification became the standard by which to incorporate racialized subjects, race would be read ironically as an abstraction divorced from historical contexts. As Butler writes, quantifying minorities "not only abstracts from the qualitative considerations of background, history, environment, opportunity, and cultural forms of expression and ideals," it also arrests and destroys the historicity of minoritized subjects by throwing the category "minority" into an "ahistorical vacuum" and "subjecting it to a logic of calculability." Quantifying minority categories negates their potential as "points of departure for interpretation" and as "ways of locating accomplishments culturally," rendering those categories instead into ontological certainties that assert, "this is what this person is."[50] This ontological move was actually a way to discipline the historic maneuvers of the antiracist movements. If those movements partly emphasized race as a mode of becoming, then discourses that quantified race, in effect, attempted to arrest its potential for transformation and rearticulation. If quantification "[destroys] the very referent it seeks to represent,"[51] quantification annihilates not only the applicant but the social movements that made the applicant possible in the first place.

By naming the ways in which race is fixed in discrete units, Butler's arguments about the quantification of minorities reveal how the university institutionalizes essentialist discourses of race, gender, class, and sexuality, reading them as discrete and calculable units rather than points of departure for locating subjects historically and culturally. We have been led to believe that essentialist discourses arise primarily as an effect of the student movements themselves, but Butler's arguments compel us to interrogate the ways in which those discourses arise as part of bureaucratic protocols and metrics. The contradictory articulation of the student movements meant that those elements that arrested the dynamism of minority difference invoked institutional hegemony rather than repelling it, inviting academic institutions to fix otherwise dynamic notions of racial difference. Fixed and stable notions of race might thus be understood not simply as epistemological constructions but as administrative procedures as well.

Applying bureaucratic metrics and protocols in matters of diversity predates affirmative action. Indeed, as Christopher Newfield explains, quantification in the American university system has historically operated as a way to deal with presumably incongruous and heterogeneous agencies. After the passage of the first Morrill Act and the establishment of big research universities composed of the humanities, the sciences, and the professions, administrators confronted the problem of how to evaluate their progress across those differences. Quantification became the answer to that question. As Newfield suggests, quantitative measures were used to contrive common denominators among fields with different and often opposing "internal assumptions, methods, goals, and standards." These measures "could be applied to any area. Better yet, they were already central to American understandings of social progress—territory controlled, size of population, level of national income, and so on."[52]

Quantitative measures were a means of dealing with "the problem" of disciplinary heterogeneity, the dilemma of how to evaluate diverse elements using a singular standard. Those measures also signified an institutional belief and commitment to ideologies of progress and their universal application—on territories, populations, and national income. By turning race into a factor, minorities would become part of quantification's jurisdiction

and its evaluation of progress. Race and eventually other modes of difference would become abstractions, just as territories, populations, and income
had been one hundred years earlier.

Yet, even while the academy was becoming the way station for minority difference, the student movements made the university a site of conflict
and possibility like never before. As Jordan observes:

> We have spent our generations in a scream that wasted in a golden ear.
> Giant, demon, clown, angel, bastard, bitch, and nevertheless, a family
> longing, we have made it to the gates: Our hearts hungry on the rocks
> around the countryside, our hopes the same: our hopes, unsatisfied.
> Now we have the choice, and we must make that choice our own. We
> are at the gates.
>
> Who are we?
>
> There has been no choice until now. Until the university, there is
> no choice.[53]

While evoking dehumanizing discourses that fashioned racialized minorities as the antithesis of rationality, Jordan ends with the academy's fragile
possibilities. We might think of that fragility as emanating from the contradictory relationship that racialized minorities have had to the academy.
Whether through the Morrill Acts of 1862 and 1890, *Brown v. Board of
Education* in 1954, the civil rights and antiracist movements of the 1960s,
the *University of California Regents v. Bakke* in 1978, the passage of Resolution SP-1 by the University of California Board of Regents in 1995 — a
move to prohibit the use of race in college admissions in California — or
Gratz v. Bollinger and *Grutter v. Bollinger* in 2003, academic formations
have always shaped and been shaped by the contours of racial projects
within and outside educational contexts. Indeed, for Jordan, the inevitability of the university has everything to do with the fact that higher education
in the United States has developed and been developed by minority existence and well-being.[54]

While the academy promises a range of conflicts — "screams in a golden
ear" — that institution is also the site where critical formations might emerge,
particularly ones that study and challenge the university's relationship to
racial formations and other modes of difference. Seeing that as precisely
the task of black studies, Jordan says: "We request Black teachers for Black
Studies. It is not that we believe only Black people can understand the Black

experience. It is, rather, that we acknowledge the difference between reality and criticism as the difference between the Host and the Parasite."[55] We might read her distinction between host and parasite as designating black critical formations within the academy as the alternative life within that institution, a life intent on using the academy for other forms of learning and subjectivization that the institution never intended. Like a parasite, black studies would produce critical formations in numbers that the host would never imagine or suspect. Black studies, in this sense, would exploit the academy for sustenance, residency, and dispersal, imagining ways to be more in the academy than of it.

Sustenance, residency, and dispersal eventually mean not an absolute eschewal of institutionalization but a desire for alternative institutionalities. We might think of alternative institutionalities as analogous to what Frankfurt School theorists theorized as the contradictory possibilities of reason. As Marcuse wrote, "Reason . . . was instrumental in creating the world we live in. It was also instrumental in sustaining injustice, toil, and suffering. But Reason, and Reason alone, contains its own corrective."[56] As Jordan argued that the university is inevitable, she was in fact converging with that understanding of reason outlined by Marcuse and others: the academy as both the object of critique and an instrument of alternatives.[57]

As reason is a site of contradiction that is responsible for both disfranchisements and their undoing, so we might think of institutions as sites of contradiction and negation. Just as producing alternatives to reason does not entail renouncing reason but involves using reason for the purposes of negation, we might infer that crafting alternative forms of institutional practice and belonging does not mean abdicating institutional life but working to negate hegemonic forms of institutional reason. Negating those forms means demonstrating how institutional contradictions might themselves suggest political and institutional alternatives. For Jordan and for the fourth demand, the possibility for such negations resided in new admissions practices that would admit subjects who could potentially negate the simultaneously demographic and epistemic hegemonies of the college itself.

Community, the essay implies, is a spirited material formation that calls for the reorganization of knowledge practices. As Butler argues, granting "concrete cultural meaning to the ideals of democracy," offering "the university as a public site of cultural exchange," compelling the academy and its constituencies to "[accept] the challenge to revise the traditional assumptions about how knowledge is circulated, produced, and received when it is practiced by communities no longer formed through discriminatory practice"[58] —these are the ingredients of an alternative engagement with institutionality. In this context, communities outside the campus yard are anything but reified and removed from academic concerns, but are the material catalysts to epistemic shifts and transformations.

Thus, Jordan designates black studies as "life studies" not out of a sentimental regard for African American life, but out of a sense that minoritized communities are forces of negation that compel the imagination to exceed the given state of institutional affairs. As "life studies," black studies, for Jordan, is committed to all possibilities of life and not simply the possibility of black lives. In the context of Harlem, it meant a commitment to black *and* Puerto Rican life as the material for a "critical logic" that "reveals modes and contents of thought which transcend the codified pattern of use and validation."[59] Emergent interdisciplinary fields like black studies were thus meant to dream horizons that might exceed the prescriptions and violations of institutional excellence as well as the boundedness of categories. In the next chapter, we will see how, contrary to notions that divide "the academy" from "the community," institutional discourses of power/knowledge would find their footing in local terrains.

The Reproduction of Things Academic

ALMOST EVERYONE CREDITS BLACK STUDIES with having led the charge of instituting the study of race. Interesting as this distinction is, its significance runs a little deeper and goes beyond the pomp of being first among the ethnic studies. More important, that field helped to midwife interest in and inaugurate the dispersion of minority difference. As racial and gender minorities demoted Western man, a people and an interdiscipline would be brought out into all quarters. During the expanding economy of the Cold War, for instance, African Americans would migrate from the southern, northern, and midwestern parts of the United States. The national and international context for this change of character, as Manning Marable notes, included "the transformation of the global status of black and third world people in the United States and internationally," a move that occasioned the rise of the United Nations and the convening of the 1956 Congress of Negro Writers and Artists in Paris.[1] As the Soviet Union pointed to the racial hypocrisies of the United States, the Cold War competition between the United States and the Soviet Union would also "[promote] an interest in black culture and history."[2] Although African American studies may have gone into the Cold War's hot spell as "a discourse and body of scholarly work confined largely to racially segregated institutions," the field came out of the fire transformed into "a vibrant curriculum [with] hundreds of programs fighting to change white higher education."[3] The intellectual context for the institutional emergence of African American studies was also cemented by academic organizations devoted to the study and promotion of black life and African heritage.[4] And with the establishment of black, Asian, Chicano, Native American, and Puerto Rican studies, ethnic studies would get its first taste of autonomy. The dispersions that led to and emanated from the institutional emergence of interdisciplines like black studies motivated brand-new sovereignties occasioned by the advance of new kinds of peoples and interests.

This chapter considers how these new types of peoples, interests, and sovereignties created links between dominant institutions of knowledge and local communities. Showing how those links made the academy and local communities overlapping formations, the chapter rebuts arguments that read the university and "the people" as mutually exclusive and counters propositions that delink the history of the interdisciplinary fields from the history of the modern academy. The chapter also analyzes how the origin tales spun by African American studies in particular would represent the first minting of another political entity and object of love, a new item called minority culture, one that would be taken up by subsequent interdisciplinary adventures. In this epic transformation, minorities would go from being members of empty-handed generations to people headstrong with histories and civilizations. Yet, for a reason, the arrival of this new object would not usher in a season of unbridled liberation but would also provide the building blocks for a new way to regulate.

As the history of black studies and the social movements implies, the interdisciplines were both the midwives and the children of affirmative and regulatory modes of power. If the modern university is, as Derrida characterized it, "responsible to a nonuniversity agency," then the student movements and the interdisciplines helped to broaden the scope and meaning of "nonuniversity agency."[5] For instance, after the social movements of the fifties and sixties, the university would begin to be responsible to minoritized populations and communities, groups previously held outside the modern academy's range of interests and connections. Indeed, we might think of the post–World War II U.S. academic environment as one characterized not only by the expansion of university structures but by the amplification of new forms of "nonuniversity" communities, communities to which the academy would establish new kinds of responsibility. In this regard, the social movements of the 1960s—along with the forms of study that they generated—helped to articulate contemporary horizons of responsibility for women, blacks, Asian Americans, Native Americans, and Latinos.

But, as the history shows, responsibility has always been a doubled-edged matter. On the one hand, responsibility—in the post–World War II moment of national liberation and civil rights—was the means to establish an ethical commitment to the well-being of communities minoritized by colonization, racial segregation, gender exploitation, and sexual regulation. Yet, as responsibility was increasingly defined through nationalist politics that idealized heteropatriarchal, able-ist, and ethnically homogeneous notions of community, responsibility—as an ideal—was often used to establish elaborate systems of regulation designed to determine what activities, interests, spaces, and experiences needed to be disciplined to the point of docility. In its regulatory guise, responsibility would ensnare a multitude of social and epistemic formations within its jurisdiction. In the Janus-faced name of responsibility, political organizations and academic programs devoted to minoritized subjects would arise in the postsixties environment, disseminating both the life-enhancing and regulatory aspects of responsibility, producing an ironic kinship with the disciplinary universes of dominant Western institutions.

As "nonuniversity agents" were brought into the purview of academic knowledge, it became more and more difficult to separate "the community" from the academy. In this new period, the academy was far from the territory conquered by well-intentioned radicals. Instead, that ivory tower would grow into a crucible for unprecedented dramas between revolution and power, the contents of which would spill into streets and neighborhoods, violating taken-for-granted divisions between the hegemonic and the marginal. The rise of African American studies in colleges and universities and in local neighborhoods would help extend minority difference into new quarters, opening up new relays for the establishment and breakdown of networks of power/knowledge.

And a New Love Arises: Black Power and the Emergence of "the Grass Roots"

To explore how a simultaneously erudite and vernacular formation like black studies opened up new relays of knowledge/power, we can turn to Toni Cade Bambara's 1971 short story "My Man Bovanne." The historical moment that saluted "My Man Bovanne" was defined by an interest in black culture and consciousness. Because of the influence of black nationalism, the 1960s and 1970s saw both the interest in and the elaboration of black culture rise to peaks that were unimaginable twenty years earlier.

Ethnic studies scholar Jane Rhodes argues that this interest in and elaboration of black culture "involved the acquisition of significant lifestyle changes—the use of African names, the celebration of African-based holidays, and the wearing of African-inspired dress." She notes how black nationalism inspired changes in popular and avant-garde cultures as well, engendering new developments in R & B music, literature, film, visual art, and theater.[6] Far from being an esoteric phenomenon, black nationalism was a powerful communicative mode that attempted to produce and proliferate the networks by which black nationalist discourses might be disseminated in black communities.

One of the primary means by which black nationalist discourses were disseminated was through underground newspapers such as the Nation of Islam's *Muhammad Speaks* and the Black Panther Party's *Black Panther.* As Rhodes notes, "these publications, made possible by the recent availability of mimeograph machines and offset printing, captured the zeitgeist of the era."[7] By 1968, the *Black Panther* was selling 125,000 copies per week.[8] Moreover, as periodicals like the *Black Panther* addressed the writings of revolutionary theorists such as Frantz Fanon, Mao Tse-tung, and Che Guevara, they became domains for the convergence of vernacular and theoretical languages as well as the dissemination of militant protest and erudite knowledge.

Bambara's "My Man Bovanne" was both the product and the examination of that dissemination. The short story was first published in the periodical *Black World* under the title "Mama Hazel Takes to Her Bed" and then later under the current title in Bambara's anthology *Gorilla, My Love.* The short story's publication in *Black World* underlines another facet of that historical juncture: the emerging communicability of minority difference. To begin with, *Black World* was part of Johnson Publishing Company, publisher of *Ebony* and *Jet* magazines.[9] Johnson's interest in basing a publication on black power aesthetics and principles revealed much about capital's own developing interest in, rather than a retreat from, minority culture and the U.S. student movements. More pointedly, the publishing world's interest in the student movements and in the Black Arts Movement testified to the fact that black culture was not simply of interest to anti-establishment radicals but to the "establishment" as well. Indeed, it was a moment in which the establishment would more and more learn how to affirm the most radical enunciations of difference, producing the conditions whereby what happened on campus yards would affect the world outside. Rather than this being a moment of estrangements between the radical and the hegemonic, it was a time of unprecedented and often unconscious intimacies.

Minorities in general, and African Americans in particular, were gaining rights and representations that would usher in new forms of independence as well as a new object that would disseminate stories of group solidarity, identity, and origin. As a matter of fact, "My Man Bovanne" gestures toward the object of love that began to change social relations within black communities in the United States. Moreover, the short story dramatizes how that object signals a moment of unprecedented agencies and dignities at the same time that the object let loose regulations that few people had ever known. The love object would go by many names, but the one that the short story uses is "grass roots." In the following section, the main character, Miss Hazel, discusses the benefit party for the black power group to which all the neighborhood folks are invited. She then introduces the reader to Bovanne and simultaneously illustrates the function of the category "grass roots":

> Nice man. Which is not why they invited him. Grass roots you see. Me and Sister Taylor and the woman who does heads at Mamies and the man from the barber shop, we all there on account of we grass roots. And I ain't never been souther than Brooklyn Battery and no more coun-try than the window box on my fire escape. And just yesterday my kids tellin me to take them countrified rags off my head and be cool. And now can't get black enough to suit em.[10]

Miss Hazel introduces the category "grass roots" as one that presumably bestows a new admiration and respect onto everyday black folks, the group-ing that expresses appreciation for working-class and poor black folks. As such, the category would serve as a rebuttal to the historic ways in which African Americans had been dismissed by whites and the U.S. government as a degenerate and dispensable population. The category would correct this dismissal and present blacks as fundamental elements to political orga-nizing and community building, offering a chance at the A-list for Miss Hazel, Bovanne, and people like them. Politically and socially, "grass roots" identified them as facets of that object of love known as minority culture.

As a character and an image we can locate Miss Hazel within efforts by black nationalist groups like the Black Panther Party and by visual artists such as Emory Douglas to—in the words of scholar and visual artist Colette Gaiter—"[construct] a visual mythology of power for people who felt powerless and victimized."[11] Constructing that mythology, for Douglas, the former minister of culture for the Black Panther Party, meant depicting black women as essential militants in black revolutionary struggle. To this end, several of Douglas's illustrations portray older black women, like Miss Hazel, as ardent supporters of revolutionary projects. Discussing Douglas's representations of those women, Gaiter notes, "In *The Black Panther* newspaper, images of poor and working class black people proliferated. Although the Panthers are perceived as a male-dominated organization, Douglas often featured women in his illustrations."[12] Despite the sexism of black revolutionary organizations, she says, black women often functioned as metaphors for "the people" in the visual and discursive production of those organizations.

In this regard, Miss Hazel is like the black women portrayed in Douglas's illustrations, women whose aprons and grocery bags become sites for advertising the party's Free Food Program and its campaign to liberate Bobby Seale and Angela Davis. As Gaiter observes, Douglas "often used 'signs within signs' in his drawings—people holding signposts or wearing buttons, tags, labels, and other integrated messages."[13] For example, in the illustrations "Hallelujah: The Might and Power of the People Is Beginning to Show" and "Thanks to the People's Free Store I Can Go Home and Mop My Floors & Feed My Children," older black women sport buttons printed with the faces of Bobby Seale, Ericka Huggins, and Angela Davis.

Douglas captures the venerable nature of black women through deeply etched facial features, through eyes closed in contemplation and jubilation, and through clothes conveying the domestic dignity of black poor and working-class women. In "Hallelujah," the button becomes a sign within the sign of the older black woman, underlining the notion that the revolutionaries arise from the body politic known as "the people," emphasizing a revolutionary ethic that totally comprises and enlists the older women's identities and bodies. In "Thanks to the People's Free Store," revolutionary ideals are integrated into everyday life and chores. The illustrations present the women as love objects whose status as grassroots entities is denoted through their real and imagined connections to the revolutionary agendas of groups like the Black Panthers.

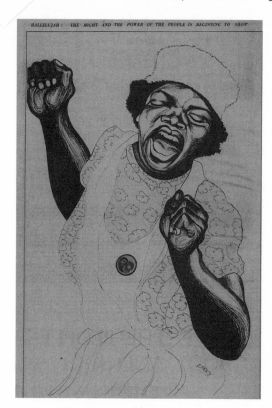

Emory Douglas, "Hallelujah: The Might and Power of the People Is Beginning to Show." This poster presents black women as the love objects of black nationalist organizing. Copyright 2012 Emory Douglas/Artists Rights Society (ARS), New York.

Yet, despite the historic exclusions and dismissals that "grass roots" is meant to correct, Miss Hazel is keenly aware of the ways in which the category actually misnames her and the other older folks from the neighborhood. In fact, she approaches the concept as a kind of partition between the time before the category's debut and the moments produced after its arrival, signifying a shift between yesterday and now. "Yesterday" marked the moment in which Miss Hazel's "countrified rags" and the other elements of vernacular culture were now part of the "democratic reign of appearance and flattery."[14] Today they and theirs are part of a radical and liberated moment in which they become the object of the young militants' dictation. Bambara's "grass roots" is one of the names of history and as such identifies a new political and disciplinary scene.

In this new love object, we can see the trace of power/knowledge and the academy. In the context of the short story, "grass roots" is the product

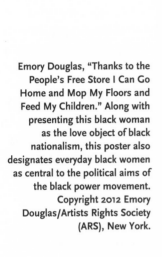

Emory Douglas, "Thanks to the People's Free Store I Can Go Home and Mop My Floors and Feed My Children." Along with presenting this black woman as the love object of black nationalism, this poster also designates everyday black women as central to the political aims of the black power movement. Copyright 2012 Emory Douglas/Artists Rights Society (ARS), New York.

of the black power movement's effort at unity, an effort mounted largely by students. But the contours of the academy are not only in the identities of the various members of that movement. The academy is also in the historical discourse where notions of "grass roots" are first sown, notions that arise from modern articulations of power/knowledge that hark back to the nineteenth century's production of republican romanticism.

In his discussion of the French nationalist historian Jules Michelet's mid-nineteenth-century text *The History of the French Revolution,* Jacques Rancière credits Michelet with having invented a way of talking about revolution in the very moment that saw the birth of "the masses," a way of simultaneously celebrating and regulating revolutionary ruptures. Rancière, in an interpretation of Hobbes, argues that the king—as a center and force of history—is "killed" by a once subjugated multitude that has found its liberation and identity as "a people" in writing. With a few well-placed strokes of a pen, the people achieve their democratic sovereignty and the king's murder with a "mass of papers," made up of "biblical prophecies and ancient-sounding harangues."[15] According to Rancière, this combination of republican ideals of popular sovereignty and romanticist notions of people and nationhood gives birth to modern history.

In this republican-romanticist circumstance, the people's affirmation and regulation came through, for Rancière, in Michelet's discussion of the Festival of Unity held in Paris on July 14, 1790, the historic event that heralded the French Revolution and the birth of popular sovereignty. Anxious about future possibilities for revolution, the French National Assembly called for the Fête de Fédération to unify the various parts of the French nation that would be turned into departments in order that they might not erupt in internecine conflict. The national festival would federate the eighty-nine departments and obligate those same departments and the festival's attendees—the National Assembly, the king, the civilians, and the soldiers alike—to pledge their allegiance to the new constitution and to the rule of law.[16] Rancière points to the ways in which the new objects of unity—"native land" and "the people"—are the effects of a republican affirmation of popular sovereignty and a romanticist elevation of national territory and the people. For Rancière, the festival was not the harbinger of an unadulterated freedom but the warning of a new kind of regulation. If the native land and the people were the love objects of a new historiography, then this love would come with handcuffs on the side.

And yet, while the land and the people are placed on pedestals as new objects of love, it is the historian who takes the platform. According to Rancière, the historian turns these pledges of allegiance, these narratives of unity, into love letters of sorts, letters that only he may hold, that only he may contrive as the proof of national unity. For the historian, the love letters are vehicles for ascendance and visibility. Imagining the people's declarations of allegiance as narratives of communal romance and unity is the historian's way of turning the people into the historian's ink. The festival's attendees—the newborn, his mother, the old man, and the young girl—will become the means of a romanticist and republican production and in the end spell out "nationalism." As Rancière implies, the narrative of unity does not create value primarily for the people but for the historian and for nationalist historiography. The festival, after all, inaugurates a mode of history that foretells of "tomorrow's heroes" who will devote themselves to the good of the native land and its romantic narration. As a historian produces a narrative of unity, so "the community" is born and contrived from the workshops of power/knowledge.

Like the festival, the benefit in "My Man Bovanne" presents its own spectacle of appreciation. The benefit was attended by the humble and the mighty—the able-bodied, the disabled, the old, the young, the lay, and the dignified. Although the festival brought together hundreds of thousands of Frenchmen while the benefit assembled only the regulars from the neighborhood, their intents were very similar. Both commemorated revolutions. Both tried to establish and contrive narratives of unity. Both had their symbols of life, growth, and death embodied in the presence of the young and the old. While many young radicals believed that they had left the West behind, their politics of liberation proved that the West yanked at their coattails every step of the way.

Although "My Man Bovanne" is only eight pages long, it would try to set black nationalism straight in the most sweeping strides. It would do so by stripping "grass roots" of its claim to innocence and by catching black nationalism in a defining deception, in which nationalism presents itself as the "first meaning," as the text that—to paraphrase Barthes—will return us to our simple and literal nature.[17] In the case of "grass roots," the term promises simple adoration and indispensability. As the symbols and justifications for the simple and the literal, the "people" became the building blocks for an evolving hegemonic system that will guarantee that innocence and purity will function for the good of dominance.

This hegemonic system was taking place in and largely inspired by a moment of national liberation struggles in which minoritized subjects were mobilized not only for the purposes of protest but for the purposes of representation as well. "My Man Bovanne" tried to interrupt that mobilization. As we will see, through the character Miss Hazel, the short story constantly evokes anterior, ulterior, and exterior meanings as a way to frustrate the romantic undercurrents of the category "grass roots." Indeed, Miss Hazel's references to "yesterday" and the ways in which black power changed social relations in the neighborhood are an example of connotation's interest in "other sites of the text." "Yesterday" is important as a way to consider the arbitrariness of black power's mode of valorization and devalorization. The short story exposes black nationalism as a formation that emanates largely from a republican-romanticist paradigm that presses the people into heroic narratives of national unity and identity. That paradigm invokes the history of republican romanticism as it tries to establish narratives of revolution and innocence as primary and straightforward, as the playthings of historical narration. As a critique of republican and romanticist gestures, the short story refuses to be determined by the presumably straightforward categories and meanings of national liberation. In fact, "My Man Bovanne" seems to ask the reader, "How did the mamas and papas of the neighborhood become the means of production for a republican and romanticist narrative, one that tried to establish the people as the serviceable material for a discourse of simplicity and innocence?" If modern history, as Rancière implies, is the name of that process by which "the people" became part of a national and nationalist story, then that process called "history" was refined as intellectuals and activists bestowed the sovereign mantle of "the people" on people who had never before been legitimized as such. Inasmuch as the militants walked step-by-step with modern history and used the people as the syntax of nationalism, they helped to expand the archives of power/knowledge and the hegemonic boundaries of the academy.

"My Man Bovanne" and the Critique of Stultification

Their similarities notwithstanding, there is a crucial difference between the Festival of Unity and the black power benefit. The love object of black nationalism did not arise out of a fidelity to liberal democracy like the object that Rancière describes in *The Names of History*. This darling item of student militants sprang from critiques of democratic capitalism's contradictions over the ideals of liberal governance and the exclusions that bedeviled those vaunted principles. But while many a radical presumed that power would be alienated by their critiques, new networks of power would find ways to subdue by affirming nationalism's analyses. In doing so, those networks would make the most of those hierarchies of knowledge ratified by the movements themselves, hierarchies that would make esteem and disfavor concurrent.

According to "My Man Bovanne," the concurrence of admiration and derision can be seen in the figure of the people, the community members who are supposed to represent the grass roots while reckoning with the young people's presumptions about their incapacities. For instance, in this scene Miss Hazel says:

> So everybody passin sayin My Man Bovanne. Big deal, keep steppin, and don't even stop a minute to get the man a drink or one of them cute sandwiches or tell him what's goin on. And him standin there with a smile ready case someone do speak he want to be ready. So that's how come I pull him on the dance floor and we dance squeezin past the tables and chairs and all them coats and people standin round up in each other face talkin bout this and that but got no use for this blind man who mostly fixed skates and skooters for all these folks when they was just kids. So I'm pressed up close and we touch talkin with the hum. And here come my daughter cuttin her eye at me like she do when she tell me about my "apolitical" self like I got hoof and mouf disease and there ain't no hope at all.[18]

In this scene, Bovanne's incapacity is figured in his blindness. Miss Hazel's is symbolized through her lack of social and sexual decorum. In this context, the category "apolitical" arises as the designation of an incapacity, but it is a designation that could only come out of the circumstances of left progressivism, circumstances that would make oppositional consciousness the basis on which to presuppose the imbecility of the grass roots. So, when Miss Hazel is dancing with Bovanne, her kids take that as the glaring sign and egregious wonder of her "apolitical" nature and thus attempt to make Miss Hazel aware of her incompetence for radical endeavors.

This may seem like a typical interaction concerning the awkwardness of a parent and the embarrassment of a child. But the tortured exchange between the elderly and the militant allegorizes what Michel de Certeau designates as Western historiography's illusory relationship to the other. As de Certeau explains in *The Writing of History,* "The other is the phantasm of historiography, the object that it seeks, honors, and buries." For de Certeau, this historiography shelters a "structure belonging to modern Western culture," a structure that stipulates that *"intelligibility is established through a relation with the other."*[19]

As guests of the benefit and as a grassroot constituency, Miss Hazel, Bovanne, and the others are sought after and honored. As people to whom the radicals condescend and dismiss as backwards, they are buried so that the young people's intelligence and intelligibility might be established. As youths who claim to break with a past of Uncle Tom-ism apparently embodied in Bovanne and of sexual looseness symbolized by Miss Hazel, the young people are the agents of a new historiography. While it alienates the old folks, this historiography, ironically, claims to give us Bovanne, Miss Hazel, and the black community as consecrated forms of knowledge. In this way, the nationalist historiography that the short story critiques is akin to its hegemonic Western counterpart in that both forms of historical writing represent the people on condition that they remain silent.

An example of this partnership between representation and silence can be found in the following scene. When the children—still smarting over their mother's flirtations with Bovanne—announce to Miss Hazel that she was "suppose to be talking with [Reverend Trent] tonight ... about giving us his basement for campaign headquarters," Miss Hazel responds:

> Didn nobody tell me nuthin. If grass roots mean you kept in the dark
> I can't use it. I really can't. And Reven Trent a fool anyway the way he
> tore into the widow man up there on Edgecomb cause he wouldn't take
> in three of them foster children and the woman not even comfy in the
> ground yet and the man's mind messed up and—[20]

Miss Hazel names the ways in which "grass roots" promises visibility, recognition, and appreciation while requiring her absolute obedience. In doing so, she identifies this requirement as a regulation enacted by radical nationalist politics.

While national liberation claims its radical alterity in opposition to Western liberalism and epistemology, this version of nationalism actually reenacts Michelet's invention by making silence the condition of representation. In a discussion of how the figure of "the poor" functions in nationalist historiography, Rancière states, "[Michelet] invents the art of making the poor speak by keeping them silent, of making them speak as silent people."[21] Ingrained in nationalist historiography is the promise of representation under certain conditions for the people and with certain opportunities for the historian. Summarizing those, Rancière argues that "the historian keeps [the people] silent by making them *visible*."[22] Here he suggests that the historiography that Michelet popularized and the one that shaped how we write modern history satisfies the democratic ideal of representation *and* fulfills democracy's implicit imperative to regulate. In like fashion, the short story questions national liberation's ideal of representation and its unspoken mandate to regulate and silence. Reading the short story in the context of Western historiography's politics suggests that the young people's radicalism is more Western than they would ever care to suppose.

In "My Man Bovanne" the folks from the grass roots represent "gods" and "goddesses" known less for their powers and more for their functions in the schemes of people half their age, called forth to be represented, on the one hand, put down to be silenced, on the other. This romance of silence and representation is what Rancière refers to as "stultification" or "the presupposition of a radical break between two forms of intelligence." Stultification is "the first knowledge that [the master] transmits to the student: the knowledge that he has to be explained to in order to understand, the knowledge that he cannot understand on his own. It is the knowledge of his incapacity."[23] Rather than being the outcome of conservative forces, stultification is the consequence of progressive forms of education that endlessly verify their "starting point: inequality."[24] In the economy of stultification, the student is the silent and ungifted muse who inspires the teacher's representation. Likewise, this "radical break" that constitutes relations between the militants and the old defines the political economy of the benefit, one in which the budding revolutionaries impart to the seniors "a knowledge of their incapacity."

Miss Hazel tried to tell them. She tried to name the distance that constituted this new economy of knowledge. For instance, when her children maligned Mister Bovanne, calling him a "tom" and referring to his eyes as "blown-out fuses," she responded by asking, "Is this what they call the generation gap?"

> "Generation gap," spits Elo, like I suggested castor oil and fricassee possum in the milk-shakes or somethin. "That's a white concept for a white phenomenon. There's no generation gap among Black people. We are a col—"
>
> "Yeh, well never mind," says Jo Lee. "The point is Mama . . . well, it's pride. You embarrass yourself and us too dancin like that."[25]

Here, Elo ruptures the relation between parent and child, fashioning her mother as the ignorant student bereft of radical consciousness and constructing herself as the master endowed with Afrocentric knowledge. Using the metaphoric relation of master and student to explain stultification, Rancière says, "The master's secret is to know how to recognize the distance between the taught material and the person being instructed, the distance also between learning and understanding."[26] In her indignation over her mother's presumably ignorant reference to the notion of a "generation gap," Elo not only calls attention to an alleged distance between a black cultural knowledge and Miss Hazel. She calls attention to that distance by first disavowing it. She disavows it because Miss Hazel and the others represent the grass roots of black politics. As such, they are the evidence of an uninterrupted relationship between young and old. But Elo's statement is not a simple declaration of fact. It is also a rebuttal to an old woman in need of explanation and correction. By associating her mother's question with white folks, she identifies her mother's own intelligence with an inferior Western logic, making Miss Hazel culturally inauthentic and intellectually deficient. While her mother, Bovanne, and the rest of the ordinary folks represent the unbroken pace of tradition and history, they are—to the children—just as much the broken-down inheritors of a grave miseducation. In the nation imagined by black nationalist historiography, the common people would be both citizens and exiles.

In a historic moment in which modes of power were working to make minority culture and difference part of various regimes of representation, knowledge of minority difference and culture would become for national liberation movements a standard by which to determine who was of superior intelligence and who was of inferior grades. In this way, a subjugated knowledge intended to bring about a new appreciation of minoritized subjects would be used by power to let loose forms of subordination. And so, within this milieu, a mother reflects on the rift between her and her children, and she wonders, "[How] did things get to this, that she can't put a sure hand on me and say Mama we love you and care about you and you entitled to enjoy yourself cause you a good woman?"[27] If we read the short story as allegory, we might say that it alludes to the institutional rise of black studies and the subjectivities that its emergence yielded. Manning Marable notes that hundreds of black studies departments and programs emerged in a three-year time span, from 1968 to 1971.[28] Indeed, thirteen hundred colleges and universities offered courses in black studies by 1974. If we place that institutional history within the contours of the short story, we get a more complicated narrative: coupled with the black studies organizations and cultural centers that emerged in that period, black studies departments and curricula helped to alter social relations not only within the academy but outside it as well. "My Man Bovanne" represents an attempt to reckon with that change at its inception. The short story did so by asking us to consider the ways in which the hierarchies that characterized the pedagogical relations in academic settings might have been transferred to the storefronts, community centers, and schools within the neighborhood.

The historical record presents the pedagogical and stultifying relationship of master and student not so much through a story of generational conflict as through the narrative of national liberation's sexism. For instance, in 1970 Bambara's *The Black Woman: An Anthology* addressed the ways in which patriarchy within African American communities and black radical organizations accounted for relations of stultification between black men and women. Eight years later, Michelle Wallace's *Black Macho and the Myth of the Superwoman* would grapple with the sexism of black radicalism during the sixties and the seventies. In the classic text *When and Where I Enter: The Impact of Black Women on Race and Sex in America*, historian Paula Giddings discusses the patriarchal affirmations of the period: "Both Black men and radical-chic White men—women, too—applauded the machismo of leather-jacketed young men, armed to the teeth, rising out of the urban ghetto. The theme of the late sixties was 'Black Power' punctuated by a knotted fist."[29] Black patriarchy would work to provide "a common ethos between northern and southern Blacks" and offer "a metaphor for the male consciousness of the era."[30] Indeed, we can say that black feminism during that period represented a critique of a particular—albeit hegemonic—genre of black male affirmation that was predicated on slotting black women into the position of "students" who, in the words of Angela Davis, were supposed to "'inspire' [their] men and educate [their men's] children."[31]

Because of the ways in which the short story analyzes the power formations that position the neighborhood folks as the students who inspire the teacherly young radicals, we can, therefore, locate "My Man Bovanne" within black feminism's critique of the "radical breaks" wrought by black nationalism. The short story is unique, though, because it names not only gender as an element of stultification but age and disability as well. Indeed, the short story is concerned with how Miss Hazel and Mr. Bovanne are regulated because of age, how Miss Hazel is disciplined according to gender and sexual propriety, and Bovanne is othered because of disability. By attending to stultification's intricate network, "My Man Bovanne" suggests that nationalism's economy of stultification was never populated with one hierarchy, but with many. Hence, we can read "My Man Bovanne" as a literary text whose aim was to clarify how black nationalist historiography as a social discourse was producing an economy of knowledge that would distribute mastery and tutelage as the basis of valorization within black communities.

In addition to underlining the intersectional character of stultification, the short story also points to a moral economy at the center of this radical break between the conscious and the unenlightened, an "obedience to custom" that constitutes its anatomy. In the following scene, for instance, the children try to convey to Miss Hazel what's at stake in her performance of gender and sexual propriety. Again Jo Lee says to her, "The point is Mama . . . well, it's *pride*. You embarrass yourself and us too dancin like that."[32] Here the keyword of national liberation and black nationalism is used to discipline Miss Hazel. Framed as a category of newfound assertion and dignity, "pride"—in this context—operates to seduce Miss Hazel into believing her own impropriety and inferiority. In the moment of black nationalism, pride, as Rhodes states, functioned as a tool to assert "masculine authority and a sexual division of labor."[33] In fact, in one issue of the *Black Panther*, an article upbraided black men and women for "failing to exhibit black pride," a failure denoted by black men's interest in pursuing white women and black women's lack of interest in supporting black men.[34]

What looked like an assertion—pride—turned out to be an instrument. As such, the category "pride" betrays a peculiar lineage, one that Nietzsche identified as the dangerous inspiration that makes up morality:

> [Morality] does not merely have at its command every kind of means of frightening off critical hands and torture-instruments: its security reposes far more in a certain art of enchantment it has at its disposal— it knows how to "inspire." With this art it succeeds, often with no more than a single glance, in paralysing the critical will and even in enticing it over to its own side.[35]

What morality could do with a single glance, it was also supposed to accomplish by evoking pride. If deployed artfully, maybe pride would inspire

Miss Hazel to restrain her sexual energies. Perhaps it would enchant her own critical will away from the wave of regulation that threatened to overtake her, beguile her away from ever recognizing nationalism's mission to use morality as a way of measuring a person's value and legibility. Pride, Bambara suggests, is a holy watchword of stultification, dividing the world between those who possess it and those who don't.

In 1968, morality was lifted as one of the main points of national struggle and black studies. At the black studies symposium that took place that year at Yale, African American studies scholar Nathan Hare said, "We have to begin to study these things, to question, perhaps to build a new black morality of our own, at the same time as we develop a new kind of educational system."[36] In this proposal, Hare helps articulate how the emergence of black studies as a critical and institutional enterprise set laws and customs over its constituency.

Women-of-color feminism in general, and black feminism in particular, arose partly as systems to critique the orthodoxies of national liberation, chief among those being the hierarchies sanctified by moral discourses. But those hierarchies were not designed by people intending evil, but were promoted by those with the best and most progressive intentions. As Rancière observes, the stultifier is not a conservative bogeyman, "not an aged obtuse master who crams his students' skulls full of poorly digested knowledge, or a malignant character mouthing half-truths in order to shore up his power and the social order."[37] The stultifier is a sympathizer—sometimes a liberal, sometimes a radical. On most occasions, he is the enlightened pedagogue trying to develop ignorance into maturity, the one for whom the accumulation of his knowledge is the verification of the other's ignorance. The critique of stultification thus interrogates the benevolent paternalism that has historically characterized not only liberal but also leftist politics. In the context of the short story, it is young people—the self-appointed guardians of culture and community—who Miss Hazel has to fight off. The relations of force that the short story dramatizes are produced by the well-intentioned and the militant. They allegorize contentions between radicals and their constituencies, quarrels safely removed from the historical archive, frictions kept on the quiet tip. To hear the progressives tell it, they are inequalities that can be obscured or even overlooked because they are the necessary practices of liberation, the appropriate conventions piled on tasks pursued in the name of love.

Institutionalization and the Distortion of Good Intentions

In those days of the student movements, good intentions made their way on breezes. Stuart Hall recalls those times. In an interview, Colin McCabe asks him, "You must have been at that period [after World War II] a totally enthusiastic backer of national liberation struggles in the third world."[38] Hall responds that he was indeed enthusiastic and recalls a dinner to celebrate the defeat of the French in Indochina. He goes on to say that with the 1950 election of the Marxist government led by Cheddi Jagan in Guyana, Kenya's independence from Britain in 1961, and Malaysia's rise from British rule in 1963, he "knew that the end of empire was a huge thing that was happening right before his eyes" (15). There was, he says, "a belief in the beyond of colonialism," a belief and confidence in decolonization as the utopia that lay beyond the borders of colonial repression (17). This was the emotional tenor of a decolonizing time, one that inspired faith in the nation form. According to this faith, the nation could be liberated from the violations of liberal democracy and Western imperialism and put to radical ends.

But the malignancies of colonialism, which worked their way into postcolonial nations, undermined that confidence. Hall states that "[the] moment of decolonisation was a moment when the deformations of colonialism had not been deeply interrupted. There'd been a shift of political power and domination. But, take the Caribbean. It remained a poor, one-crop, economically dependent region" (16). Hall describes here the realities of neocolonialism, the fact that the dismantling of the colonizer's ensigns might ordain a new hegemony. This shift, in Hall's words, would "show why Fanon was right. You have to have your nationalist moment. But the nationalist moment can never be enough. It can never be enough" (ibid.). Similar to Rancière's critique of the unity promoted by republican romanticism and Bambara's critique about the presumptions and functions of grass roots, Hall elaborates his interpretation of Fanon, stating, "The attempt to build a unity for developing the nation leads to the emergence of single figures or one-party states. No contradictions, no place in the ideology for opposition" (ibid.). Hall indicates, here, that as the nation form became the goal and end point of liberation, the autocracies of the colonial era would take hold of anticolonialism's epic experiment.

We can think of "My Man Bovanne" as a prophetic critique of that era's enthusiasm for institutional transformations. Miss Hazel, for instance, critiques the young radicals' presumption that they will endow the folk with unprecedented agencies and usher in Freedom Land. Her agnosticism is roused because the young people's radicalism evokes prior institutional histories and formations that were presumably put down by black nationalism. Still discussing her children's response to her flirtations with Bovanne, she says, "And here come my youngest, Task, with a tap on my elbow *like he the third grade monitor and I'm cuttin up on the line to assembly.*" During this exchange, her daughter Elo compares Miss Hazel to "a bitch in heat." And Miss Hazel thinks to herself, "Terrible thing when your own children talk to you like that. Pullin me out the party and hustlin me into some stranger's kitchen in the back of a bar *just like the damn police.*"[39] Both of these instances are significant for the ways in which they call to mind prior institutional entanglements. Task's tap and the children's ambush remind Miss Hazel of grammar-school regulations and police encounters, clashes that are presumably the antitheses of a revolutionary movement. Yet Miss Hazel's memories of school and police harassment point to the ways in which black nationalism operates as a palimpsest inscribed with the images of various institutions. Rather than being innocent of the institutional restrictions and exclusions that it sought to overcome, revolutionary nationalism often reproduced those restrictions and exclusions within its own day-to-day practices. Like its anticolonial counterpart, black power proved to be very often a weak interruption of power.

"My Man Bovanne" demands an analysis, then, of how institutions roam across political and cultural practices, how institutions enjoy mobility because they are — as Derrida puts it — "always and already the structure of our interpretation."[40] Touching on institutions and their itinerant natures, Gayatri Chakravorty Spivak argues that there is no "non-institutional environment." Rather, institutions do not "exist in isolation," a fact that obliges us to analyze our frameworks and modes of interpretation.[41] Spivak, therefore, rebuts the notion that institutions can be thought of as entities discretely removed from the spaces outside their walls. Instead, we get a picture of institutions as not only material objects but also discursive edifices characterized by promiscuous interactions. As such, we are obliged to look at frameworks and structures of interpretation if we are to understand those promiscuities that compel institutions to do anything but stay put, those affairs that betray institutions' interests in and desires for seemingly noninstitutional terrains.

In the historic context that motivates Bambara's short story, the non-Western happenings that occasioned the institutional rise of black studies are the national liberation struggles of the fifties and sixties. "My Man Bovanne" observes how the rise of black studies and black power helped to disseminate various institutional logics and practices to the presumably noninstitutionalized landscapes of African American communities. Indeed, the short story seems to say, "There is no noninstitutional environment" that will guarantee our radical innocence.

The short story and the struggles that occasion it point to the need to engage international frameworks as we narrate the history of ethnic studies, the practices of the black power movement, and ultimately the changes to the American academy. In fact, as Spivak argues, the history of institutionalization in the West since the seventeenth century has referred and continues to refer to happenings in non-Western environments. As she states, we are caught within the institutionalized fiction of "the West as West, or the West as the world"[42] if we assume that we can narrate institutionalization in the West without addressing what is happening outside that region. Turning our attention to cultural texts like "My Man Bovanne" and to the antiracist movements becomes one way of anchoring our critiques of the university within the histories of non-Western struggles and formations.

Briefly gesturing toward the rising institutional promiscuity of black nationalism, John H. Bracey Jr., August Meier, and Elliott Rudwick wrote in their introduction to the 1970 anthology *Black Nationalism in America,* "Racial solidarity or black consciousness has pervaded all strata of Afro-America." Noting how forms of black solidarity inspired groups such as "teachers, social workers, priests, lawyers, scholars, and athletes" and how "blacks are more highly visible in government, private industry, and the mass media than ever before," the authors argued, "Paradoxically, this increasingly effective display of racial solidarity has actually *produced more integration than advocates of separatism perhaps realize.*"[43] We might read Bracey, Meier, and Rudwick's arguments as more than a straightforward historical observation. We can say that they are acknowledgments of a new discursive context for minority difference and culture, one that establishes subjugated differences in general, and minority nationalism in particular, as the ironic resources for rather than the obvious weapons against institutional absorption. In a similar passage from the introduction, the three observe, for instance: "In the sixties with the combination of successes and failures of the civil-rights movement, some younger middle-class blacks turned more and more to a nationalist rhetoric in an attempt to gain wide support for their essentially assimilationist goals and to maximize any gains from the annual summer rebellions of the lower-class blacks."[44] Here, they point to an operation of power in which the adversarial rebellions associated with urban uprisings and student movements become techniques of upward mobility. This passage and the one before it indicate a shift in power as it turns toward rather than away from subjugated differences and cultures. In this context and shortly after the student rebellions, forms of power looked out on an agitated landscape and wondered how best to institutionalize differences as a way to better manage them.

In contrast to national liberation's acceptance of Western institutional models, sixties and seventies black feminism deliberated upon how institutional logics and practices insinuated themselves into African American communities. In *The Black Woman,* for instance, one contributor after another addresses how black power revivifies Western institutional concepts and practices. More specifically, the volume is filled with contributors who discuss how patriarchal practices of black nationalism recall and promote the gender and sexual regulations of bourgeois institutions, promoting those regulations as part of the black woman's responsibilities. For instance, in Kay Lindsay's "Poem" from that volume, she writes:

> I'm not one of those who believes
> That an act of valor, for a woman
> Need take place inside her.
>
> My womb is packed in mothballs
> And I hear that winter will be mild.
>
> Anyway I gave birth twice
> And my body deserves a medal for that
> But I never got one.
>
> Mainly because they thought
> I was just answering the call of nature.
>
> But now that the revolution needs numbers
> Motherhood got a new position
> Five steps behind manhood.

> And I thought sittin' in the back of the bus
> Went out with Martin Luther King.[45]

What is striking about the poem besides its lyricism is the fact that it presents a "shift" from one discourse around motherhood as a natural occurrence to reproduction as a revolutionary strategy. While the word *revolution* signifies a "new position," Lindsay's elaboration of both those categories exposes how the revolution reenacts the not-too-distant hierarchies of Jim Crow segregation. As a call to nature and a call to revolution, motherhood exists "five steps behind manhood." As such, the poem questions the idea that "the revolution" represents social rupture and instead aligns its gender and sexual politics with social reproduction. The revolution becomes the vehicle for the conservative institutions from which it ostensibly diverges, namely, the patriarchal family form.

Black feminists during and after that period identified the ways in which black nationalism as an institution possessed interpretative structures consistent with white racial formations. For black feminists of the day, the institution of patriarchy undergirded much of black nationalist political and community organizing. Indeed, if the late sixties into the seventies were noted for the chauvinism of black nationalist politics, then black feminism responded to that chauvinism by illuminating and analyzing how the ghosts of Western institutionality gave breath to black nationalist organizations.

The short story and the larger context of black feminism in the late sixties and seventies identify how hegemonic institutional formations and practices were inscribed on black nationalism. As such, they underline Spivak's argument about the omnipresence of institutionality. Another way of saying this is to say that "My Man Bovanne" allegorizes the critical and interpretative function of black feminism—that is, by using the character Miss Hazel to present black feminism as an analytic enterprise designed to comprehend institutional logics and practices and to provide alternatives to them.

It used to be that black feminism was a way of framing and interpreting institutional overlaps and promiscuities. In this aspect, black feminism shares kinship with Derrida's notion of deconstruction and its relation to institutional analysis, a notion that defines that analytic mode as having never been "a technical set of discursive procedures" or even less "a new hermeneutic method working on archives or utterances in the shelter of a given and stable institution." Deconstruction, he argued, was a "taking of a position, in the work itself, toward the politico-institutional structures that constitute and regulate our practice, our competences, and our performances."[46] Inasmuch as black feminism addressed heteropatriarchy as an institutional model at work in black nationalism, it intersected with the interests and aims of deconstruction.

Like black feminism and like deconstruction, "My Man Bovanne" illustrates that an institution is more than a set of walls and structures. Miss Hazel, as one among the ignorant, bears witness to the interpretative structures that try to make the home folks into the tools of progressive regulations, regulations that call to mind the restrictions of school, police, and family. The picture that she gives us of national liberation is that of a collage made up of various disciplinary regimes. In opposition to those regimes, the short story—perhaps even against Bambara herself[47]—takes a position against the restrictions of nationalism and attempts to undermine any notion that black nationalism is the appropriate representative of black communities. In doing so, the short story revises the subjects that constitute the "masses" and signals politico-institutional structures that are alternative to the ones that black nationalism mandated.

Sexuality, Responsibility, and the Paternal Purpose

One way of understanding the short story is to say that it contends with the young people's narrative of responsibility, their sense of what one is obligated to do in order to establish and preserve a nationalist community. That question was at the forefront of the sixties student movements. For instance, in "The Justification for Black Studies," drafted by the San Francisco State Black Student Union, the statement listed one of the goals as the preparation of "Black students for direct participation in Black community struggles, and to define themselves as responsible to and for the future success of that community."[48]

The student movements did not ask the question of responsibility in a vacuum. They did so within an institutional context that was also posing that question. For instance, in 1945 a Harvard committee made up of eleven eminent faculty members would—at the request of then president James Bryant Conant—release *The Harvard Report on General Education*, also known as the "Red Book." The Red Book would attempt to outline the responsibilities that a liberal arts education had to a functioning democracy, attempting to secularize a then Christian-oriented American higher education and to clarify higher education's relationship to the public good in a "challenging era of global responsibility."[49] Arguing, in particular, for the responsibilities that a liberal arts education had in the U.S. context, the Red Book stated that a liberal arts education was necessary to inspire innovation and to pass on a sense that "We are part of an organic process, which is the American, and more broadly, the Western evolution."[50] While "religious education, education in the great books, and education in modern democracy may be mutually exclusive," the report went on to argue that "they work together to the same end, which is belief in the idea of man and society that we inherit, adapt, and pass on."[51] As the Red Book suggests, the liberal arts transformations to American higher education were defined in terms of responsibility to the nation and were organized around the figure of Western man.

We can locate the Red Book's investment in connecting the liberal arts to the state, again, within *The Conflict of the Faculties*. In his letter to Kant, King Frederick William upbraided the philosopher for "[misusing] your philosophy to distort and disparage many of the cardinal and basic teachings of the Holy Scriptures and Christianity," and scolded Kant for his "irresponsibility," demanding that he *apply [his] authority and [his] talents to the progressive realization of our paternal purpose.*"[52] Kant, of course, responded by reassuring the king that in keeping philosophy and Christianity separate and by keeping the people away from scholarly debates he is indeed behaving responsibly to the paternal purpose, a purpose denoted through an extension of the nation-state form and national ideals through disciplinary and epistemic means. No wonder, then, that the university would emerge as the site of a unique responsibility—one that tries to foster subjects accountable for and to the nation-state and nationalist ideals, subjects who would feel obligated to a paternal purpose.

Recognizing this aspect of the university through his reading of *The Conflict of the Faculties,* Derrida identifies the modern Western university as a powerful and historic domain for the production of the paternal purpose and our responsibility to it. Hence, if the modern university begins with Kant,[53] then the modern university begins with the theme of responsibility and the set of questions that it launches: "*What* do we represent? *Whom* do we represent? Are we responsible?"[54] Kant's conversation with the king made the question of responsibility a powerful constitutive feature of Western intellectual life and the Western academy; it also measured responsibility in terms of how well the intellectual and the academy realized paternal purposes.

The student movements would reimagine this aspect of the university and redistribute it to minoritized populations. They would reimagine the university as the place in which minoritized subjects might articulate forms of responsibility that challenged and contested the state. Yet, while the civil rights and black power movements may have objected to the paternal purposes set down by U.S. liberal capitalism, those movements had no quarrel with the intellectual and institutional edict to realize a paternal mission. In fact, they had a profound belief in that mission. We might think, therefore, of the social movements of the sixties and the seventies as ones that both contested the paternal purpose of liberal and colonial capital and replaced those purposes with others that called for disciplinary identifications with minority nationalism. While those movements questioned the authority of the bourgeois state and colonial governments' paternal missions, they left the idea of the paternal purpose and its necessity intact. In doing so, they failed to inquire about the discursive and ideological architecture of responsibility and the ways in which that architecture resembled the blueprint that Kant evolved in his correspondence with the king.

The U.S. student movements and the birth of the interdisciplines hail from this discourse of responsibility, and in that discourse we can find the histories of sexuality. Indeed, the civil rights and black power movements fostered paternal purposes that legislated sexual hegemonies. This fact obtained not only in the context of the black power movement, as was previously discussed, but described that movement's more liberal predecessor and peer, the civil rights movement. Discussing the ways in which a paternalistic civil rights movement became a forum for disciplining sexuality in general, and homosexuality in particular, historian Thaddeus Russell writes that the civil rights era of the 1950s was one in which an agitated black middle class pressured African Americans in general, and a more sexually tolerant African American working class in particular, to conform to the sexual ideals of the American nation-state. Russell argues that "The civil rights ideology of the black middle class rose in tandem with a new racial liberalism among white elites that was born out of the discourse of ethnic and racial tolerance during World War II."[55]

In addition to the explicitly homophobic writings and sermons of civil rights leader Adam Clayton Powell Jr., Russell discusses Martin Luther King Jr.'s implicit and sometimes explicit theories of African American integration. In his theory of the "integrated personality," for example, King counseled against "those who are giving their lives to a tragic life of pleasure and throwing away everything they have in riotous living" and recommended that they "lose [their] ego in some great cause, some great purpose, some great ideal, some great loyalty."[56] In correspondence with a young gay man who wrote to King's advice column in *Ebony* magazine about the young man's homosexuality, King noted that the problem of homosexuality "was not an uncommon one" but required "careful attention." King ended his response by recommending that the young man "'seek a good psychiatrist' in order 'to solve it.'"[57] Through leaders such as King and Powell, the student-led civil rights movement became a site for the production of modes of responsibility that were antagonistic to sexual freedom and homoerotic agency and that evoked the historic function of the university as the domain for defining responsibility according to the dictates and errands of national identity. Put plainly, the genealogy for articulating responsibility in the way that the civil rights movement did lies partly in the regimes of power/knowledge put in place in the name of the Western academy.

While the Western academy has been a powerful domain for the production of responsibility, the student movements did not simply reproduce this aspect of the university. They helped to revise the objects of responsibility, presenting minority cultures as the new aim of responsible oppositional politics. The student movements ushered in exciting new social contracts between minoritized subjects and marginalized communities, but they also disregarded the complex ideological and discursive foundations of responsibility, fostering unwitting alliances between radical activism and nationalist regulations. Hence, as they revised and recontextualized such founding questions as "What do we represent? Whom do we represent? And are we responsible?" the civil rights and black power movements helped to make sexual regulation a substructure of minority responsibility. Because of this aspect of the antiracist movements, this regime of regulation became an integral part of the American academy's affirmation of ethnic studies, helping to pave the way for a new interdiscipline's restrictive affirmations.

We can see the genealogy of responsibility even more directly in the black studies movement. For Nathan Hare and for many other proponents of black studies, erecting an interdiscipline organized around the study of black cultures was an academic enterprise geared toward the simultaneous and deliberate establishment of a moral discourse for which scholars trained in black studies would be responsible. Writing in 1998, scholar and cultural critic Barbara Smith pointed to that establishment in her remarks about black history and queer sexualities. Discussing how African American history provided little acknowledgment that "Black lesbian and gays ever existed," Smith attributed that absence not only to homophobia and heterosexism but also to "the reality that Black history has often served extrahistorical purposes that would militate against bringing up 'deviant' sexualities."[58] Smith traced those extrahistorical purposes to a bourgeois nationalist imperative: "Black history's underlying agenda frequently has been to demonstrate that African Americans are full human beings who deserve to be treated like Americans, like citizens, like men."[59]

At the Yale conference, Maulana Karenga argued that black history was foundational to black studies because black history is "the most accessible subject and that's really the place where one is 'inspired' and 'informed.'"[60] As black history provided the foundations for black studies, it also authorized a discourse of responsibility that obliged the agents of black studies to demonstrate the full humanity of blacks and their equivalence with American citizenship and masculinity. In doing so, this sense of responsibility alienated black queer sexualities and identities from the epistemic and institutional purviews of African American studies. Black studies would thus be the fulfillment of another type of paternal purpose, one presumably originating in black cultures and one that would produce discourses of responsibility that had direct bearing on sexual agency and diversity as topics for research as well as institutional protection and fulfillment. As it inherited the civil rights and black power notions of responsibility, black studies would lift up black cultures only by offering institutional models for disciplining gender and sexual eccentricity.

"My Man Bovanne" goes to the very heart of this aspect of the black power movement and power/knowledge by bringing the architecture of responsibility into stark relief. The short story exposes the sexual restrictions of that architecture and advances sexual agency as an alternative to responsibility's edifice. After Miss Hazel has gone through round after round of her children telling her what her responsibilities are to the movement, to the neighborhood, and to the people, she devises a plan to sneak My Man Bovanne away. She begins to let her mind wander and run:

> And I'm thinking I'll have him change the lock on my door first thing. Then I'll give the man a nice warm bath with jasmine leaves in the water and a little Epsom salt on the sponge to do his back. And then a good rubdown with rose water and olive oil. Then a cup of lemon tea with a taste in it. And a little talcum, some of that fancy stuff Nisi mother sent over last Christmas. And then a massage, a good face massage round the forehead which is the worryin part. Cause you gots to take care of the older folks. And let them know they still needed to run the mimeo machine and keep the spark plugs clean and fix the mailboxes for folks who might help us get the breakfast program goin, and the school for the little kids and the campaign and all. Cause old folks is the nation. That what Nisi was sayin and I mean to do my part.[61]

To the nationalist, Miss Hazel's bath with "Epsom salt on the sponge" and her "rubdown with rose water and olive oil" will seem like "naïve knowledges, located low down on the hierarchy, beneath the level of cognition or scientificity."[62] These vernacular refreshments and titillations will seem to the kids "inadequate to the task" of nation building. But rather than submit to a logic of stultification that imagines local practices around sexuality as empty amusements, Miss Hazel reaches into some other archive and calls forth subjugated knowledges that refuse docility and banishment. And so she reactivates carnal knowledges from regional cultures, knowledges that defy stultifying hierarchies of superior and lower intelligences, hierarchies that are—quiet as it's kept—indispensable to liberation.

In the passage from "My Man Bovanne" just quoted, sexuality is not only a proxy for local knowledges. It is a principle of distillation, the foundation for separating the things that are worth our time from the things that aren't worth the trouble. Mimeo machines, rubdowns, spark plugs, cups of tea, and breakfast programs—these items deserve some care and attention, but sexual regulation? Of all the yokes to take upon them, why be responsible for that one? We can think of the passage as Miss Hazel's formula for emancipation, what Rancière defines as the process by which "every common person might conceive his human dignity, take the measure of his intellectual capacity, and decide how to use it."[63] For Miss Hazel, sexual expression is a way of consummating the will, a method for asserting corporeal as well as intellectual and political capacities. In such an understanding of sexual agency, participating in the political campaign and supporting the school follows from seemingly apolitical gestures like face massages and sponge baths. For this old and ignorant woman, sexual agency denotes the broad program for "[transforming] all [the lowly people's] works into ways of demonstrating the humanity that is in them as in everyone else."[64] Sexuality names a refusal to think under the sign of inequalities that divide the world between those who have radical politics and consciousness from those who don't. And by this route, the people "[will] discover unsuspected intellectual [and political] powers that will put them on the road to new discoveries."[65] And so she ends the story with another name, one different from and seemingly inferior to the name "grass roots," but a name that is closer to the will and attention responsible for her and the people's emancipation: "I imagine," Bovanne says, "you are a very pretty woman, Miss Hazel." "I surely am, I say just like the *hussy* my daughter always says I was."[66]

My (Main) Man Bovanne: Disability, Ethical Development, and the Responsible Subject

As the short story uses Miss Hazel to sunder logics that contrive hierarchies of lower and higher intelligences, "My Man Bovanne" uses Bovanne himself to disrupt the able-ism of national liberation. In doing so, the short story exposes the ways in which national liberation in general, and black nationalism in particular, not only naturalized heteronormativity but able-bodiedness too. As such, we can read the character Bovanne as a metaphor for the debilities caused by U.S. racial projects and the dominant response of antiracist social movements to those debilities. Elaborating on the historic function of disability as a metaphor for minority status, disability studies scholar Douglas C. Baynton observes, "Disability has functioned historically to justify inequality for disabled people themselves, but it has also done so for women and minority groups."[67] Historically attributed to U.S. minority groups, disability has also justified discrimination against those groups, becoming "a significant factor in three great citizenship debates of the nineteenth and early twentieth centuries: women's suffrage, African American freedom and civil rights, and the restriction of immigration."[68] In the context of the extension and denial of citizenship, disability was used to "clarify and define who deserved, and who was deservedly excluded from, citizenship."[69]

In terms of the short story, Bovanne refers both to the discrimination and paternalism suffered by disabled persons within the United States and to disability's role in the grammar of African American citizenship. If disability justified exclusions from citizenship, then Bovanne stands for an inaugural loss that founds African Americans' historic exclusions from the rights and privileges of U.S. citizenship. Explaining the function of disability in the racialized exclusions of citizenship, Baynton notes that "arguments for racial inequality and immigration restrictions invoked tendencies to feeble-mindedness, mental illness, deafness, blindness, and other disabilities in particular races and ethnic groups."[70] Within a context in which disability has structured racial inequality, Bovanne is the figure of abjection that disturbs the order, identity, and system of citizenship and national identity.

As citizenship and national identity depend on regulatory discourses about sexuality, Bovanne also represents a disturbance to national identity's regulation of sexuality. Theorizing the relationship between heterosexuality and disability, Robert McRuer argues that "the system of compulsory able-bodiedness, which in a sense produces disability, is thoroughly interwoven with the system of compulsory heterosexuality that produces queerness: that, in fact, compulsory heterosexuality is contingent on compulsory able-bodiedness and vice versa."[71] In the short story we see heterosexuality's relationship to compulsory able-bodiedness precisely through the drama around Miss Hazel's sexual interest in Bovanne, a drama narrated by the children as a matter of "pride." Just as the kids try to force Miss Hazel's heterosexuality in directions that conform to the party's goals, they also attempt to steer her sexual interests away from Bovanne because of his disability. For her interest in Bovanne, Miss Hazel's children chastise her for being "not too discriminating" and behaving like a hussy. In fact, Elo says, "His feet can smell a cracker a mile away and go into their shuffle number post haste. And them eyes. He could be a little considerate and put on some shades."[72] For Elo, Bovanne's disability symbolizes the antithesis of revolutionary progress and nationalist pride. Whereas the children's feet lead them to the community and the nation, Bovanne's feet and apolitical nature, symbolized by his blank eyes, run back to Mr. Charlie. In doing so, the short story allegorizes how national liberation—with its idealization of black heterosexual masculinity—operates as a simultaneous regime of sexuality and able-bodiedness, in the process using race pride to manage disability and desire.

As the antithesis of nationalism's emphasis on black masculine prowess, Bovanne is not only the symbol of an inaugural loss. He is also the metaphor for an originary denial resting in the bosom of African American liberation movements. Discussing this founding refutation in relation to minority movements in the United States, Baynton writes: "[Disability] figured not just in arguments *for* the inequality of women and minorities but also in arguments *against* those inequalities. Such arguments took the form of vigorous denials that the groups in question actually had these disabilities." Historically, aggrieved groups have denied their purported disabilities by arguing that they were able in mind and body and therefore "not the proper subjects of discrimination." As Baynton says, "Rarely have oppressed groups denied that disability is an adequate justification for social and political inequality."[73]

As an early example of how black liberation struggles invested in ability, we might only remember Frederick Douglass's claim that "the true basis of rights was the capacity of individuals."[74] In such a formulation, disability becomes not only the sign of incapacity but also the obstacle to an appeal to rights, for bourgeois nationalism, as well as the impediment to national embodiment, for revolutionary nationalism. In the context of the short story, the young activists deny Bovanne in an effort to refute any charge that they and their people are disabled. While Bovanne may be "an adequate justification for social and political inequality," they are not. As the story shows, this denial does not arise from generic circumstances and formations. It is launched from that variety of rights- and nation-based social formations that characterize much of grassroots politics. Before national liberation, Bovanne's disability was agency: he repaired what was broken and everybody liked him. After black nationalism, Bovanne became a pariah whose disability was stripped of any properties that might sustain community. Bovanne stands for a completely new way in which community began to function with the advent of black nationalism. As a discursive formation, community began to operate according to able-bodiedness, the short story implies. Through Bovanne, the short story illustrates a constitutive but little acknowledged part of the turn toward revolution.

As a figure of disability, Bovanne's blindness foils nationalism's project of ethical development. Bovanne in the children's eyes is the Uncle Tom shuffler who is antithetical to revolutionary and cultural nationalism's model of ethical development, a development predicated on radical consciousness and self-determination. We see those mandates in the children's exhortations to dance and dress in ways that are culturally appropriate and therefore respectable, to conduct oneself in a manner becoming of a mother of the nation. To court Bovanne is to forfeit not only respectability but also a nationalist future of self-determination and capability, to give up the nation for a set of blank eyes and shuffling feet.

But Miss Hazel is a hussy, and that's exactly what allows her to refute Bovanne's illegibility as a disabled subject. Her sexual interest in him is part of an economy of knowledge that remembers Bovanne as the one who "fixed skates and scooters," as someone who had a place in the neighborhood.[75] Her desire for him, therefore, refutes an able-ist construction of Bovanne as socially useless and puts her at odds with the children's nationalism. Miss Hazel accesses local memory to rebut the sexual regulations imposed on her by the kids *and* to reframe disability.

In addition to functioning as the metaphor for an inaugural loss and an originary denial, Bovanne also symbolizes that historic shift in power to which this book is devoted. Knowing that minority struggles within the United States are haunted by the specter of disability, forms of power/ knowledge devised ways to exploit the anxieties inspired by that haunting. Those forms would solicit minoritized subjects by ascribing ability in some instances and disability in others. Ethical development, for minorities, in this moment of regulatory affirmations, would become the constant negotiation with the specter of disability and the persistent promise and deferral of ability and recognition. In this way, Bovanne allegorizes the entrance of minoritized subjects onto a new historical scene in which those people and communities disabled by minority status would have to straddle their position as enfeebled intelligences and their chance at joining the ranks of higher intellects who know things by "reason," "method," "training," and "study." These are the relations of power appropriate for a world that must now make concessions to minority demands for access and inclusion, a world in which the mechanisms of power would promise to turn disabling differences into able-bodied cultures and identities—that is, if minoritized subjects would only agree to identify with its institutions and belong.

The Epistemological Propositions of the
Post–Civil Rights Academy

If "it is in discourse that power and knowledge are joined together," as Foucault argued, the minority movements of the 1960s and their instantiation in neighborhoods, on campuses, in businesses, and in the state demonstrate how minority discourse occasioned a new union for power and knowledge.[76] This new union would help to rewrite the ingredients for social reproduction, making minority difference, culture, and identity much more than isolated acts, showing them to be the means by which new social relations were produced. "My Man Bovanne" and the social changes that brought about these new relations encourage us to assemble a theoretical apparatus that can account for the rise of social relations explicitly shaped by discourses of minority difference.

The oldest critical apparatus that we have for thinking about social relations and how they are managed through affirmation is historical materialism. Indeed, historical materialism has frustrated a constitutive and hegemonic affirmation of capitalist relations of production—the laborer who is "contracted as [a free person], who [is] equal before the law."[77] We might recall that, for Marx, capital makes its mark on personhood through labor power and labor, targeting labor power because it is capital's source of value, granting it the possibility of reproduction. Discussing the conditions by which labor power circulates as a commodity, Marx says, "[Labour-power] can appear on the market as a commodity only if, and in so far as, its possessor, the individual whose labour-power it is, offers it for sale or sells it as a commodity."[78] Labor power is thus the laborer's difference that might be consumed by the money owner, the deceptively affirmative property within all subjects. With this theorization of labor power, Marx posited capital as that political and economic operation organized around the use and manipulation of a form of difference, one that seems to proclaim the laborer as free and in charge.

In the post–World War II moment, various social institutions would reorganize themselves around the use and manipulation of the forms of difference promoted by insurgent social movements. In this historic period, minority differences would emerge as properties inherent within minoritized histories, subjects, and cultures. In the age of the student movements, these emergent differences would be like labor power because they too were capacities that hegemonic forces would try to pick up and gather. The scene of this appropriation was not so much the one made up of factory floors and labor strikes but the theater produced by student protests and academic negotiations. This scene, rather than the other one, pushes us to redefine the point and horizon of materialist analysis.

This is what Miss Hazel began to see. And hence, she started to wonder how the value of a head rag could change overnight, how it could be a point of embarrassment on Monday and switch into a declaration of pride come Tuesday morning. She began to notice the shift that came when black power blew in. Understanding that shift means that we must turn our attention to the academic struggles of the sixties and thereafter, especially to the ways in which those struggles provided the conditions that made minority difference and culture generalizable beyond the academy. If we take "the academy" to be not simply the literal institutions of postsecondary education but that set of relations organized around giving new value to minority culture and difference, then we might see the ways in which that shift comprised new collections of social and subject formations. The "academy" names that mode of institutionality and power that delivers those marginalities over for institutional validation, certification, and legibility, bringing them into entirely new circumstances of valorization.[79]

It is important to remember that minority culture and difference are managed in the very moment that Western democracies believed that student protests and antiracist movements would throw civilization into crisis. "Whether by way of psychoanalysis, culturalism, or economism," Spivak argues, valorizing marginality "is still part of [a] crisis-management" involving powerful institutional forces.[80] The Nixon administration and American capital's investment in minority difference should by themselves caution us away from the idea that the entrance of minoritized subjects and knowledges into spheres of representation and valorization signaled a new Eden for minority culture and identity. Indeed, that entrance was part of a larger effort by modes of power to keep minoritized grievances from compromising the itineraries of state, capital, and academy.

The 1970s especially represented the moment of the valorization and disfranchisement of marginality. For African Americans, the decade witnessed the upward and downward expansion of black social structures.[81] At the same time that there was unprecedented access to education and employment, for instance, there was also growing economic disfranchisement for

African Americans. This phenomenon was part of an economic trend beginning in the 1970s in which income was reallocated more and more among the wealthy, so much so that between 1973 and 2000, the share of income going to the top 1 percent of American taxpayers would rise by 91 percent, growing by only 31 percent for the top 10 percent of taxpayers.[82] During this thirty-year period, the average income of the poor and the working class would increase by only 16 percent.[83] African American culture would be absorbed into processes of valorization—as evidence of U.S. racial progress and as a convenient tool for affirming diversity—while more and more blacks would be incorporated into an expanding prison-industrial complex and thrown into escalating levels of poverty.[84] This contradictory social landscape would help to give birth to contexts in which the valorization of minority cultures would be dialectically tied to processes and conditions of devaluation.

In the last part of the story again Miss Hazel plans a regimen of jasmine leaves, Epsom salt, rose water, and olive oil. We might read this regimen as the metaphor for an intervention needed for subjects who are devalued not only by social processes outside the neighborhood but by political formations within it as well. It is as if the upward and downward expansion of social structures found their discursive counterpart in indigenous efforts to affirm and manage difference. When the children try to affirm and manage the folks from the neighborhood, they thus operate within the spirit of that expansion.

But Epsom salt, olive oil, rose water, and mimeo machines are not about retreating from institutional contexts because of their overwhelming complexity. They are about calling for modes of valorization and responsibility that are not wedded to management and regulation. More specifically, they call for the articulation of new projects and practices within the specific crisis that academy entails—ventures that will meet the management and hegemonic valorization of difference with alternative inflections of minority particularity and culture, and that can name and challenge even the absorption of minority difference.

Like June Jordan's essay "Black Studies: Bringing Back the Person," Bambara's short story directs us to critical practices that must take place *within* the crisis of institutionalization. If we follow the story's lead, we have an opportunity to construct a materialist analysis that engages the academy and its duplicitous valorization of minority difference and culture.

We also have a chance to fashion a politics that wrestles with academy's means of making difference valuable. In that effort, we might even achieve more radical versions of democracy. An immanent critique of this sort is necessary now more than ever. Such a critique acknowledges that minority difference and culture have the potential to be sites of resolution and rupture and are therefore the objects of dangerous negotiations. In Ethiopia, I hear, they tell a story of a cow that gave birth to a fire. Being a mother, her first instinct was to lick it, but she knew the baby—despite itself—would burn her. It occurred to her to leave it, but she could not do that either. That fire was her own. That burning thing is to the mother what minority culture is now to those of us who work with subjugated modes of difference. We are like that heifer who is trying to figure out how to handle a flame.

Immigration and the Drama of Affirmation

IT'S NOT OFTEN THAT THE HISTORY OF IMMIGRATION is taken up in discussions of the antiracist movements. The social movements of the sixties are imagined typically as having to do with domestic minorities, civil rights, and affirmative action. Such frameworks tend to imagine the immigrant as an international entity inadmissible to the taken-for-granted histories of minoritized subjects within the United States.[1] Rather than being the exception to U.S. racialization, the immigrant is deeply implicated in the transformations to the racial state and to racial capital in the years following the 1960s. Indeed, during the post–World War II period, immigration in general, and foreign student migration in particular, were priorities for the U.S. nation-state, a fact that drew the U.S. government and the American academy into a new relation, one that helped to attune the expansions of both the U.S. economy and the American university in the years after World War II. Thus, the history of immigration, at least in the period after World War II, is partly underwritten by the transformations in the American academy and vice versa. In such a context, immigration and international student migration became new elements in power's affirmative development that would be looked at and worried over in an effort to determine their suitability for hegemonic absorption. As the history of immigration to the United States suggests, power's ability to absorb immigrant difference—like power's capacity for other forms of minority difference—was formidable without being total.

Similar to the ways in which domestic minorities were being enfolded into new regimes of affirmation, a strategic situation was developing by making foreign subjects recognizable through their regulation. Indeed, we might think of the post–World War II moment as one in which the dominant institutions of the United States were replenishing themselves by absorbing the immigrant as a figure of minority difference and culture. The immigrant would thus become a national subject for U.S. institutions and, as such, would be taken through the regulatory gauntlet of legibility and recognition. Assessing that passage necessitates what Kandice Chuh has termed "subjectless critique" or the creation of "the conceptual space to prioritize difference by foregrounding the discursive constructedness of subjectivity." For Chuh, such a critique "points attention to the constraints on the liberatory potential of the achievement of subjectivity, by reminding us that a 'subject' only becomes recognizable and can act as such by conforming to certain regulatory matrices. In this sense, a subject is always an epistemological object."[2] We might contextualize the significance of Chuh's theorization by framing the post–World War II moment as one in which state, capital, and academy turned, not to subjectlessness, but to subjectfulness. In the post–World War II moment, the university and the American nation-state would mount efforts to install the immigrant as one of the discursive persona within the imaginative life of American institutions, producing the immigrant as part of the subjectfulness of those institutions and their dominance. In doing so, the American academy from the Cold War period until the present would help shape the meaning and direction of the international, using international students and immigrant communities to do so. More specifically, the American academy would attempt to use international students to shape the contours of liberal capitalism in the post–World War II period. During the Cold War period, the international student emerges as a tool to foster U.S. dominance, that is, as an alibi for the racial benevolence of a U.S. nation-state that knows how to develop and recognize immigrant subjects. As such, elite students from foreign countries would study at U.S. universities in order to assist in the redevelopment of their own countries after graduation. For American colleges and universities, those students would be trained to export liberal capitalist ideologies to their communities abroad. Through its training of foreign students, the American academy would become a principal author of the meanings and directions of the international, working with state and capital to articulate the international as a safe haven for capitalist property relations.

With the passage of the 1965 Immigration Act and the emergence of the antiracist movements, the U.S. academy would continue its efforts to use elite immigrants to shape the direction of capitalism. Thus, immigrant communities would become targets for power's archival operations, making the racial, cultural, and ethnic differences of those communities into raw materials for hegemonic affirmation and regulation. But the academy would also become a site in which to deliberate on the hegemonic deployment of immigration processes, a deliberation that would help to illuminate immigrant communities as contradictory and heterogeneous formations that simultaneously engage and disrupt networks of power.

Immigration, Foreign Students, and the Growth the American University

For American colleges and universities, the post–World War II moment was a period of unprecedented growth as well as a time of substantial rises in foreign student migration. Indeed, as historian Paul A. Kramer states, "The immediate postwar decades saw the explosive growth of student migrations to the United States measured along every axis: in the sheer scale of student numbers, in the breadth of sending countries, in the proliferation of sponsoring programs, and in the numbers of receiving colleges and universities."[3] Just as the American academy was being diversified in terms of racial groups and women, it was also being transformed because of international student migration. After the war's destruction of European and Asian centers of higher education, governments in war-ravaged countries were looking for educational options for their young people in an effort to rebuild what was so brutally torn down. The United States provided the educational answer to the infrastructural needs of foreign governments. As Kramer notes, "The massive expansion of American higher education during these years presented foreign students with an appealing array of programs and fields of specialization."[4]

As a matter of fact, the Cold War period of the 1950s and 1960s placed foreign students on the national radar. As Kramer states, "[Increasing] investments by the U.S. state, expanding student numbers, global decolonization, and Cold War rivalry" helped to promote foreign students as possible advocates of democratic capitalism and American power within their respective countries.[5] Seeing the education of foreign elites as part of a Cold War strategy to promote democratic capitalism, the political commentator and intellectual Walter Lippman argued in 1954, during the moment of decolonization:

In any true estimate of the future of the enormous masses of mankind who are awakening, who are emerging *from bondage and from ancient darkness, from foreign and native domination* . . . , we must presume that the educated class can be, and will be, certain to decide their direction. From these elites will come the politicians, the civil servants, the military commanders and the industrial managers of these new countries. What these key people know, and what they believe about themselves and about the rest of the world, is the inwardness of the whole vast movement of historical forces.[6]

As Lippmann suggests, a hegemonic discourse was emerging that would frame foreign students as heirs to both a discourse of inferiority and the historic triumph of decolonization, a combination that could ultimately serve the needs of American dominance by positioning recently liberated elites as beneficiaries of American political and institutional benevolence.

In the post–World War II moment, decolonization in Africa and Asia would significantly impact the direction of American higher education. Students from recently independent nations would seek out an American education in hopes of learning "technical, policy, and institutional frameworks suited to the building of modern, robust nation-states," sometimes electing American colleges and universities over institutions in colonial metropoles (792). For many American political leaders, decolonization would raise anxieties about the threat of communism and its appeal to people from newly independent states, a worry that would help define "international education's geopolitical stakes" (ibid.).

Framing the foreign student as both an opportunity and a national anxiety, the Cold War period would attempt to maneuver foreign students as levers for U.S. authority. But maneuvers of this sort preceded the Cold War. As a matter of fact, international students were very much on the minds of U.S. citizens even before the postwar period. As Kramer notes, "[International] students in the United States have been imagined by American educators, government officials, journalists, and many ordinary citizens as potential instruments of U.S. national power, eventually on a global scale" (781). According to Kramer, the foreign student was the focus of a set of foreign-policy questions in the early twentieth century that involved "how best to cultivate, direct, and delimit their movements to and from the United States, how best to craft their experiences while in residence, and how to measure their impact upon the societies to which they returned" (ibid.). Although national interest in international student migrations was nothing new, it was only in the postwar period that the number of international students grew because of decolonization as well as state and academic expansion, an increase that would underline the foreign students' potential to facilitate the global aspirations of the U.S. nation-state.

Perhaps the most famous instance of the international student as the linchpin between the aspirations of the postcolonial state and a globally-invested United States was what became known as the "Kennedy Airlift." In 1960, the Kenyan labor leader Todd Mboya and the American businessman William Steinman led a plan to bring 250 Kenyan students to U.S. colleges and universities. Anticipating the fall of colonialism, Mboya conceived of an exchange program that would allow promising students from Kenya, Tanganyika, Uganda, and Rhodesia to fill government positions upon independence. But Mboya soon realized that there were not enough funds for the endeavor. Faced with the dilemma of getting the students to U.S. institutions, he decided that he would approach presidential rivals Richard M. Nixon and John F. Kennedy, with Nixon making overtures to the State Department only to have the request dismissed. But Kennedy was not beholden to the U.S. government for resources and used his own personal wealth to fund the airlift, doing so as a way to curry favor with civil rights advocates and send a message abroad about the country's commitment to internationalism.

As the Kennedy Airlift suggests, the foreign student—as an entity to promote democratic capitalism and as a device to help establish U.S. global dominance—inspired institutional expansions of all types within both public and private realms. In 1942, for example, the State Department, the U.S. Office of Education, and the Office for the Coordinator for Inter-American Affairs would partner with the Institute of International Education (IIE) to facilitate the birth of foreign student advisers, an alliance that would produce the National Association of Foreign Student Advisers or NAFSA (788). With the help of those advisers and NAFSA, international students would not have to navigate by themselves the bureaucratic labyrinth that would await them once they arrived on American campuses (795–96).

The Fulbright program was part of that institutional expansion. In 1945, Senator J. William Fulbright of Arkansas started the program by amending the Surplus Property Act of 1944, which used the monies from the sale of war surplus to fund student exchange in education, culture, and science. Noting the impact of the Fulbright program, Kramer writes, "By 1964, the program stretched to forty-eight countries, and had involved the participation [of] over 21,000 Americans, and over 30,000 citizens of other countries" (796).

As a figure, the foreign student was constitutive of academic policy and state policy at the very moment that the U.S. academy and nation-state were undergoing massive expansion. The foreign student was the nexus of several geopolitical formations—war, decolonization, immigration, academic development, Cold War containment, and state development. As the preceding chapters have attempted to demonstrate, minority student formations helped to bring academy, state, and capital into an unprecedented confederacy. To that end, the foreign student would become yet another item in the archive that power was assembling, providing the material foundations for producing what would later become an economy of affirmation and regulation around this particular genre of minority difference. As foreign student migration, the Kennedy Airlift, the emergence of foreign student advisers, and the Fulbright program illustrate, the foreign student would become the muse of statecraft and academic bureaucracy, a personage that would later on become part of a new strategic situation built around the simultaneous regulation and affirmation of the minor and the foreign. The institutional changes motivated by and productive of international student migration would help make elite migrants, in particular, part of the pageantry of minoritized subjects who could purportedly replenish American institutions as domains affirming national culture and independence, obscuring the ways in which foreign peoples and communities were articles not only for affirmation but for regulation as well.

War and the Ambiguities of the Foreign Student

The beginnings of the Cold War did not spell the start of the hegemonic affirmation of foreign and immigrant cultures, but those beginnings did indeed provide the prehistory for that affirmation, as the 1950s laid the groundwork by which new immigrant subjects would be absorbed into the U.S. nation-state. In particular, the circumstances of war furnished the settings by which immigrants would become students in and administrative objects of American institutions, and of American colleges and universities in particular. We might look to Susan Choi's 1999 novel *The Foreign Student* as an allegory of the drama by which the international student entered into an expanding system of American higher education and became part of the internationalist efforts of a militarizing U.S. nation-state. As a dramatization that links the U.S. role in the Korean War to the changing nature of American colleges and universities, the novel allegorizes how the figure of the foreign student was shaped by Cold War anticommunism, making the foreign student both an element of interest and an item of suspicion for the U.S. government and its citizenry.

Indeed, *The Foreign Student* allegorizes this strategic deployment of international students through the main character Chang or "Chuck," as the people at Sewanee—the elite liberal arts college in the Tennessee Mountains—call him. The novel takes place in the mid-1950s, shortly after the start of the Korean War and during the expansion of the U.S. nation-state and the American academy. Through the novel, Choi dramatizes the large and small means by which Chang becomes a target for power, engaged as a figure to be cultivated, directed, and delimited by an assortment of social entities, all the while revealing the foreign student as a figure marked by the politics of security and counterinsurgency.

The novel uses Chang to emphasize how the meaning of Asian racial difference in particular had to negotiate with the uncomfortable but persistent specter of U.S. occupation in South Korea. In doing so, *The Foreign Student* dramatizes the ghostly nature of the war through the mystery that hovers around the mysterious Chang. For instance, when Katherine, the novel's female protagonist, tells Chang that she doesn't "know anything about the war," he replies by saying, "There is not much to know."[7] But Chang's dismissal is interrupted throughout the novel by memories of and flashbacks to his own traumatic ordeals during the occupation. Despite that, he works to hide the devastation of the war from the community at Sewanee.

In fact, Chang only talks about the war when he makes presentations to the Episcopal Church Council, the church group that sponsored his immigration. On one such occasion, he begins his talk with MacArthur's Inchon Landing, saying to the audience, "I'm not here if this doesn't happen." The Inchon Landing was the military maneuver in which General Douglas MacArthur landed his troops at Inchon, a port city located behind enemy lines. By landing in that harbor city, MacArthur was able to surround the North Korean army, which had been occupying South Korea. Because of this maneuver, some North Korean soldiers fled, but others remained and blended in with the population, engaging in guerrilla warfare and inspiring the United States and South Korea to attack civilian populations. Rather than emphasizing the civilian massacres waged in the name of anticommunism, Chang affirms the idea that the war was a humanitarian intervention for freedom on the part of the United States. In doing so, Chang telegraphs the benevolence of the war, leaving parishioners with the sense that it created opportunities for foreign students like him.

Framing national benevolence in regional terms, Chang produces a narrative for the Episcopalians that equates anticommunist South Korea with not only the democratic-loving United States but the tradition-loving South as well. As the novel states, "He would groundlessly compare the parallel to the Mason-Dixon Line, and see every head nod excitedly."[8] In Chang's rendition of the Inchon Landing, South Korea and MacArthur represent the confederacy trying to protect its traditions and privileges from the violence of the encroaching antislavery and "communist" North. In doing so, Chang associates anticommunism not simply with the United States but with the lost freedoms of the slave-owning classes in the United States. As a result of this narrative in which democracy becomes the confederacy and South Korea becomes the Southern United States, a foreign student like Chang becomes the equivalent of the white Southern citizen as well, contriving (Southern) U.S. culture as tantamount to South Korean.

As we soon learn, Chang's talent at manipulating detail and contriving equivalences is not a skill extemporized for the Tennessee Episcopalians. Indeed, this skill was part of his training as an interpreter for Lieutenant General John G. Hodge, the military governor of South Korea. In order to win compliance from South Korean soldiers, Hodge instructed Chang not to "bother him with nuance" but to teach the Korean soldiers to "give and receive orders, as if they were really American."[9] As Hodge's orders imply, making the soldiers like Americans means turning them into subjects primed for discipline and docility. For Hodge, equating South Koreans and Americans was a means of enforcing conformity rather than producing distinction among this occupied people.

Translation, in this sense, was a means not simply of revealing meaning but of developing relations of power that would foster U.S. occupation and Korean compliance. Discussing the use of translation in the context of occupation, Tejaswini Nirañjana writes, "Translation as a practice shapes, and takes shape within the asymmetrical relations of power that operate under colonialism."[10] Nirañjana goes on to state that as translation takes shape within the relations of power, it sets out to "[form] a certain kind of subject."[11] In the context of *The Foreign Student,* that subject is one that will give and receive orders . . . like an American.

In addition to producing subjects who will be interpellated by the American military, the novel shows how translation also strives to produce a reality that is "unproblematic [and] 'out there,'" all the while yielding representations that promise "direct, unmediated access to a transparent reality."[12] Attempting to provide the churchgoers with a presumably unmediated access, Chang spins an Elysian tale about the war:

> He genuinely liked talking about MacArthur. It all made for such an exciting, simple-minded, morally unambiguous story. Each time he told it, the plot was reduced and the number of details increased, and the whole claimed more of his memory for itself and left less room for everything else. He punched the slide-changer now, and Korea after 1945 was replaced by the U.S. Infantry coming out of the Seoul Railway Station, a soap-scrubbed and smiling platoon marching into the clean, level street.[13]

The "exciting, simple-minded, morally unambiguous story" of the U.S. occupation in South Korea was translation's gift, an achievement mobilized by what Gayatri Chakravorty Spivak calls "the logic of language" — that part that "allows us to jump from word to word by means of clearly indicated connections."[14] Those clear connections are, according to Spivak, precisely the mechanisms for translation's deception, making translation more than a "matter of synonym, syntax, and local color."[15] As hegemonic translations present reality as transparent and unmediated, they, in Nirañjana's words, "completely occlude the violence that accompanies the construction of the colonial subject."[16] This particular logic of translation holds the unsaid of Korean occupation at bay and delivers the Episcopal listeners to an unsullied destination, complete with soldiers arising out of a battle-torn scenery looking well ordered and clean.

But plot reductions and easy translations are nevertheless pressed by the weight of war and its atrocities. While the war may have set the conditions for Chang's arrival at the college, it also laid the foundations for the deaths of millions of people. So Chang will leave out of translation the fact that—even as MacArthur's landing drove parts of the North Korean army from South Korea—the maneuver led to the massacre of innocent civilians, all in the name of communist cleansing. Neither will he reveal that MacArthur "[launched] massive rooting out operations against 'bandits' dispersed around the Jiri Mountain (Jirisan) region of Southern South Korea," operations that would in turn lead South Korean commanders to suspect the local people of being North Korean collaborators.[17] He will not tell the good people of the church how this would result in the killing of tens of thousands of unarmed civilians.

He will leave unpublished the fact that when the North Korean army mounted a surprise attack that caused civilians to flee toward the south, the U.S. army fired upon hundreds of refugees, fearing that they might be potential collaborators with the North, handing down a tragedy that would become known as the No Gun Ri massacre. As if this were not enough, U.S. soldiers would also destroy two bridges that were crowded with refugees and attack a railway station in the South, killing three hundred or so civilians there.[18] Chang will withhold from the worshippers the fact that the South Korean and Princeton-educated leader Syngman Rhee would support the killing of innocents all in the name of "'exterminating traitors,' 'rooting out the reds,' and 'removing the Soviet puppet.'"[19] There, among the Episcopals, he will translate the war as a benefit to the Korean people, emphasizing a certain logic that would only affirm U.S. hegemony, doing so in the name of recognizing the South Korean right to democratic and capitalist sovereignty. With the prowess that only a native informant can muster, he will draw the Episcopals' attention away from the fact that the logic they are spoon-fed is alive with silences about his own travails involving rice mixed with feces and skin feverish from lice, a relatively small bit of the humiliations caused by war, displacement, and occupation.

As student and military agent, Chang symbolizes the union of academy and militarization during the postwar moment of international student migration. As Kramer comments:

> In strictly numeric terms, the largest number of exchanged persons—
> if not exactly "students"—were military trainees. After World War II,
> the U.S. government's education of foreign military personnel . . . was
> greatly expanded, streamlined, and systematized, some of it taking

place at the U.S. military academies but the majority at other military schools, bases, and facilities inside and outside the United States.[20]

Although Sewanee is not a military college, we can read Chang's hidden history of militarization as part of the overlap between the academy and the military in the post–World War II moment. As the history of the U.S. occupation of Korea suggests and as Chang illustrates through his service for the occupation, military trainees were part of the U.S. government's efforts to educate foreign military personnel in tactics of counterinsurgency and to "shore up American global power" by providing client states with not only military education but arms as well.[21]

It is important to remember that maneuvers like the Korean War were not simply about the containment of communism. They were also designed to further U.S. and capitalist economic expansion. To this end, the post–World War II moment was also the era in which "production began to shift to Asia and Latin America where export-oriented economies were emerging."[22] Lisa Lowe observes that this productive shift was directly related to U.S. war campaigns: "Insofar as the United States sought to address the imperatives of capital through the expansion of markets and labor supplies, it also sought hegemony internationally through foreign wars in Asia."[23] Seen in this light, international student migrations were a way to foster anticommunism *and* capitalist economic relations abroad.

Aesthetic culture proved to be a crucial lever in that project. In fact, one of the tasks of the United States Information Agency (USIA) was to deploy aesthetic culture for the good of the U.S. government's political and economic imperatives. As Choi's novel states:

> With the arrival of the State Department as the presiding agency in South Korea had come the United States Information Service, overseas purveyor of American news and American culture, Gershwin and *Time* and democracy, and after the press conference with Ho, he applied for work there. The prospect of selling the U.S. to South Korea suddenly seemed much more attractive than that of selling South Korea to the U.S. He crossed over. He knew he couldn't get out of the loop. He thrived there, in the zone of intentional misinformation, the way the disaster throve in the breach.[24]

As the passage implies, culture was part of the state's business, especially during the period of occupation. Part of that business entailed dressing up

U.S. culture as a commodity for non-Western consumption, as fare that would conform to the foreign diet. The passage provides a glimpse into the workings of the United States Information Agency, pointing to the ways in which American culture was a propaganda tool for U.S. foreign policy. Indeed, the passage's reference to Gershwin recalls how in the 1950s the USIA would institute a program to promote American jazz as a vehicle to convince the rest of the world that the United States "was a melting pot of opportunity."[25] As part of the government's hegemonic interest in aesthetic culture, the USIA would—through its international radio service, the Voice of America—introduce the world to such jazz greats as Duke Ellington, Dizzy Gillespie, and Louis Armstrong. The USIA deployed aesthetic culture, and jazz in particular, as Nicholas Cull argues, to "[submit] evidence to peoples and other nations . . . that the objectives and policies of the United States are in harmony with and will advance their legitimate aspirations for freedom, progress, and peace."[26] Or, as Penny von Eschen puts it, spreading jazz around the world would be a way "to win converts to 'the American way of life.'"[27]

Inasmuch as jazz is an art form originating from a minority community, the use of jazz in the power plays of the United States represented, perhaps, a seed of hegemonic affirmation. Another seed was the 1955 and USIA-sponsored photographic exhibition titled The Family of Man. The exhibition was composed of "503 pictures by 273 photographers" from all over the world. Discussing the global range of the exhibition and the USIA's interest in it, Cull writes: "Visitors saw a snapshot of the Warsaw ghetto; a photograph of rioters confronting tanks in Berlin in 1953; pictures of apartheid in South Africa; a dead soldier in Korea; and a glorious giant panorama of the general assembly of the United Nations as the exhibition reached its end." He underlines the role of the United States as a facilitator of global knowledge: "By sponsoring such an exhibition the USIA became a bridge, introducing the individual viewer to the rest of the planet." Inasmuch as the exhibition "[introduced] the individual viewer to the rest of the planet," it implied that the United States was a trusted domain for presenting information about the rest of the world; far from the United States being an isolated nation, it was the cosmopolitan representative of humanity—its struggles and its ideals.[28] Put simply, the exhibition was a means for the USIA to present the United States as the respecter of human diversity and, in doing so, it foreshadowed the strategic and hegemonic use of minority difference.

Indeed, Barthes gestured toward the germ of such a use in a critique of the exhibition. In his 1957 *Mythologies,* he wrote that The Family of Man exhibition was one in which "the difference in human morphologies is affirmed, exoticism is stressed, the many variations of the species are manifested, the diversity of skins, skulls, and customs and notions of Babel are extended over the image of the world." The most insidious part, Barthes implied, was that "from this pluralism, magically enough, a unity is derived: man is born, works, laughs and dies in the same fashion everywhere." In other words, the diversity of the photographs notwithstanding, "there is underlying each one an identical 'nature,'" a diversity that "is only formal," one that "does not belie the existence of a common mould."[29]

As Barthes implies, the exhibit was a means of affirming the world's dazzling diversity and corroborating a humanist claim about the essence and unity of humanity—that "man is born, works, laughs and dies in the same fashion everywhere." The exhibition repeats the maneuvers of Chang's lecture to the Episcopals—taking incommensurable formations and arguing for an inherent and universal identity. Rebutting this deployment of difference as an alibi for humanist articulations, Barthes asks, "Why not ask the parents of Emmett Till, the young Negro assassinated by the Whites, what *they* think of *The Great Family of Man?*" In addition to pointing to a nascent mode of hegemonic representation that uses diversity to buttress a universal identity, Barthes's question leads us to ask how articulations of difference might be maneuvered to disrupt hegemonic power's own utilization of difference.

The fullness of that inquiry would have to wait until later. Years would pass before the immigrant would be regarded as an internal entity, before migrant communities from other nations would become part of that archival pantheon that would take shape in the sixties and thereafter. In the next section, we will see how the affirmation of immigrant communities took place within the context of a newfound acceptance of minority difference, an acceptance born of student protests, changes in immigration law, and transformations to American universities and colleges.

The Namesake *and the Quest for Legibility*

While *The Foreign Student* allegorizes a period of international student migration in which power had not yet learned to affirm minority difference,

Jhumpa Lahiri's 2003 novel *The Namesake* covers the moment in which power was establishing a facility with minority difference and identifying the immigrant as an item for archivization. The novel begins in 1968 and goes up to the year 2000, commencing with the story of yet another foreign student to the United States—Ashoke Ganguli, a Bengali man from Calcutta who migrates to the United States with his wife Ashima, in pursuit of an education. Whereas Chang Ahn found himself in a United States that had little to no framework for understanding the presence of immigrants of color, the United States in which Ashoke found himself was one quickly developing systems for grappling with a growing immigrant presence.

Like *The Foreign Student, The Namesake* addresses the management of immigrant and foreign difference through the contradictory practices and conditions of racialized inclusion and affirmation. As such, *The Namesake* critiques the growing conditions of subjectfulness, that is, the ways in which hegemonic institutions demanded and objectified immigrant subjectivity, demanded immigrant subjectivity to be the alibi for U.S. neocolonialism, objectified international migrants so that immigrant communities could be absorbed into an expanding ideal of U.S. culture. As *The Foreign Student* demonstrated how war brought international students into greater political focus, *The Namesake* indicates how immigration policy changes and the antiracist movements helped produce the conditions by which immigrant communities were absorbed into regulatory regimes of recognition, archivization, and affirmation.

The context for that absorption lies partly with the Immigration Act of 1965, which abolished quotas on immigration to the United States. Inspired by the civil rights struggle as well as national ideals around democracy and brotherhood, the U.S. government would begin to revise prior immigration exclusion acts, leading Senator Edward Kennedy, floor manager for the original bill, to comment in 1964: "The reform accomplished in Public Law 89-236 broadens a central theme in American history—equality of opportunity. It stands with legislation in other fields—civil rights, poverty, education, and health—to reaffirm in the 1960's our nation's continuing pursuit of justice, equality, and freedom."[30] In addition, Senator Philip Hart of Michigan told the Senate subcommittee, "Discriminatory provisions against immigrants from eastern and Southern Europe, token quotas for Asian and African countries, and implications of race superiority in the Asian-Pacific Triangle concept have no place in the public policy of the United States."[31] As the passages suggest, the Immigration Act of 1965 was intended as part of a large body of measures that would cast the 1960s as a period of sweeping racial reforms that would extend from civil rights to the abolition of the national quota system for immigrants, a system that Senator Kennedy, Senator Hart, and others asserted was rooted in notions of racial superiority.

But whether the country lived up to its own ideals was far from the only matter at stake. In truth, the international reputation of the United States was also at issue. For instance, President John F. Kennedy, in a message to Congress in 1963, invoked the specter of negative international impressions as a motivation for immigration reform:

> The use of a national origins system is without basis in either logic or reason. It neither satisfies a national need nor accomplishes an international purpose. In an age of interdependence among nations, such a system is an anachronism, for it discriminates among applicants for admission into the United States on the basis of the accident of birth . . . But the legislation I am submitting will insure that progress will continue to be made toward our ideals and toward the realization of humanitarian objectives.[32]

If the passage of civil rights legislation in the 1960s was part of the United States' attempt to establish itself as a Cold War superpower, then the Immigration Act of 1965 was another link in the nation's effort to bolster its standing globally.

We can get an appreciation of how the Immigration Act of 1965 functioned for the good of U.S. hegemony from the act's provisions. While the language of the act was about the perfection of freedom as a national and transnational ideal, the act was written in such a way as to meet the labor needs of the country at the time. For example, even though the act established seven preference categories—"four for the purpose of family reunion, two for professional and skilled or unskilled workers, and one preference for refugees, including those displaced by natural calamity"—it emphasized technical labor, in particular, as a way to compete with Soviet advancements in air and space technology. As Vijay Prashad explains, "[President Kennedy] informed the legislature that he wanted to see the immigration system overhauled so that 'highly trained or skilled persons may obtain a preference without requiring that they secure employment here before emigrating.'"[33] The Immigration Act provided the conditions whereby technical labor during the years 1966 to 1977 came mainly from India, with "83 percent [entering] under the occupational category of professional and technical workers (roughly 20,000 scientists with Ph.D.'s, 40,000 engineers, and 25,000 doctors)."[34] Hence, the Immigration Act of 1965—because of the new racial demographic that it promoted—enhanced the nation and other countries' understandings of the United States as a democratic and diverse society.

The Immigration Act of 1965 impacted and shaped Asian American communities in particular ways. As historian Sucheng Chang notes, "The law ushered in a resurgence of immigration from Asia."[35] Lisa Lowe asserts that the law paved the way for "dramatic shifts in Asian immigration to the United States," shifts that abolished former national origins and exclusions and "widened the definition of Asian American."[36] Writing in the mid-1990s, Lowe argued that the law shaped Asian American communities as follows:

> Because of the many historical and political economic changes of which the act of 1965 is an expression, the majority of Asian Americans are at present Asian-born rather than multiple-generation, and new immigrant groups from South Vietnam, South Korea, Cambodia, Laos, Thailand, the Philippines, Malaysia, India, and Pakistan have diversified the already existing Asian American group of largely Chinese, Japanese, Korean, and Filipino descent.[37]

The act extended a series of maneuvers around Asian immigration enacted in the period from 1850 to World War II and in the period after 1965, maneuvers in which "U.S. interests . . . [would recruit and regulate] . . . both labor and capital from Asia."[38] These material changes in Asian American communities would produce the conditions by which powerful institutions would strategize over the incorporation of Asian and Asian American subjects. Inasmuch as the law was designed to correct years of immigration exclusion, it provided the conditions by which the forms of difference produced by immigrant communities would be included into the national body.

The figure of the immigrant, therefore, is not only the subject of U.S. policy and lore; that figure has also stood as an ideal for the ethical development of the U.S. nation-state, allowing for the production of a strategic system of power organized around the integration of difference. Implying this use of the immigrant in the managerial ethos of U.S. political culture, Eqbal Ahmad wrote in 1981 that "American political culture was management oriented," a fact that he attributed to "its immigrant character." As he put it, "Historically, group demands have been met through the process of political bargaining and selective rewards. Ideological and political dissent has been managed by the co-optation both of individuals and ideas." According to Ahmad, the conditions for bargains and rewards were partly "made possible by expanding resources (largely through territorial aggrandizement and colonial exploitation) and an extremely mobile social structure."[39] In many ways, we can say that Ahmad is reinterpreting the axiom that understands the United States as a "nation of immigrants." While that axiom understands itself as a historical observation about how the history of various migrations has shaped the country, Ahmad approaches the history of immigration to the United States as one genealogical starting point for the management of diversity. Immigration, for Ahmad, has been one phenomenon that has inspired the United States to devise ways to regulate dissent through the absorption of new peoples and ideas. A "nation of immigrants," then, has to be understood as a nation of diversity management.

The American academy has been integral to the management of immigrant subjects. As Aihwa Ong puts it, the American university would become "an extension of world trade," training elite migrants, particularly from China and South Asia, in science, engineering, and computer technology.[40] In doing so, the academy would help to position Asian labor for the good of a postfordist and globalizing economy. Furthermore, the American academy would also help to clarify and elaborate the meaning of Asian American culture and identity. As such, Asian American communities and subjects would be immersed in a discursive context in which racial and cultural meanings were being rearticulated on virtually every campus. Discussing how those contexts promoted the rise of Asian American studies and impacted Asian American communities, Asian American activist Mike Murase wrote in 1976:

> the history of development of ethnic studies is in itself a significant part of Asian American history. It marks the first organized effort within the context of the formal educational system to reinterpret the history of Third World Peoples in this country to accurately reflect our

perspectives: as an ideal it represents an honest attempt . . . to disseminate the life stories of millions of non-white people in America.[41]

Therefore, during this period the academy facilitated the inclusion and regulation of Asian labor and enabled the designation of Asian Americans as
both epistemological subjects and objects.

Lahiri's *The Namesake* recalls these two axes of the American academy's relationship to Asian subjects—one in which American universities
facilitated the incorporation of elite Asian labor and the other in which colleges and universities provided critical and institutional formations to analyze Asian subjects and cultures. Indeed, the novel begins in 1968, the year
that the Immigration Act of 1965 was officially enacted. Ashoke is a doc-
toral candidate in fiber optics at MIT, and Ashima is pregnant with their
first child. Beginning in that meaningful year, the novel invokes 1968 as a
year with several formations inscribed upon it—as the period of the Immigration Act, as the era of new racial meanings, and as the time of power's
strategic incorporation and representation of those meanings.

In addition to the other weight that 1968 carries, Ashoke and Ashima's
son is born that year, and his birth brings together the various inscriptions
etched on '68: He is a symbol of the newfound diversity among Asian
American subjects, a diversity that emanated from the Immigration Act of
1965; he is, also, symbolic of how those new Asian American communities
entered a national laboratory in which novel interpretations of race and
minority difference were being invented and assembled; moreover, the baby
is a sign of the ways in which various institutions would try to shelve and
deploy an interest in Asian American cultural difference.

The world in which the Gangulis find themselves is one that is quickly
being rearticulated by the meaning of immigrant culture. In many ways,
the novel allegorizes how such rearticulations take place within the very
moment in which institutions of power claimed to be accommodating
minority desires for new designations. But we see how those accommodations leave much to be desired as the Gangulis decide which two names to
give the little boy. The narrator explains the Bengali practice of endowing
each person with not one, but two names:

> [A] practice of Bengali nomenclature grants, to every single person, two
> names. In Bengali the word for pet name is *daknam*, meaning, literally,
> the name by which one is called, by friends, family and other intimates,

at home and in private, unguarded moments. Pet names are a persistent remnant of childhood, a reminder that life is not always so serious, so formal, so complicated. They are reminder, too, that one is *not all things to all people.*

Every pet name is paired with a good name, a *bhalonam*, for identification in the outside world. Consequently good names appear on envelopes, on diplomas, on directories, and in all other public places.[42]

The conflict over names begins with what is a seemingly stock narrative about immigrant adjustments to American life—that is, how to reconcile foreign cultural practices with American institutional protocols. The first such conflict comes when the Gangulis learn that they must officially register the baby's name in order for him to be released from the hospital:

The fourth day there is good news and bad news. The good news is that Ashima and the baby are to be discharged the following morning. The bad news is that they are told by Mr. Wilcox, compiler of hospital birth certificates, that they must choose a name for their son. For they learn that in America, a baby cannot be released from the hospital without a birth certificate. And that a birth certificate needs a name. (27)

After some back and forth between Mr. Wilcox and the Gangulis, the parents give the baby the pet name Gogol, because that is the name of Ashoke's favorite author and the one that he was reading right when his life was almost ended. Once, when he was a young man living in Calcutta and fresh into adulthood, he had taken a train trip to see his grandfather who was living in Jamshedpur. On the way to his grandfather's the train derailed, killing many of the passengers and leaving Ashoke's body broken and almost left for dead. His only salvation was that one of the rescuers saw him holding a page of Nikolai Gogol's *The Overcoat.* Ostensibly, the conflict between the Gangulis and Mr. Wilcox has to do with a hospital that needs a name immediately and a cultural practice that renders a name gradually, but the conflict is less about a clash of cultures and more deeply about the minoritized complexities that cannot be sustained by dominant U.S. institutions. After all, the hospital does not worry over the likely foreignness of the name, just over its actual existence. And so, the parents give the boy a pet name that will suffice until the good name comes along.

But, as it turns out, the good name never arrives because the great-grandmother who was to give it dies unexpectedly, and so her letter—like the good name—never makes it to the Ganguli household. Years pass before the parents have to think of a good name for Gogol, but the day comes, not surprisingly, when Gogol has to enter school, and on that morning another conflict arises over what complexities an institutional culture can oblige. Gogol's parents prepare him for the good name that he is to use with his teachers and friends. That name is Nikhil. But, of course, Gogol is only used to being called Gogol and finds it strange that he would have to suddenly adopt a new name. Ashoke tries to explain to Gogol's new teacher— a woman by the name of Mrs. Lapidus—that Gogol is called Gogol at home but his good name is now Nikhil. Not familiar with the custom, Mrs. Lapidus responds by opening up Gogol's immunization records and birth certificate and says, "There seems to be some confusion, Mr. Ganguli . . . According to these legal documents, your son's legal name is Gogol" (58). In response, he reassures Mrs. Lapidus that the boy will grow into his name, taking his leave by saying, "Be good, Nikhil." But Mrs. Lapidus is still discomfited and notices that Gogol is as well. And so she asks Gogol if he wants to be called Nikhil. He signals "no" and the pet name is confirmed by a letter tied to Gogol's neck that announces, "Due to their son's preference he will be known as Gogol at school" (60).

Through the great-grandmother's death and the scene at the school, the novel sets up an antinomy between the two letters—the familial one that never came and the administrative one that arrived uninvited. In doing so, *The Namesake* puts Bengali culture in tension with the changing culture of American institutions, "changing" because—like Mr. Wilcox at the hospital—the teacher is less concerned with the peculiarity of the names themselves. Eight years after the Immigration Act of 1965, there were bound to be Indian children in the school system, "Jayadev Modi in the third grade and Rekha Saxena in fifth" (57). As the passage suggests, this was an institutional culture sensitizing itself to different cultures and foreign names. Indeed, the tension over Gogol's official name is not about the strangeness of the name but about the complexity of the cultural practice that requires one name and then another. The tension demonstrates the attentions and limitations of an emergent institutional culture poised to achieve hegemony through the incorporation of minority difference.

As such, the incident at the school inaugurates Gogol's struggle with and the novel's meditation on a growing institutional need for legibility, particularly the legibility of minoritized subjects. In doing so, the school stands as a metaphor for a mode of power that begins to declare that it knows how to place and recognize immigrant culture in ways that can rival even parental cultures. Thus, institutional recognition, in the moment after the student movements and the Immigration Act of 1965, becomes less predicated on the erasure of immigrant difference than on its inscription—an inscription tied around a little boy's neck, no less.

As the school makes Gogol's pet name into his good name and thus enters it into official records, that maneuver symbolizes a kind of institutional encroachment in which administration seems to have access to every bit of him—no part withheld, every part made available. That encroachment violates the function of Bengali nomenclature, its deliberate withholding of certain parts of identity from official documentation. While the Bengali practice of nomenclature adheres to a separation between those parts of identity that are admitted into official realms and those parts that are reserved for intimate spheres, the novel allegorizes how institutions of power work in the sixties and thereafter to overwhelm the complexities of minority culture.

But while the school seemed to manage the desires of a bewildered child by giving him the name he wanted, Gogol—as young people are wont to do—grows increasingly dissatisfied with the name he favored, as the narrator explains:

> [By] now, he's come to hate questions pertaining to his name, hates having constantly to explain. He hates having to tell people that it doesn't mean anything "in Indian." He hates having to wear a nametag on his sweater at Model United Nations Day at school. He even hates signing his name at the bottom of his drawings in art class. He hates that his name is both absurd and obscure, that it has nothing to do with who he is, that it is neither Indian nor American but of all things Russian . . . Other boys his age have begun to court girls already, asking them to go to the movies or the pizza parlor, but he cannot imagine saying, "Hi, it's Gogol" under potentially romantic circumstances. He cannot imagine this at all. (76)

As his budding sexuality becomes the context for renaming himself as well as rearticulating his identity, the novel frames Gogol's awakening to social recognition as simultaneous with his incitement to and management of sexual desire. While still a high-school student, he attends a nearby college party with two friends from his class. At the party he meets a young first-year student named Kim, who asks him his name. He is reluctant to tell her his real name. In fact, he

> wishes there was another name he could use, just this once, to get him through the evening. It wouldn't be so terrible. He's lied to her already, about being at Amherst. He could introduce himself as Colin or Jason or Marc, as anybody at all, and their conversation could continue, and she would never know or care. There were a million names to choose from. But then he realizes there's no need to lie. Not technically. He remembers the other name that had once been chosen for him, the one that should have been.
>
> "I'm Nikhil," he says for the first time in his life. (Ibid.)

Rearticulating himself as "Nikhil" emboldens him to kiss the girl:

> It is the first time he's kissed anyone, the first time he's felt a girl's face and body and breath so close to his own. "I can't believe you kissed her, Gogol," his friends exclaim as they drive home from the party. He shakes his head in a daze, as astonished as they are, elation still swelling inside him. "It wasn't me," he nearly says. But he doesn't tell them that it hadn't been Gogol who'd kissed Kim. That Gogol had nothing to do with it. (Ibid.)

In this passage above, the rearticulation of identity is, for Gogol, rooted in the incitement to sexuality. The passage allegorizes the libidinal undercurrents of the race-based movements of the 1960s, particularly their investments in gender and sexual normativity. In such a context, reinventing the meaning of minority identity often meant reinventing the sexual identities of men of color.

As the rearticulation of identity for national liberation movements meant confronting and appealing to the state, Gogol's sexualized rearticulation becomes immediately a juridical imperative. In fact, the kiss and the "new" name form a turning point within the novel so that after kissing the girl, Gogol goes to court. More specifically, after the kissing scene, the novel has Gogol visit the county courthouse to change his name. The clerk calls him forward, and after Gogol approaches the judge's dais, "a middle-aged, heavy-set black woman wearing half-moon glasses" asks, "What is the reason you wish to change your name, Mr. Ganguli?" (101). He makes his way around to telling the judge that he "[hates] the name Gogol" (102). "'Very well,' the judge says, proceeding to stamp and sign the change-of-name form that Gogol brought with him." Afterwards,

> he is told that notice of the new name must be given to all other agencies, that it's his responsibility to notify the Registry of Motor Vehicles, banks, schools. He orders three certified copies of the name change decree, two for himself, and one for his parents to keep in their safe-deposit box. No one accompanies him on this legal rite of passage, and when he steps out of the room no one is waiting to commemorate the moment with flowers and Polaroid snapshots and balloons. In fact the procedure is entirely unmomentous, and when he looks at his watch he sees that from the time he'd entered the courtroom it had taken all of ten minutes. (Ibid.)

We might think of the scene in the courthouse as an allegory of minoritized subjects appealing to the state for recognition and redress, recalling that part of the civil rights struggle, for instance, that engaged the state as the domain of political emancipation. Theorizing the civil rights movement's relationship to that mode of emancipation, Lisa Lowe writes, "In focusing the struggle in the political domain, the civil rights project extended the opportunities of some segments of minority communities and made substantial gains."[43] Michael Omi and Howard Winant add that the state became the "chief movement target" because the state had "historically maintained and organized racial practices" and because the state "was traversed by the same antagonisms which penetrated the entire society."[44] But, as Lowe contends, focusing on political emancipation—as the mode of freedom and recognition offered by the state—was not without significant limitations: "the civil rights project confronts its limits where the pursuit of enfranchisement coincides with a refortification of the state as the guarantor of rights and precludes the necessary critique of the state as the protector of liberal capitalism, steadily dividing the racialized labor forces it continues to exclude from those rights."[45] Here, Lowe identifies a powerful and genealogical instance in which minority emancipation corresponds with the state's own protocols. Indeed, we can look at Gogol's day in court as part of that genealogical moment inasmuch as he too encounters the state as the certifier of his identity and the guarantor of his right to it.

But the state's status as the certifier and guarantor of minority rights and identity is untrustworthy ground, to say the least. As Lowe argues, the state guarantees liberal capitalism and, therefore, the racialized exclusions on which it depends, assuring that there will be widespread exploitation in the midst of opportunity. Hence, the letdown that Gogol experiences in the latter part of the scene is a metaphor of the eventual impotency of political emancipation. As such, the scene challenges the idea that the state is the ideal supporter of and audience for minority identity and recognition.[46] While the kiss promised a form of acknowledgment that would be endless in its pleasure, the courthouse granted a recognition that was anemic and frustrated in its consummation. Locating this anemia and frustration within the state's absorption of civil rights struggles, critical race theorists Kimberlé Crenshaw, Neil Gotanda, Gary Peller, and Kendall Thomas note that "the reigning contemporary American ideologies about race" were organized around an "implicit social compact" in the sixties and seventies that promoted racism as exceptional rather than systemic and that thereby "excluded radical or fundamental challenges to the status quo."[47] Part of the implicit social compact between the state and the antiracist movements of the fifties and sixties was over the issue of identity. Discussing how identity shaped powerful segments of the race-based movements of those two decades, Omi and Winant explain that the "enduring legacy of the racial minority movements" was the "forging of new collective racial identities." While civil rights gains were being retrenched, "the persistence of the new racial identities developed during this period stands out as the single truly formidable obstacle to the consolidation of a newly repressive order."[48]

Yet, contrary to movement claims, if political emancipation during that period was executed through the state's support for minority recognition and formal representation, then identity was not by definition antithetical to that emancipation offered by the state in the 1960s and afterwards but fundamental to that emancipation. As Crenshaw, Gotanda, Peller, and Thomas note, "the mere recognition of race" and the promotion of diversity without ensuring equal opportunity were strategies by which the state withdrew from antiracist redistribution.

For the modern nation-state, recognizing identity as a way to circumvent redistribution is not a phenomenon that arose in the moments after the student movements. Indeed, its genealogy lies in the liberal-capitalist United States. In fact, Marx's 1843 article "On the Jewish Question" is, in many ways, about the modern nation-state's relationship to identity and redistribution. The essay is, in part, a rebuttal to the German philosopher Bruno Bauer's assertion that Jewish emancipation is inconsistent with state emancipation, an assertion based on Bauer's assumption that the Jew has no right to demand political emancipation as defined by a Christian state. Marx counters Bauer's assertion by arguing that the modern nation-state is not Christian but secular and best exemplified by the Union states in the secular United States. According to Marx, the secular nation-state engages the question of religious diversity not as a religious issue but as a social one and—in the spirit of political emancipation—demonstrates a certain openness to religious diversity: "[What] is the relation between complete political emancipation and religion? If we find in the country that has attained full political emancipation, that religion not only continues to exist but is fresh and vigorous, this is proof that the existence of religion is not at all opposed to the perfection of the state."[49] According to Marx, religion is not opposed to the state's perfection or to political emancipation because in the secular state religion becomes part of the "general presuppositions" and "elements" of the state, taking its place alongside private property, birth, rank, and education. As they become part of the state, these "effective differences" are not abolished but are allowed to act "after their own fashion" and "particular nature," as the very items that the state archives in the terrain of civil society and that the state recognizes as part of civil society.

In such a configuration, the state, for Marx, acts as the intermediary between man and his liberties and emerges as the entity that will allow man to have access to the freedoms of religion, property, education, occupation, rank, and birth: "[By] emancipating himself politically, man emancipates himself in a devious way, through an intermediary, however necessary this intermediary may be . . . The state is the intermediary between man and human liberty."[50] The state thus becomes the condition of those freedoms and positivities that man takes as fundamental to his various identities. Seen in this light, political emancipation through the modern nation-state has always been a way to manage diversity—indeed, to mediate the subject's relationship to diversity. Said differently, political emancipation defines the processes by which the state conceives and domiciles identity.

By archiving modes of difference in the halls of civil society, the state manages diversity through political emancipation and in doing so, narrows the breadth of that diversity. In his discussion of religion's own emancipation as a private identity, for instance, Marx says, "Religion no longer appears as the basis, but as the manifestation of secular narrowness."[51] The state "narrows" the elements and presuppositions of civil society by relegating them to that terrain, turning them into freedoms only secured through the state, and then making them alibis for the privatization of the individual: "But liberty as a right of man is not founded upon the relations between man and man, but rather upon the separation of man from man. It is the right of such separation. The right of the circumscribed individual, withdrawn unto himself."[52] Politically emancipating the various items of civil society, for Marx, means using those elements to further the economic mode of private property, "narrowing" items for the good of an economic mode.

Because of the antiracist movements of the fifties and sixties, the U.S. nation-state would achieve new levels of freedom and secularity. Indeed, the transformations that took place on campus yards would help to make the rearticulations of minority difference into the general presuppositions and elements of U.S. liberal capitalism, but these presuppositions would not sit and wither on the vine of the private sphere but would change the identities of academy, state and capital, making them the intermediaries between minoritized subjects and minority difference.

Indeed, we might even look at the passage in the courthouse as a metaphor for the changed nature of U.S. institutions. In addition to the courthouse, Lahiri's novel highlights the academy as a new site for unpacking minority difference and culture. In a scene that takes place while Gogol is an undergraduate at Yale, he encounters minority difference as not simply a personal and private struggle that he alone engages but as an institutional discourse emerging within the academy. Lahiri describes the scene:

> One day he attends a panel discussion about Indian novels written in English . . . Gogol is bored by the panelists, who keep referring to something called "marginality," as if it were some sort of medical condition. For most of the hour, he sketches portraits of the panelists, who sit hunched over their papers along a rectangular table. "Teleologically speaking, ABCDs are unable to answer the question, 'Where are you from?'" the sociologist on the panel declares. Gogol has never heard the term *ABCD*. He eventually gathers that it stands for "American-born confused deshi." In other words, him. He learns that the C could

also stand for "conflicted." He knows that deshi, a generic word for "countryman," means "Indian," knows that his parents and all their friends always refer to India simply as *desh*. But Gogol never thinks of India as desh. He thinks of it as Americans do, as India.[53]

We can situate the panel within that period of the American academy known as multiculturalism. Discussing that period in "Postcolonial Studies in the House of U.S. Multiculturalism," Jenny Sharpe situates multiculturalism's emergence within the ethnic studies movements of the sixties and seventies and observes: "Inasmuch as racial minorities and their cultures were excluded from the curriculum of traditionally white colleges, the campuses were a microcosm of segregated America."[54] Like the formation of ethnic studies programs, centers, and departments and the antiracist movements that inspired them, the panel grapples with the meanings of a minoritized constituency. In doing so, the panel allegorizes how the academy has become an important site for the articulation of an inquiry around the nature of South Asian cultures and identities within the United States. Hence, the scene points to how marginality—as "some sort of medical condition"—takes on the status of an object that demands a will to knowledge about the impact that decolonization and migration have had on immigrant subjects and communities that settle and form in the United States. Gogol's "dis-ease" with his name is, therefore, symptomatic of a larger conflict having to do with how to live as the racialized outcome of immigration to the United States.

Multicultural education was the product of the student movements of the fifties and sixties, the rise of the ethnic studies in the seventies and eighties, and the changes in immigration policy. As Sharpe explains, "multicultural education was not simply a response to the historical underrepresentation of racial minorities but also the presence of new immigrant groups. The sudden emergence of these new ethnicities was the result of immigration laws introduced since the mid-sixties."[55] This mixture of historical forces would help the ascent of postcolonial studies within U.S. colleges and universities. As an institutional formation that arose out of the simultaneously domestic and global circumstances of the U.S. nation-state, multicultural education would give birth to modes of inquiry that would attempt to apprehend the marginalities of citizen and noncitizen subjects alike.

And yet multiculturalism and postcoloniality became part of the general elements and presuppositions of U.S. political economy—that is, ones constituted by the intersections of academy, state and capital—and became part of the protocols of an affirmative mode of power. This sort of incorporation would work to narrow multiculturalism and postcoloniality's possibilities. For Sharpe, multiculturalism's narrowing could be seen in the lack of redistributive practices in the academy:

> Constituted around diversity and difference rather than racism and the unequal distribution of power, liberal multiculturalism weakened the original goals of multicultural education, which were to redress the debilitating effects of racial (and sexual) discrimination. In short, it disassociated multicultural education from questions of affirmative action.[56]

In her own critique of how the concept of Third World marginality was narrowly incorporated into the academy, Spivak discusses how that incorporation presumed a hegemonic intermediary that would offer validation and recognition: "When a cultural identity is thrust upon one because the center wants an identifiable margin, claims of marginality assure validation from the center."[57] According to her, the Western academic world of the 1980s was responding to First World diversity by demanding "an identifiable margin" that constructs a "new object of investigation" as well as offering a new item for validation and certification. As such, Spivak suggests that "marginality" becomes the effect of power/knowledge and therefore answers the call to make difference legible and admissible within institutional realms.

After the student movements, the Immigration Act of 1965, and the emergence of ethnic and postcolonial studies in the seventies, eighties, and nineties, political emancipation would name the process by which postcoloniality would be affirmed and managed to the benefit of dominant social relations, providing the conditions by which institutions of power would mediate the relationship between diasporic subjects and a new thing called "marginality." Political emancipation would become the spirit of hegemonic institutionalization—in which modes of minority difference would be selectively incorporated, but not for the good of social redistribution. Indeed, the selective incorporation of immigrant populations can be seen in the immigration acts during and after the sixties. For instance, while the 1965 act may have eased immigration policies, the Immigration and Nationality Act

Amendments of 1976 and the Health Professionals Education Assistance Act of 1976 demanded that migrants and immigrant health-care providers demonstrate proof of employment before migrating, a move that slowed down the immigration of technical professions. At the same time, the family reunification portion of the 1965 act remained active, producing a situation in which the number of family members who migrated to the United States increased while the number of technical professionals who migrated decreased. The increase in family member migration would introduce increasing numbers of immigrants into the working and petit bourgeois classes, causing class stratification among immigrants to rise.[58] The selective affirmation and enhancement of some immigrants' lives would take place alongside the diminishment of other immigrants' circumstances, a process that would be part of a larger, "international division of humanity grounded in the capitalist reproduction of 'monstrous' economic disparities."[59]

Minority Culture and the Critique of Affirmation

After the 1960s, U.S. institutions were raised as sites of resolution for the very exclusions that they had helped to enact, offering themselves as the answers to minoritized needs. But as *The Namesake* and *The Foreign Student* suggest, the power of those institutions to placate, to make right, and to identify was never total. Both novels counsel us toward the creative and critical horizons that might be opened up if minority difference would read its own complex architecture—its implications within and its rebellion from the conformist affirmations of U.S. institutions. In the compromised terrain of culture is precisely where we might find alternatives to how culture is narrowed in regimes of affirmation.

Gogol's own moment comes at the end of *The Namesake*. His father has died; his marriage has ended, and his mother has decided to halve her time between two locations—six months in India and six months in the United States. It's Christmas Eve and the last time that she will hold a party in the house that she has known for twenty-seven years. She sends Gogol upstairs to fetch the camera. After retrieving it, he goes to his room to find a fresh battery and "a new roll of film." And there he notices the book that saved his father's life and occasioned the name that gnawed at him since his youth:

then another book, never read, long forgotten, catches his eye. The jacket is missing, the title on the spine practically faded. It's a thick clothbound volume topped with decades-old dust. The ivory pages are heavy, slightly sour, silken to the touch. The spine cracks faintly when he opens it to the title page. *The Short Stories of Nikolai Gogol.* "For Gogol Ganguli," it says on the front endpaper in his father's tranquil hand, in red ballpoint ink, the letters rising gradually, optimistically, on the diagonal toward the upper right-hand corner of the page. "The man who gave you his name, from the man who gave you your name," is written within quotation marks . . . The name he had so detested, here hidden and preserved—that was the first thing his father had given him.[60]

The inscription on the book provides a key to the universe of problems laid out by the novel—"The man who gave you his name, from the man who gave you your name." Throughout its chapters, *The Namesake* points to the inability of institutions to accommodate the plurality and complexity of minority cultural practices even while nominally affirming minority difference. The novel points to how Bengali nomenclature is affirmed only by reducing it to the insufficient protocols of school and hospital. To use Chuh's fitting theorization, the novel demonstrates how minoritized subjects achieve subject status by having their particularities and differences regulated in the name of legibility and coherence, a maneuver that could only read the unruly breadth of minority formations as unlawful occurrences.

In contrast to the various ways in which plurality is read as a debilitating, estranging, and immobilizing incoherence, Ashoke's inscription solemnizes the plural nature of Gogol's identity. Indeed, the inscription implies that Gogol has more than one paternity—one Russian and the other Bengali. In doing so, *The Namesake* suggests that minority difference hails from histories and social formations that are infinitely plural and from systems and orders whose essences are ultimately unreachable. The plurality confirmed in the inscription stands against the singular and univocal identity required by Gogol when he is born and imposed by Mrs. Lapidus when he enters school. As such, that insistence to plurality stands against the very maneuvers of Euro-American university education—the ways in which the academy makes identity into a cottage industry for power-knowledge, an industry that offers difference as a domain of authenticity that will give birth to coherence rather than the location of pluralities that will defy final summations. As such, the inscription opposes an institutional ethos that makes minority difference into an official matter and urges us to use minority culture as a critical lever to alienate the institutionally legible ways in which we are put into action and representation, causing the novel to end where it begins—with the necessity of retaining and cultivating the unofficial.

The Foreign Student also points us to the productive nature of the unofficial. Toward that novel's conclusion, Chang has left Sewanee to get away from Katherine and what seems like an unattainable future with her. At a Japanese Noodle House in Chicago, where he has become a bit of a fixture, he reflects on how he was rendered into an official subject as a student in Sewanee and as a translator for the U.S. military:

> He remembered the time he had felt that his future depended upon performing flawlessly at a succession of gates, and being judged, and allowed to advance. This idea was no longer his. He knew what he was meant to do, and wasn't he doing it? He was surrounded by people who struggled mightily and viciously and independently each day and they took him for the thing he dreamed of being, a scholar. "Ask Einstein," they said. "He should know." At the Belmont Noodle House he was allowed to sit for hours with his books, his empty bowl shoved aside, his teacup kept endlessly full, although the restaurant had just a handful of tables. His very presence transformed the place into a library. So he was a scholar, because that was what he did. He'd discovered the power to make himself, to throw away what he hated and say what he was.[61]

There in the unofficial terrain of the noodle house, Chang authorizes himself to administer his own development. In that context, "No threshold loomed ahead, demanding to be crossed. Nothing measured and valued his progress."[62] As a site that cultivates forms of agency and recognition that are not premised upon "conforming to certain regulatory matrices,"[63] the noodle house represents a critical alternative to the processes by which Sewanee College and the military make recognizable subjects. As the passage evokes the evaluative systems of the military and the academy, it gestures toward what Max Weber described as the dominance and influence of "the kind of 'education' that produces a system of special examinations and the trained expert that is increasingly indispensable for modern bureaucracy," a dominance and influence that characterized educational institutions in Europe and would come to typify schools and universities in the U.S. as well.[64] As Chang realizes that his future does not depend on "performing flawlessly at a succession of gates," the passage suggests that the American academy is not the guaranteed site of harmonious self-making for immigrant students, the presumed laboratory in which they are completed.

In *The Foreign Student* and *The Namesake,* minoritized sites become locations from which to engage in an archaeological expedition, one aimed at determining how minoritized subjects became recognizable and measurable and how minority culture might be used to throw off the yoke of hegemonic validation and appraisal. In *The Foreign Student,* the noodle house allegorizes the potential of minority culture to illuminate the anatomy of neocolonial subjectification. In *The Namesake,* Gogol's bedroom becomes the place to pore over his own historical and cultural formation and to identify what official narration leaves out, those unofficial elements waiting to be created and embellished, the very resources needed to hold the tyranny of official legibility at bay.

In both scenes, reading becomes the practice of a creative negation, a practice that unravels the established standards of coherence and recognition: a noodle house is turned into a library, and a young Bengali man learns of how he was born from a Russian book. The novels advance a theory of reading much like the one that Barthes promotes in *S/Z,* which posits reading as more than "the reactive complement of a writing which we endow with all the glamour of creation and anteriority," a practice that understands that "[to] read is to find meanings, and to find meanings is to name them; but these named meanings are swept toward other names . . . ," a method that insists that "[reading] does not consist in stopping the chain of systems, in establishing a truth, a legality of the text, and consequently in leading its reader into 'errors'; it consists in coupling these systems, not according to their finite quantity, but according to their plurality."[65] As Barthes's theorization makes clear, a critical reading practice does not privilege official and institutionalized meanings. In the context of the novels, Chang and Gogol realize in the act of reading that they do not have to yield to the institutionalized systems of dominant legibility, valorization, and recognition—that they can create themselves in ways the institutions did not intend.

As we negotiate a political economy that deploys minority affirmation to rebuttress institutional power, we might make this critical reading practice part of our epistemological and institutional methodology. Indeed, the two scenes symbolize the possibilities that await minoritized subjects who are willing to engage the naming, unnaming, and renaming of minority difference, willing to engage how minority difference is imprinted both by marginality and hegemonic institutionality all at the same time. Indeed, we might think of Gogol and Chang as metaphors for minoritized subjects who are prepared to work and create beyond the names offered by state, capital, and academy. Reading minority difference's archival history in this way allows us to refuse the fiction of minority innocence and compels us to develop methodologies for challenging institutional efforts to "pin down" the meaning of minoritized lives, efforts that strive to put into law singular and univocal definitions of formations that are endlessly and vitally plural. This is a story about how, despite power's greatest efforts, there will always be remainders—moments of unrecognizability—where minority difference is concerned. Indeed, part of our job in the wake of hegemonic absorption is to promote and encourage those moments, developing new ways of entering minority difference, encouraging modes of agency that will make that difference legible and liminal at the same time. Our journey might begin where *The Namesake* ends: "He leans back against the headboard, adjusting a pillow behind his back. In a few minutes he will go downstairs, join the party, his family. But for now his mother is distracted, laughing at a story a friend is telling her, unaware of her son's absence. For now he starts to read."[66]

The Golden Era of Instructed Minorities

FOR AN EXTREMELY LONG TIME, the academy was the place where things stayed the same—where today would yield only begrudgingly to tomorrow. It was the domain where content was assumed to be stable and where student and faculty bodies were presumed to be eternal. As the preceding chapters have tried to make clear, the student movements of the fifties and the sixties would help to change all of that, not only for college and university campuses but for government and economy as well. Indeed, we might say that the race- and gender-based movements would overturn the distribution of "the sensible," to use Jacques Rancière's formulation, and disrupt the confidence of everyday meanings. In doing so, the student movements would attempt to introduce new political orders within all spheres of American society, presuming a notion of politics as that which "revolves around what is seen as and what can be said about it, around who has the ability to see and the talent to speak, around the properties of spaces and the possibilities of time."[1] The student movements introduced a new historicity into U.S. society, forcing institutions that snubbed time and alteration to wake up and see that things could change.

As preceding chapters have suggested, the antiracist movements of the sixties and seventies were conversing with national liberation struggles in other parts of the world. Antiracist and anticolonial struggles helped to locate culture within "the sphere of power, contest, and negotiation," charging culture with the task of addressing culture as both a revolutionary and a manageable social formation.[2] Culture thus arose as a site of study within intellectual institutions in the West generally, and in the United States in particular, reconfiguring—as Brett Benjamin indicates—"the disciplinary structures of the university and [reshaping] radical thought through engagements with New Left social movements."[3] The movements "associated with the rights revolution of the 1960s and 1970s," as Wilson Smith and Thomas Bender explain for the U.S. context, "pressed universities to establish inter-disciplinary centers that would address issues of race, ethnicity, and gender."[4] This institutional alteration was accompanied by disciplinary transformations as well:

> Other disappointments with the "normal" practices of the disciplines and their withdrawal from pressing public issues prompted many humanities scholars and social scientists to turn to a variety of theories, mostly identified with France, that went by a variety of rubrics, including "poststructuralism," "postmodernism," or, more generally "cultural studies."[5]

As I observed in chapter 2, culture was not only a site of political and academic engagement but also of economic interest. Indeed, national liberation movements in Africa and Asia especially would inspire global capitalist agencies to turn their attention to the uses of culture, helping to produce the conditions by which an engagement with minority and non-Western cultures would become a site for the disruption and resolution of social hierarchies. The American academy and global capital were, therefore, the means of production for a strategic use of minority culture, a strategic use in which the changing meanings of minority culture might be used by entities that had for years held them at bay.

In this area of timely change, an affirmative mode of power would mount its programs of regulation. This chapter analyzes how that change was regulated as power responded to the interventions of anticolonial, feminist, and antiracist movements. It looks at how the American academy and global capital adopted and renovated the regulations of representative democracy, how those institutions disciplined the critical formations and subjects that the race and gender movements inspired, and how capital and academy attempted to close the social universes that those movements worked to open up. If the American university was the inheritor of histories of colonialism and formations of capital, as Grace Hong has argued,[6] then the closure of those universes was part of the transformations of academy and capital as well, making global capital and the post–civil rights academy articulations of a new mode of power, one that would selectively incorporate minoritized subjects so that a broad and radical redistribution of social relations could be indefinitely held at bay.

Political Theory, the Aesthetic, and the Regulation of Minoritized Subjects and Epistemes

The social movements of the sixties and seventies are widely credited with having made the American academy more "representative." Indeed, as Christopher Newfield has noted, the American public research university attempted to prevail over a system of social stratification that worked to restrict middle-class attainment along the lines of race and class.[7] That democratic vision of the public research university was "the product of the economic 'golden age' that followed the global chaos and destruction of the Great Depression and World War II."[8] This was a vision that was "defined by massive public works and publicly subsidized industrial development in North America, Japan, and Europe. It was propelled by widespread social activism and the various civil rights movements that sought universal access to its ideals of social development," a

> vision of publicly funded social development [that would result] in the creation of the first middle class in the United States—a middle class that included blue-color production workers, unionized service workers, public-sector employees and members of construction trades, to name just a few of the groups that were enjoying the most egalitarian access to prosperity in recorded history.[9]

The public research university, as an institution, took as its goal the production of middle classes, to such an extent that it became the "institution where blue- and white-collar, children of both workers and managers, citizens of every racial background were being invited into a unified majority."[10] According to Newfield, that vision would incur its severest wounds from a conservative elite that would use the "cultural wars" to discredit this increasingly diverse middle class as well as the public research institutions that gave birth to it.

If the public research university invited new constituencies into its realms, what was the anatomy of that invitation? If the American academy became the place—real or exaggerated—in which minoritized subjects would gain representation as students and faculty and where minoritized and previously subjugated knowledges would achieve circulation through the study of culture, what was the genealogy of the academy's standard of representation and circulation for those minoritized items? As we will see, during its "golden age" the American academy would take its cues about minority representation from the Western nation-state, especially from the political theories that occasioned representative democracy.

Discussing the nature of representative democracy in his 1861 text *Considerations of Representative Government,* for instance, John Stuart Mill observed:

> In a really equal democracy, every or any section would be represented, not disproportionately, but proportionately. A majority of the electors would always have a majority of the representatives; but a minority of the electors would always have a minority of the representatives. Man for man they would be as fully represented as the majority.[11]

For Mill, liberal democracy is based on proportional representation; electors will receive representatives that are only proportionate to their size. As such, the liberal definition of representative democracy calibrates representation according to the inequalities that already exist within a given society, preserving those inequalities through its very nature and definition.

For Mill, preserving the differences between majority and minority also means disrupting the local institutions and cultures that constitute the minority: "One of the strongest hindrances to improvement, up to a certain advanced stage, is an inveterate spirit of locality."[12] That spirit of locality works against the maneuvers and criteria of unity proposed by representative democracy:

> [Portions of mankind] may not yet have acquired any of the feelings or habits which would make the union real, supposing it to be nominally accomplished. They may, like the citizens of an ancient community, or those of an Asiatic village, have had considerable practice in exercising their faculties on village or town interests, and have even realized a tolerably effective popular government on that restricted scale, and may yet have but slender sympathies with anything beyond, and no habit or capacity of dealing with interests common to many such communities. I am not aware that history furnishes any example in which a number of these political atoms or corpuscles have coalesced into a body,

and learnt to feel themselves one people, except to a previous subjection to a central authority common to all.[13]

Mill contrasts the presumed social and political inferiority of local and minoritized communities to the universal and cosmopolitan appreciations of representative democracy. In contrast to that cosmopolitanism, the minor "portions of mankind" seem parochial and limited as best, and modernizing them requires the discipline of and subjection to representative democracy and its authorities.

As David Lloyd states in his discussion of Mill's text, "the initial subordination of localities by centralized power . . . is an historical precondition of representative government on which it continues to draw and which it furthers." This subordination is necessary for state augmentation: "This dismantling of local centers of power by central government implies accordingly the incorporation into the state of a variety of laterally and vertically differentiated class and/or ethnic groups."[14]

For Mill, that differentiation resolves itself through the subordination of the local and through the incorporation of local subjects, an incorporation that will be secured though a feeling of national identity and that may be caused by racial heritage, common language, shared religion, or regional identification. Of all of these affective possibilities, political identity is, for Mill, the most compelling: "[The] strongest of all is identity of political antecedents; the possession of national history, and consequent community of recollections; collective pride and humiliation, pleasure and regret, connected with the same incidents in the past."[15] Lloyd sums up Mill's theorization of political identity's role in the establishment of national unity: "[History] for Mill is the narrative of the ethical development of the race, defined precisely by the ever-widening capacities for identification."[16]

According to Lloyd, this ethical development of minority communities depends on aesthetic theory. In fact, aesthetic theory is what transforms at least certain members of minority communities into "a minority of instructed minds," an elite cadre of minoritized subjects who have achieved a certain level of detachment and worldliness and are thereby fit to be representatives of their communities: "This concept [of the aesthetic] is fundamental to Mill's whole argument; hence, the cultural importance for him of the 'instructed minoritity,' that is, the intellectuals regarded as ethical subjects. In this ethical subject, the political and aesthetic spheres intersect" (379).

Aesthetic theory also works to help that subject to reconcile the contradictions between liberal ideals and the exclusions and regulations that those ideals obscure: "The domain of aesthetic culture provides a site of reconciliation which transcends continuing political differences and accordingly furnishes the domain of human freedom promised in theory by bourgeois states but belied in all but form by their practices" (ibid.). According to Lloyd, the aesthetic can act as a site of reconciliation because it can "prefigure and produce an ethical subjectivity restored to identity within universal human essence," doing so even as civil society is characterized by exclusion and alienation (380). As a tool of reconciliation, aesthetic culture acts as a kind of peacekeeping force that obscures the significance and inevitability of material inequalities and exclusions. In this capacity, aesthetic culture strives to smooth over whatever dissonance is caused by the contradictions between state ideals and material exclusions, promising opportunities for representation to those subjects dogged by those contradictions. Hegemonic aesthetic culture means that aesthetic and political theories officially understand minorities as objects of development *and* incorporation, even while the material practices of the modern nation-state and capital regulate and exclude subjects on the basis of a variety of social differences. In a discussion of the bourgeois revolutions of the eighteenth century, for example, Lloyd states: "Given the claim that these revolutions establish universal equality of rights for all men, the provision for proper representation of minority interests within the constitution becomes essential to the theoretical legitimation of bourgeois hegemony" (371). In sum, aesthetic culture's emphasis on development and political theory's emphasis on the citizen presume the representation of minorities as ethical subjects who might one day be reconciled with the ideals of modern citizenship.

As it offers the possibility of citizenship, aesthetic theory deploys the canon as a means of recruiting people to the cultural ideals of the Western nation-state. As a means of subordinating local culture, dominant aesthetic theory separates major cultural traditions and forms from minor ones. Lloyd argues that the Western canon "can . . . be conceived in two interconnected aspects," a historical aspect that "consists of the ordering of an evolution of genres . . . in relation to the historical development of the species" (380). Examples of this aspect would be the song, the ballad, the epic, the drama, and the lyric. The other aspect of the canon "is evaluative and concerns the discrimination between major and minor writing" (ibid.).

As such, the canon is the aesthetic analogue to political theory's classification of social groups into majorities and minorities, and, like political theory, aesthetic culture delivers preeminence to the majority while offering restrictions and hard evaluations to the minority.

To use Jacques Rancière's language, dominant aesthetic theory and political theory are ways of "distributing the sensible." Defining this idea, Rancière says, "I call the distribution of the sensible the system of self-evident facts of sense perception that simultaneously discloses the existence of something in common and the delimitations that define the respective parts and positions within it."[17] As Rancière makes clear, such a distribution has broad social implications: "A distribution of the sensible therefore establishes at one and the same time something common that is shared and exclusive parts. This apportionment of parts and positions is based on a distribution of spaces, times, and forms of activity that determines the very manner in which something in common lends itself to participation and in what way various individuals have a part in this distribution." In a summation of the earliest definition of the citizen as a political and cultural being, he states: "Aristotle states that a citizen is someone who has a part in the act of governing and being governed. However, another form of distribution precedes this act of partaking in government: the distribution that . . . determines those who have a part in the community of citizens."[18] Aesthetic culture would determine who has a part in the community, and political culture would provide a field for their public participation. In doing so, both worked to establish certain regimes of the sensible.

Although the vast history of aesthetic and political cultures in the West excluded minoritized subjects from notions of citizenship and culture, the post–World War II moment was one in which various social movements throughout the globe worked to redistribute the presumed sensibilities around modern community. Largely because of the national liberation and antiracist movements of that period, the world would discover—in the words of Michael Denning—that "the masses had a culture."[19] Minoritized actors throughout the world would reshape the relationships of aesthetic and political cultures to the major and the minor in a moment in which minoritized and colonized subjects were putting culture to new and insurrectionary uses in which culture would increasingly be used as a lever for reclaiming and redefining modern community and participation in the name of historically subjugated populations. As Grace Hong notes, radical student movements in the United States followed the examples of national liberation movements and challenged a distribution of the sensible that racialized people of color as culturally inferior. Hence, in the U.S. context, the university became an "important site where the social movements of the 1960s and 1970s challenged this narrative of racialization and abjection."[20]

The "golden age" after World War II would also be characterized by national and global regimes of resolution that would try to discipline revolutionary aspirations. More specifically, hegemonic institutions would begin to solicit minoritized subjects for selective participation and incorporation. Discussing the World Bank's influence on the Asian African Conference, popularly known as the Bandung Conference, Brett Benjamin observes that "the Bank made concerted efforts to court a number of the African postindependence leaders, even some with socialist leanings, most notably Leopold Senghor of Senegal . . . , Julius Nyerere of Tanzania, and Kenneth Kaunda of Zambia." The bank praised Jomo Kenyatta for his "astute leadership" of "capitalist Kenya" and for holding "latent tribalism in check."[21] As with Nixon's interest in national liberation, the World Bank's investment in the Bandung Conference signaled the hegemonic cultivation of bourgeois minority classes, a cultivation that would—in the words of Mill—yield "a minority of instructed minds" that would cast hegemonic institutions as the resolution of minority aspirations. Concerned about their own well-being and realizing how much of it was tied to "material improvements in living conditions for its expectant, newly independent populations" (123), elite nationalists would work toward an expanded role for the World Bank. During the post–World War II moment, hegemonic appeals to minority elites would cultivate minority middle and elite classes as comprador entities rather than revolutionary ones.

One of the ways in which that resolution was achieved was through culture. Discussing the bank's deployment of culture, Benjamin writes: "Culture became the common, if contested, ground through which the [Bandung] conference attendees attempted to resolve fundamental economic and political divisions" (98). In the final communiqué of the conference, culture became the mechanism of resolution. As the document stated, "among the most powerful means of promoting understanding of culture among nations is the development of cultural cooperation" (ibid.). Although defined as an idiom of resolution, this articulation of minority culture was not the one imagined by Mill, the minority culture that had to be repressed and held at bay. This articulation of culture would enjoy a new prominence as legitimate in its own right, as a site of resolution that would not shy away from its history of colonial subjugation. In fact, the communiqué promoted culture to critique the divisions caused by colonialism, arguing that colonialism "not only prevents cultural cooperation but also suppresses the national cultures of the people" (ibid.). As Benjamin brilliantly shows, by marking culture as a lever for cooperation, the communiqué "[adopted] a language strikingly similar" to World Bank officials who promoted international trade and investment as catalysts for "wider understanding, exchange of ideas, and mutual respect" (124), an official promotion that would underline the bank's investment in rather than its retreat from culture. This rendering of culture would diverge from those theorizations wrought by such anticolonial intellectuals as Aimé Césaire and Frantz Fanon, for whom culture was a way of promoting redistribution and "[insisting] that movements, not states, provide the means, and that democracy and equity, not independence, remain the ends of struggle" (117). Thus, in a new phase of global trade and investment, culture would become a contradictory site, on the one hand consistent with the development of global capital and neocolonialism and, on the other, rooted in a desire for widespread material redistribution and change.

This global engagement with the cultures of anticolonial nationalism would also shape the responses that U.S. social institutions had toward minority difference. As Cynthia Tolentino indicates, professional classes of intellectuals of color emerged during the Cold War period not as "representative subjects" or "exceptional classes" but as formations that helped to illuminate "[shifts] in the concept of U.S. global power."[22] She argues that race began its "cultural moment" in the United States through sociological discourses that professionalized the study of race and encouraged African Americans and Asian Americans in particular to become race professionals. For many in the United States, the production of the intellectual of color became evidence of the state's investment in antiracist work and its rebuttal to Soviet charges of American hypocrisy and government-supported white supremacy. The professionalization of intellectuals of color as researchers and informants would also allow the United States to anesthetize critiques of its own imperial history in regions like the Philippines.

The springtime of American universities would dovetail with the rise of decolonization, producing the conditions whereby minority social and cultural formations would become contradictory sites for both critique and reconciliation. Because of the student movements, political, economic, and academic institutions would have to confront charges of material inequality and exclusion, responding to those charges by representing minority interests. Hence, in the mid-to-late twentieth century, the university arose as a prominent site of minority reconciliation. In fact, the American academy was in a favorable position to refine the procedures of democratic representation. It was responsible not only for incorporating racial, gender, and ethnic minorities but also for giving the world a language for how to engage and tolerate the respective differences of those minorities.

As anticolonial movements put certain pressures on Western man as a viable standard for modern civilization, the student movements disabled certain claims about what counted as major and minor cultural forms and practices, disrupting the reigning cultural and epistemological hierarchies in the process. In response to U.S. insurgencies and in an attempt at reconciliation, the American academy had to reorder the canon's capacities for identification. Aesthetic culture had to become a space of possibles for minoritized subjects rather than the simple terrain of exclusion for minority development.

As the U.S. nation-state responded to those insurgencies by wrestling over the incorporation of minorities into American society, American colleges and universities would become the places that might educate minoritized subjects into the political identities and protocols of the nation—this time with a revised canon in hand. With the incorporation of minoritized subjects, the academy would bring together political theory's interest in the development of the citizen and aesthetic culture's role in the cultivation of the cosmopolite like never before. And yet the minorities that engaged American institutions would be different from the minorities that Mill worried over. The racial, gender, sexual, and class differences of U.S. minorities would stretch the academy and the state's capacities for identification in ways that Mill would never have dreamed of.

Multiculturalism and the Resurrection of Western Man

Yet, with the widening of state and civil society's capacities for identification came the expansion of regulatory regimes. As those various movements helped to enter minoritized and colonized cultures into social articulation, minority culture and difference also became items for the development of a new phase of global capital, a phase that would engage elite minorities as its facilitators. In this context, minoritized subjects and practices would enter on the condition that they be regulated, making state and academy within the years after civil rights contradictory sites that claimed democratic representation at the same time that they disciplined minoritized subjects as local, parochial, and undeveloped constituencies or as the fragile embodiments of canonical and state ideals. The entrance of minoritized subjects into the academy, the rise of ethnic and women's studies departments, and the emergence of multiculturalism were part of a context geared toward the development of regimes of identification, incorporation, and regulation, developments that ensured that all things organized in the name of minority difference—people, programs, departments, and centers—would be subject to an ever-present danger.

In her book *Represent and Destroy: Rationalizing Violence in the New Racial Capitalism,* Jodi Melamed argues that the period in which regimes of identification, incorporation, and regulation developed was one in which the U.S. nation-state attempted to absorb antiracism into the state's machinery. According to Melamed, the U.S. nation-state's engagement with official antiracism began in the 1940s and lasts until the present day, and before World War II, "white supremacy justified economic inequality within the U.S. and European nations and between colonizers and their colonies." After World War II, U.S. global ascendancy and leadership for transnational capitalism required new strategies that "[construed] and [calculated] difference in ways that represent and settle social conflict on liberal capitalist political terrains that conceal material inequalities."[23] Discussing the years from 1970 to 1990 and the state's incorporation of antiracist social movements, she states: "[Liberal] multiculturalism would incorporate and abstract the anti-racist materialisms of the new race-based movements. Liberal multiculturalism would likewise deploy literary discourse as a cultural technology to make anti-racist knowledges productive for the next phases of capitalism development."[24] Liberal multiculturalism would signal the moment in which state and capital would use antiracism to forestall the redistribution of resources to economically and racially disfranchised communities. In this moment of liberal multiculturalism, redistribution would be dismantled while minority difference wore the garb of independence and realization.

Touching on the internal contradictions of multiculturalism, Avery Gordon and Christopher Newfield state in their introduction to *Mapping Multiculturalism:* "[Multiculturalism] promised independence to various cultures to negotiate their own relations to the national whole, *and* it looked like a cornerstone of national union in a more flexible guise,"[25] but promising independence in this context meant aggressively forgetting movement goals of material redistribution. For example, in a discussion of multiculturalism's role in the evasion of civil rights during the 1980s, Gordon and Newfield say that "multiculturalism in the 1980s sponsored renewed protests against white racism, and yet it appeared to replace the emphasis on race and racism with an emphasis on cultural diversity."[26] In sum, diversity arose as a way of preempting redistribution, making the hegemonic incorporation of minorities and minoritized knowledges into dominant institutions not only part of an affirmation but a preemption as well.

As part of that preemption, liberal multiculturalism would institutionalize those movements through the regulated incorporation of minorities and minoritized intellectual and cultural production. In this context, the main U.S. institutions would begin a new archival pursuit, making state, capital, and academy the places where minorities and minoritized knowledges could make "institutional passage from the private to the public."[27] While never achieving dominance, and while many people from socially and economically disfranchised communities would experience deeper levels of impoverishment, many women and people of color would become politicians, business executives, students, and professors in predominantly white institutions, becoming in many ways what Mill had theorized as the "instructed minority."

Yet, as Mill's theorization suggested, the development of "instructed minorities" during the years after civil rights would take place within a context that was disfranchising, to say the least, one that would work against the very social and epistemological maneuvers that introduced opportunities for minorities in the first place. For instance, in the 1980s, the state would begin to withdraw federal support from social services and higher education.[28] In a climate of state disinvestment, academic work on culture would be read more and more as antithetical to market imperatives, even as culture continued to be the face of modern institutional identity. As a result, American colleges and universities would become hotbeds of contention around the importance of the liberal arts versus the necessity of managerial training, a necessity that many believed was crucial for the development of global capital.

As Lisa Duggan explains, this debate would become one of the hallmarks of a "new liberalism" in which "various 'third way' parties and leaders labored to combine pro-market, pro-business, 'free trade' national and global policies with shrunken remnants of social democratic and social justice programs of Western welfare states."[29] This new "neoliberal" skyline was characterized by "attacks on downwardly redistributive social movements, especially the Civil Rights and Black Power Movements, but including feminism, lesbian and gay liberation, and countercultural mobilizations during the 1960s and 1970s."[30] As a result, neoliberalism worked toward an upward redistribution spurred by a pro-business ideological climate and by a "multicultural neoliberal 'equality' politics—a stripped-down, nonredistributive form of 'equality' designed for global consumption during the twenty-first century." This new liberalism was, therefore, a means of using difference to foster capitalist distribution while curtailing social redistribution for underrepresented folks.

The family took on a special ideological role, helping to justify the continued denial of federal support to higher education and disfranchised communities. As Duggan explains, "Third way proponents argued for smaller, more efficient governments operating on business management principles, and appealed to 'civil society' (or the voluntary sector) and 'family' to take up significant roles in the social safety nets."[31] Family would become a way of forgetting prior struggles around redistribution and social transformation. Indeed, the discourse of family became a metonym in the eighties and nineties for the closure of critical universes that were opened by feminist social movements, one critical opening exemplified through efforts to redistribute wealth downwardly. The family became the ultimate cultural value and as such functioned in the regulatory spirit of aesthetic culture—that is, to foster identification with the interests of state and capital, thereby becoming one of the instruments used to close the very universes that various social movements worked to open up.

An anxiety about the closure of those universes within a seemingly middle-class and cosmopolitan Eden appears in Zadie Smith's 2005 novel *On Beauty*. Set in a fictional college town named Wellington, the book tells the story of two families who must share space within the town and the college—also named Wellington—despite the contentious rivalry between the families' patriarchs. Monty, a conservative Afro-British academic, heads the all-black Kipps family and a progressive white British poststructuralist named Howard heads the interracial Belseys. The novel and the families in it represent the world that has been reordered and the commonsensical discourses that have been redistributed because of the antiracist and feminist movements and because of the rise of poststructuralism and postcolonialism. The book allegorizes how the multicultural academy embodied the overlap between aesthetic and political theory and as such became the scene of various closures that keep former possibilities at bay.

On Beauty seems to eschew a narrative of the culture wars as the trials of a noble but compromised Left that must defend its ideals against a cynical and regressive Right. In the conservative rendition of the culture wars, the academy is a secular Sodom and Gomorrah, exhibiting no respect for values around family and work. In the liberal depiction of the culture wars, the academy is for values of tolerance and diversity—our beacon on the hill. We are introduced to both from the start of the novel. Indeed, the novel opens with an e-mail from Howard's son Jerome to his father in which the young man underlines the differences between the Belseys and the Kipps:

> Now, listen to this bit carefully: in the morning THE WHOLE KIPPS FAMILY have breakfast together and a conversation TOGETHER and then get into a car TOGETHER (are you taking notes?)—I know, I know—not easy to get your head around. I never met a family who wanted to spend so much time with each other.[32]

Seemingly, the novel capitulates to this dichotomy embodied in the conservative Kipps family and the progressive Belsey household. But already we have indications even in the e-mail that the dichotomy is a false one, more performative than authentic. "THE WHOLE FAMILY" and "TOGETHER" are written in capital letters, suggesting hyperbole rather than accuracy, frustrating a discourse that casts conservative and progressive renditions of the culture wars as polar opposites.

In fact, there is an irony between the fantastic presence of family and the reigning discourse that casts the Left as above familial entanglements and identifications. In contrast to that looming discourse, the novel presents the family form as a constant and overarching presence even while the narrative of the culture wars poses the family form as either absent in or insignificant to liberal and Left contexts. The hyperprominence of family in *On Beauty* allegorizes both the preeminence of the family in U.S. social discourse during the eighties and nineties as well as the looming one-dimensionality of social thought and practice in the age of neoliberalism, a one-dimensionality that—as Herbert Marcuse argued—attempts to cancel the critical intent of oppositional formations.[33]

Driving at that restrictiveness, *On Beauty* not only narrates the investments that conservative and progressive subjects have in restrictive discourses of the family; it also points to a mode of power that charges the academy with the task of recapturing potentially recalcitrant social forces. For instance, the novel frames Howard initially as the symbol of a critique of the dominant modes of Western knowledge and as the renewal of Western man. As a matter of fact, Howard represents the poststructuralist revolution, the moment when the grand narratives of modernity were aggressively called into question, the time when origins and ends would be disrupted as matters and measures of truth. Howard explains his work to a group of listeners at a faculty party, for instance:

> "Well," he said loudly, hoping to finish it off with a daunting display of academic pyrotechnics, "what I meant was that Rembrandt is part of the seventeenth-century European movement to . . . well, let's shorthand it—essentially *invent the idea of the human*," Howard heard himself saying, all of it paraphrased from the chapter he had left upstairs, asleep on the computer screen, boring even to itself. "And of course the corollary to that is the fallacy that we as human beings are central, and that our aesthetic sense in some way makes us central—think of the position he paints himself in, right between these two inscribed empty globes on the wall."[34]

As his analysis of Rembrandt illustrates, Howard is the poststructuralist subject who refuses the discourse of genius and the figure of the human as the anchor and motor of history. Howard's analysis of Rembrandt resembles Foucault's theorization about Western man, a theorization that for Foucault begins in the seventeenth century as well, that time in which "things become increasingly reflexive, seeking the principle of their intelligibility only in their own development," the moment when "man enters . . . the field of western knowledge."[35] The irony, of course, is that Howard himself is privately and deeply narcissistic. As one of the characters says to him, "you're not the only person in this world." To use Foucault's language,

Howard takes himself and his development as the "principle of intelligibility." We might read Howard's narcissism as allegorical for the ways in which, despite the very real and significant revolutions that poststructuralism wrought, our present moment does not denote the abolition of the subject of man but his reconstitution through not only conservative projects but progressive ones as well.

In the context of the late-twentieth-century United States, Western man was reconstituted ironically through the state's *administering* of civil rights. In their discussion of how liberal and conservative understandings of civil rights frame racial discrimination as the unfortunate aberration within an otherwise rational system, Kimberlé Crenshaw, Neil Gotanda, Gary Peller, and Kendall Thomas observe:

> What we find most amazing about this ideological structure in retrospect is how very little actual social change was imagined to be required by the "civil rights revolution." One might have expected a huge controversy over the dramatic social transformation necessary to eradicate the regime of American apartheid. By and large, however, the very same whites who administered explicit policies of segregation and racial domination kept their jobs as decision makers in employment offices of companies, admissions offices of schools, lending offices of banks and so on.[36]

The history of retrenchment means that the post–civil rights United States was not only constituted by the upheaval of prior racist formations and the insurgency of minority difference but also by the reconstitution of racial domination—this time through an ostensibly reformed mode of whiteness invested in its own centrality rather than the material redistribution of resources.

It is important to note that these retrenchment practices are not only national but global in their reach and significance. As Howard Winant explains in his description of how racial projects changed in the post–World War II moment, "The global racial situation . . . is fluid, contradictory, contentious. No longer unabashedly white supremacist, for the most part the world is, so to speak, *abashedly* white supremacist."[37] As a formation that would deny material redistribution to racially marginalized communities, Western man was alive and well, precisely because of the preservation of structurally racist conditions.

This mode of whiteness, one born of critique but still invested in its own material centrality, has a long history in U.S. intellectual and political movements. For instance, in a 1969 interview James Baldwin identified the white liberal as a formation that—despite its explicit intentions to enact racial reform and dismantle racial segregation—ended up reinscribing white racial privilege. Baldwin described a dispute he had with the white liberal radio host Barry Gray:

> When it was over I began to feel there was involved in all this—in the case of a great many people who think they are on our side of the fence— a will to power that has nothing to do with the principles they think they are upholding. They are operating in this part of the forest because this is where they find themselves, and it is easy for them—but it has nothing whatever to do with love or justice or any of the things they think it has to do with. And when the chips are down, it comes out. Their status in their own eyes is much more important than any real change. If there were no real Negro problem, I don't know what in the world they would do.[38]

Baldwin points to the ways in which the "Negro problem" operates as the resource by which whiteness can enact a "will to power," demonstrating how a certain investment in minority difference and its crises renews the hegemonic possibilities of whiteness.

Baldwin's remarks recall Saidiya V. Hartman's analysis of white abolitionists in *Scenes of Subjection: Terror, Slavery, and Self-Making in Nineteenth-Century America*. About the abolitionist John Rankin's concerted attempt to imagine himself as a black slave, Hartman writes: "While this flight of imagination enables a vicarious firsthand experience of the lash, excoriates the pleasure experienced by the master in his brutal exercise of power, and unleashes Rankin's fiery indignation and resentment, this phantasmic vehicle of this identification is complicated, unsettling, and disturbing."[39] For Hartman, the disturbing component in this empathetic drama is precisely how Rankin's identification takes the psychic and ethical development of the white sympathizer as the principle by which slavery is made intelligible, an opportunity made available by the slave system itself: "Rankin begins to feel for himself rather than for those whom this exercise in imagination is presumably designed to reach . . . [The] ease of Rankin's empathic identification is as much due to his good intentions and heartfelt opposition to slavery as to the fungibility of the captive body."[40] As Hartman suggests, slavery was not only a political economy that distributed black bodies for exploitation; it was also a political economy that provided the corporeal resources for white identification and radicalism. Her argument implies that a political economy that distributed minority difference—as a totem for empathy, identification, desire, and criticality and as a medium for the reconsolidation of white hegemony—dates back at least to the nineteenth century and stretches into our present. Indeed, the late twentieth century, in addition to providing opportunities for insurgent minority subjectivities and social formations, also rendered new chances for the revival of Western man. As such, the post–World War II era gave birth to new and extraordinary contradictions in which the incorporation of minoritized subjects was also part of an evolving social system that would work to renew racial hierarchies.

Redistribution and Non-redistribution: The Contradictions of Minority Existence

We might frame the social transformations wrought by the radical movements of the 1960s as contradictory occurrences that, on the one hand, ushered in a new dawn of minority culture and difference and, on the other hand, shipped "new" forms of racial hegemony onto shore. This contradiction would account for the new character of U.S. institutions, one that would solicit, regulate, and exclude minorities all at the same time. In the divergent circumstances of minority difference, the hegemonic foundations of aesthetic culture would rear their audacious heads and take minorities as objects for whom institutional preparedness would need to be determined. With the rise of this new historical contradiction, evaluative systems would emerge that would compromise and prevent various modes of redistribution geared toward the supplying of material resources, the transformation of discursive arrangements, and the reorganization of social relations and formations.

In this tragedy of redistribution and non-redistribution, the contradictory elements that inhere within the concept of the "minority" would shine as never before. Because the minority is founded in notions of development, suppression, and exclusion, the category makes institutional access not simply a question of admission and privilege but one of discipline and exclusion as well. When we leave the sphere of institutional admittance, we observe that minoritized subjects and knowledges risk a bale of measurements and limitations. In the years following the civil rights movement, the question of how minorities were made into theoretical, political, and cultural categories would begin to share space with the question of how minorities were discursively constituted as *institutional* categories, simultaneously fit for and excluded from a whole host of social institutions.

The entrance of minoritized subjects into the dominant institutions of U.S. society provided the conditions for the reassertion of evaluative discourses. Crenshaw, Gotanda, Peller, and Thomas discuss how those discourses resulted from a narrowing of the civil rights movement's vision for social reorganization:

> In institution after institution, progressive reformers found themselves struggling over the implementation of integrationist policy with the former administrators of segregation who soon regrouped as an old guard "concerned" over the deterioration of standards . . . Even more dramatic, the same criteria for defining "qualifications" and "merit" used during the period of explicit racial exclusion continued to be used, so long as they were not directly "racial."[41]

As the authors suggest, evaluative ideals like "qualifications" and "merit" bridged the racial state organized around segregation to a racial state organized around racial reform. Those ideals would mediate between the inclusion and exclusion of the minority, arbitrating between the disciplining of those that were included and the exclusion of those that were not. As the question of the political and cultural constitution of minorities necessitated thinking through the genealogy of state and capitalist formations, so the question of the institutional constitution of minorities requires a similar genealogical move.

Because of its constant practices of evaluation and certification, the academy arose as a testing ground and model for the disciplines and exclusions that would attend institutional discourses and protocols for inclusion. In the context of the post–civil rights academy, certain models of ethical development have been produced as the condition for admission. In her essay "An Affirmative View," Judith Butler, for example, argues that in the period of the dismantling of affirmative action, a "morally sanctified individualism" counters analyses of institutional discrimination that "once supported the rationale for affirmative action." As a result, "The drama of the heroic individual is reaffirmed as the proper replacement for affirmative action policies, where the latter are understood as remedial actions."[42] Not surprisingly, the figure of the heroic individual recenters the hegemonic authority of academic institutions to articulate minority life: "The institution is under no obligation to give special consideration to those who have suffered discrimination; on the contrary, the institution will now reward those who have overcome their adverse circumstances with the resources of individual character."[43]

If we read Butler's comments about affirmative action alongside David Lloyd's theorizations about minorities and representative democracy, we see that the American academy derived much of its grammar for institutional representation from theorizations of representative democracy, making the ethical development of the abstract individual into the measurement of achievement and capacity. The academy also inherited and revised representative democracy's regulatory engagement with and construction of minoritized subjects. As the academy engaged the modern nation-state's understanding of representative democracy, perfecting that understanding in relation to racial and gender minorities, it also offered the minority as the embodiment of a permanent inadequacy whose development is precarious at worst and uneven at best. In addition to narrowing the transformative potential of the civil rights movement by shirking a "broad scale inquiry into why jobs, wealth, education, and power are distributed as they are,"[44] the academy, along with other social institutions, narrowed the potential of those transformations by continuing to articulate the liberal individual as the horizon of cultural value and development, and in doing so refortified rather than displaced Western man.

As the liberal individual is taken as the major ideal for institutional inclusion, the minority is rendered as its antithesis. Lloyd discusses this discourse in the context of representative democracy: "[Whether] a minority group is defined in terms of gender, ethnicity, or any other typology, its status is never merely statistically established, but involves the aspersion of 'minority' exactly in the sense of the common legal usage of the term for those too young to be out of 'tutelage.'"[45] This definition of the minority as neither fully excluded nor fully entitled is precisely what a hegemonic formation built on regulatory inclusions as well as rationalized exclusions requires. As Lloyd argues, "The hegemonic exercise of power replaces violent and exclusive apartheids with the concept of the 'minority' defined no longer as bestial or subhuman, but as not yet fully developed, childlike, and subject to tutelage until assimilation is accomplished."[46]

The category "minority" implies that procedures of inclusion are not transparent and wholly benign. To be a minority means that procedures of incorporation are hegemonic ones as well. In fact, the regulatory regimes that constitute representative democracy and the discourse of the minority mean that we must determine the ways in which inclusion is also an operation of power. In relation to the institutional transformations inspired by the civil rights movement, the post–civil rights moment suggests historic formations that prove the inseparability of inclusion and exclusion, undermining the presumption that they are diametrical opposites. As an institution that helped to reconcile inclusion with exclusion and regulation, the post–civil rights academy simultaneously ascribed primitiveness and advancement to minoritized subjects, particularly to people of color.

This discursive horizon that intertwined inclusion with exclusion necessitated that ideals of excellence, merit, and standards would be etched not only on institutional structures but on subjective formations as well. Turning institutionalization into a mode of subject formation was established very early on. For example, Wilhelm von Humboldt said that institutionalization in the academy had to take place as an "inward development" as well as an external one:

> The means which are legislatively applied to promote the moral education of citizens are appropriate and useful only the degree to which they favor the inward development of people's capacities and inclinations. For all educational development has its sole origin in the inner psychological development of human beings, and can only be stimulated, never produced by external institutions.[47]

Here, Humboldt identifies institutionalization as a psychic enterprise as well as an external one. To this end, the university is not just a structural institution but a psychic and hermeneutic one as well, a social formation that constitutes subjectivity and interpretation, an entity that is both a material and psychic mode of power. After the civil rights years, the American academy would not only increase the possibilities for minority enrollment but expand the capacities for minority identification with power as well, an identification that would discipline knowledge and subjects within the academy and reconstitute hegemony in new racialized, gendered, classed, and sexualized arrangements.

On Beauty attempts to dramatize the regulations of incorporation. We can see this through an encounter between Claire, a white poet and literature professor at Wellington and the woman with whom Howard had an extramarital affair, and Carl, a gifted African American spoken-word artist who she has informally admitted into the class:

> "Are you serious about this class, Carl?"
>
> Carl looked around himself cautiously. This was a strange question to ask in front of everybody.
>
> "I mean, do you want to stay in this class? Even if it gets difficult?"
>
> So that was the deal: they thought he was stupid. These early stages were fine, but he wouldn't be able to manage the next stage, whatever it was. Why'd they even ask him, then?
>
> "Difficult how?" he asked edgily.
>
> "I mean, if other people wanted you not to be in class. Would you fight to be in it? Or would you let me fight for you to be in it? Or your fellow poets here?"[48]

We can read the exchange as an example of the regimes of evaluation that were informed by aesthetic culture and political theory's understanding of the minority's place within representative government. We might also read it as an allegory of the systems of evaluation that formed around a discourse of "standards," "merit," and heroic individualism, systems that arose in the aftermath of civil rights retrenchment, institutional modes that Claire has internalized. Part of Claire's question is whether or not Carl will take the mantle of the heroic individual and rise above that anonymous assemblage of opponents who do not want him to be in the class. Claire, in this instance, is also metaphoric for the reconsolidation of Western man in a progressive and minority-identified mode of whiteness.

After Carl agrees, Claire responds:

> "Oh, I'm so glad," she said and practically smiled her face off. Then she stopped smiling and looked businesslike. "Good," she said firmly. "That's decided. Good. Then you're going to stay in this class. *Anybody who needs this class,*" she said fervently, and looked from Chantelle to a young woman called Bronwyn who worked at the Wellington

Savings Bank, and then to a mathematician boy called Wong from BU, "is *staying* in this class."[49]

In this passage, Claire prods Carl to perform the rhetoric of development, to place himself within a racialized idiom of progress as a condition of his, Chantelle's, Bronwyn's, and Wong's inclusion in the classroom. Through this rhetoric of development, Claire can again claim centrality as a white subject responsible for minority uplift. As the American academy became the site in which aesthetic and political theory overlapped and the location in which minority difference was represented, the academy also became the place in which whiteness was rearticulated through its engagement with minority difference, the institution where the majority was reestablished in relation to the representation of the minority. The scene in the classroom symbolizes, therefore, the ways in which the redistribution of the meanings of minority life was snuffed out before they reached their full potential, extinguished as that redistribution worked not toward the unshakable presumptions about racial minorities and their capacities but for the ironic centrality of whiteness and its investors.

In the 1990s, affirmative-action programs at campuses in Maryland, Texas, and California came under fire for allegedly favoring people of color over more qualified white applicants for admission.[50] In Proposition 209 in California and the *Hopwood* cases in Texas, the pitched rhetoric of reverse discrimination, people of color were inscribed as the living embodiments of mediocrity, undeserving of university admission. As Christopher Newfield notes, inscribing black and Latino students in this way created a general stigmatization of black and Latino youth and became a way to fashion them as the reserve of an expanding prison-industrial complex. Indeed, "As U.S. society increasingly solved deindustrialization with layoffs and imprisonment rather than employment, and three-strikes discourse spread images of inner city youth as criminally defective, the war against affirmative action cast those neighborhoods' college-bound members as academically defective."[51] With the simultaneity of prison expansion and academic exclusion, a new level of dispensability for blacks and Latinos was being born that would create opportunities for penal institutions and omissions for academic institutions. The political and economic circumstances of the 1960s—which fostered the expansion of prisons and the closing of colleges and universities to minority students and relied on discourses of mediocrity

to open penal universes and close academic ones—were historical formations written on the bodies of black and Latino youths. In many ways,
Claire's exchange with Carl is a reminder of how his body stands as a metonym for a presumably mediocre body politic, one that justified new practices
of institutional and intellectual exclusion while it insinuated new processes
of criminalization.

The novel also points to the ways in which a hegemonic affirmation of
minority difference fetishizes certain minoritized subjects as both undeveloped and authentic, an affirmation that again resituates the status of white
subject formations. For example, Claire reflects on Howard's African American wife, Kiki, and is awash with a kind of feminist affirmation for her:

> Claire remembered when Howard first met his wife, back when Kiki
> was a nursing student in New York. At that time her beauty was awe-
> some, almost unspeakable, but more than this she radiated an essential
> female nature Claire had already imagined in her poetry—natural, hon-
> est, powerful, unmediated, full of something like genuine desire. A god-
> dess of the everyday. She was not one of Howard's intellectual set, but
> she was actively political, and her beliefs were genuine and well ex-
> pressed. Womanish, as they said back then, not feminine. For Claire, Kiki
> was not only evidence of Howard's humanity but proof that a new kind
> of woman had come into the world as promised, as advertised.[52]

As the passage implies, aesthetic culture—symbolized through Claire and
through her poetry, which had "already imagined" Kiki—has presumably
prepared a place for Kiki and, by extension, other black women and women
of color. That place is authenticity as Claire constructs Kiki as "[radiating]
an essential female nature." Constructing Kiki's authenticity is also crucial
to Claire's own racial subjectivity—that is, as benevolent and feminist white
woman who esteems women of color.

For contemporary social actors, the institutional appreciation of minority difference goes by that dubious designation "diversity." M. Jacqui Alexander discusses how the institutional discourse of diversity has shaped life
within the academy:

> Institutional claims within the "diversity" discourses become the claims
> within which people of color are understood. They represent people of
> color . . . Discourses, which on the surface appear benign, become

quite aggressive in the context of an ideological struggle to transform the relations of representation, for the institution would want its definitions to stand as the only legitimate claims relating to the subjects whom diversity is ostensibly about.[53]

Diversity, Alexander argues, becomes the horizon of institutional representation, addressing the minority in the constrictive standards of hegemonic institutions. As such, diversity—despite its claims to just and fair representation—becomes a contentious locale for framing the institutional circumstances of minoritized subjects and knowledges. As an attempt by the American academy to assert dominance over the representation of minority difference and as a mode for compelling minorities to conform to institutional discourses around difference, diversity enacts the regulatory procedures of aesthetic culture. Diversity thus works to manage the redistribution of sensible notions of minority existence—particularly ones that frame minority incorporation as institutionally possible and beneficial, thereby limiting the redistribution of material and social relations involving minoritized subjects and thus secreting tactics for minority exclusion.

We can locate the contradictions of diversity both within the contemporary American academy and within present-day globalization. Indeed, as the relationship between the World Bank and the Bandung Conference implies, the nonredistributive and regulatory properties of affirmation are part of the unfolding of contemporary globalization. As the rise of state, economic, and academic practices organized around newly discovered diversities suggests, this mode of affirming minority difference was quickly becoming the face of social reproduction. Grace Hong notes, with regard to the global politics of diversity and its bearing on black feminists, that "racialized and gendered management currently does not occur solely through the denigration of black feminism and black feminists, but also simultaneously through a form of valorization and fetishization, albeit of a limited and facile type."[54] For Hong, the contemporary neoliberal moment "allows for, and indeed requires, the nominal valorization of black feminism as a way to deflect charges of racism and misogyny, which does not preclude and in many instances facilitates the exclusion and extinguishing of black feminists."[55] Addressing this deployment of diversity, black feminist writing of the eighties and nineties worried over the ironic persistence of "racist and sexist structures despite [a] seeming disavowal of overt racism and white supremacy."[56] In terms of the novel, Claire's fetishization of Kiki symbolizes neoliberalism's fetishization of minority difference in general, and black feminism in particular, a fetishization whose hypocrisy is denoted in a variety of maneuvers—the dismantling of affirmative action, the decline in the numbers of blacks entering graduate programs, the increased incarceration of blacks and Latinos. As the years from the post–World War II moments to the present show, the hegemonic affirmation of minority difference has produced regulatory and nonredistributive social formations that have transcended national and institutional boundaries, affecting various bodies at the micro and macro levels, dispatching tactics characterized by the most astonishing variation.

The Closing of Critical Universes

Framing the postwar period as a moment in which hegemonic forces worked to narrow and forestall the redistributive efforts of social movements, Herbert Marcuse says in *One-Dimensional Man*: "Under the rule of a repressive whole, liberty can be made into a powerful instrument of domination. The range of choice open to the individual is not the decisive factor in determining the degree of human freedom, but *what* can be chosen and what *is* chosen by the individual."[57] Marcuse theorizes how the democratic offerings of industrial society manage social change: "Contemporary society seems to be capable of containing social change—qualitative change which would establish essentially different institutions, a new direction of the productive process, new modes of human existence. This containment of social change is perhaps the most singular achievement of advanced industrial society."[58] Marcuse worries over how advanced industrial society contains the social change called for by the student movements, making advanced industrial society part of representative democracy's regulations of minority difference.

Marcuse's interest in containment as a social formation is reflected in the following scene from *On Beauty*. In a conversation that takes place between Kiki and Carlene, Monty's wife, Kiki discusses her marriage and acknowledges the alienation that she feels as a wife and the resentment that she feels toward her husband. In a gesture of understanding, Carlene says to Kiki, "You've been disappointed." Kiki responds,

"Oh, I don't know about disappointed . . . it's not really a surprise. Stuff happens. And I *did* marry a man."

Carlene looked at her curiously. "Is there another option?"

Kiki looked straight back at her hostess and decided to be brazen. "For me, there was, I think . . . yes. At one point . . .

"I guess I mean, there was a revolution going on, everybody was looking at different lifestyles, alternative lifestyles . . . so whether women could live with women, for example."

"With women," repeated Carlene.

"Instead of men," confirmed Kiki. "Sure . . . I thought for a while that might be the road I was going to go down. I mean, I went down it some way."[59]

Kiki's remarks touch on the deception at work here, that admission into the family form, with its gendered structures and its promises of normativity, is a deceptive liberty; so often narrated as an admission free of compromise and charged with unprecedented possibilities, Kiki's own admission into that life belies this narrative. Indeed, her entrance into the academy as the spouse of an academic has meant the closing of a universe to which she once belonged, flying in the face of the picture that we have of the academy as the site that can bring alternative imaginings to the height of embodiment.

The reader is never privileged with the particulars of Kiki's former life, that gender and sexual universe closed down by the maneuvers of a mode of power that said it cared. We might hazard that the revolution that she's referring to is the one that took place in the seventies and eighties with groups like the Combahee River Collective of 1974, or Samois, the lesbian S/M group founded in San Francisco in 1978. Or perhaps she was calling to mind Lesbian Sex Mafia of 1981 and its promotion of "politically incorrect sex"? It's possible even that she, like so many other African American women, was inspired by the gender and sexual creativity exhibited in Alice Walker's *The Color Purple.* Maybe she read Audre Lorde's *Sister Outsider* and happened upon that now classic chapter titled "Uses of the Erotic: The Erotic as Power," the manifesto in which Lorde talked about the erotic foundations of joy: "[That] deep and irreplaceable knowledge of my capacity for joy comes to demand from all of my life that it be lived within the knowledge that such satisfaction is possible, and does not have to be called *marriage,* nor *god,* or an *afterlife.*"[60] To call it a "revolution" is not at all to flirt with hyperbole. A conflicted and precarious upheaval was going on, a commitment to enlarging the boundaries of sexual and domestic possibility, a queer imagination that reached into but beyond sexual freedom, an imagination that Lorde seemed to capture: "Recognizing the power of the erotic within our lives can give us the energy to pursue genuine change within our world, rather than merely settling for a shift of characters in the same weary drama."[61] As the scene with Kiki and Carlene implies, alternative forms of sexuality were part of a variety of closures that resulted from state, academy, and capital's responses to prior social movements, closures that prevented the redistribution of material resources, deactivations that limited alternative sexual and gender formations in every way they could, all the while claiming that they—and we—would be satisfied.

As an institution that brought together aesthetic culture and political theory's solicitation and regulation of minority difference, the multicultural and post–civil rights academy helped to produce the broader conditions for a political economy of affirmation and loss, of representation and exclusion, of redistribution and retrenchment, a political economy that would characterize relations within state and capital as well. In this light, the academy was never simply a domain of minority opportunity. The academy was also the terrain of minority diminishment, a reduction that would take place in the epic time of incorporation. Hong captures this sense of the academy: "If we are to center the U.S. university as the object of our analysis, we must understand the regulation and disciplining of the study of race and gender as centrally and constitutively organizing its mechanisms of power."[62]

Christopher Newfield argues that the social movements of the sixties helped to imagine the public university as a site of democratic change, one in which "blue- and white-collar, children of both workers and managers, citizens of every racial background were being invited into a unified majority."[63] According to Newfield, conservatives attacked the public university precisely because of the potentials of this middle-class vanguard. But if academy, state, and capital were part of a new strategic situation in which social institutions were affirming minority difference and culture for regulation and exclusion, then an enlightened middle class was also implicated in that drama, requiring us to look at how the seeds that would close critical universes were planted in conservative *and* progressive soil.

The golden years of academic transformation, state reform, and capitalist expansion were shaped within this new mode of power. If academy, state, and capital were part of a new strategic situation in which social institutions were affirming minority difference and culture for regulation and exclusion, then the very middle classes produced within this time of change were implicated in that drama. Those minoritized classes were formed in contradiction, simultaneously eccentric to and customary for power. As such, disrupting power's newest mode has to come from itineraries—like the ones set by the Lumumba-Zapata movement—that are willing to disrupt the historic functions of the middle class.

Almost as an extension of the conversation between Kiki and Carlene, the next chapter examines the ways in which queer sexuality has become one of the latest articles in power's archive of affirmation and how queer practices and identities have inspired an administrative ethos that attempts to manage the desires and hopes of minoritized subjects. As another illustration of Kiki's complaint and this book's observation, the chapter will, it is hoped, show us how a mode of power that has affirmed minority difference while negating a will to redistribution has been our grammar and logic of practice for a very long time.

Administering Sexuality;
or, The Will to Institutionality

THE PRECEDING CHAPTERS have dealt with the ways in which race, nationality, and gender have been maneuvered by hegemonic affirmation. This chapter turns to sexuality's journey in power's latest mode. In particular, it looks at sexuality to ask, What changes does a mode of difference undergo in administrative contexts? The chapter poses this question about minority difference and administration out of a belief that "the administrative" defines more than discrete institutions but an entire historical ethos involving the state's deployment of rights and capital's interest in difference. We might think of sexuality's engagement with the twists and turns of administration as archival power's latest affair with minority culture and difference. As such, sexuality inherits the universe of problems outlined in the preceding chapters, a universe established out of power's negotiations with the upheavals of the student movements around race and gender. With sexuality's entrance into power's archive, the histories of the gay and lesbian movement were brought into the purviews of institutional consideration, representation, and management. As power sought to institutionalize race and gender, power in this moment works to determine how best to subject queer sexuality to its managerial calculus. In this sense, sexuality's particular "institutional passage from the private to the public"[1] yields special revelations about the metastases of affirmation, recognition, and legibility.

The contemporary administrative ethos has special bearing on how we conceptualize sexuality as an object of knowledge and as a historical formation. First, it means that sexuality at this historical juncture is a mode of difference that resonates with administration and with power's archival and managerial project. Hence, queer sexuality is not so radically eccentric and extravagant that it is insulated from the hail of power. Second, conceptualizing sexuality as a mode of difference entangled in administrative discourses and systems means that we should exploit and elaborate all the ways to enter a text, even the ones whose main doorways seem tried and true. And so, let us begin with *The History of Sexuality*.

Worrying over Affirmation: The History of Sexuality

The world in which queer sexuality finds itself is characterized by the most spectacular affirmations in the form of rights, benefits, and visibility. To address these technologies and effects of affirmation, we might revisit Foucault's groundbreaking text to appreciate the mechanisms of sexuality's confirmation and excitation in this era of power. We can begin to assemble such a critique by reviewing Michel Foucault's theorizations of power and sexuality, by ruminating a little on well-trodden territory. In the first volume of *The History of Sexuality,* he re-theorizes power as a potentially productive rather than exclusively negative force. Power is not only that which says "no." For Foucault, power is also that which says, "Yes, tell me more. Yes, say that. Say that and say much more than that." Power is that which speaks in the affirmative. Foucault elaborates on this aspect of power and its appeal to subjects in an interview titled "Truth and Power":

> If power were never anything but repressive, if it never did anything but to say no, do you really think one would be brought to obey it? What makes power hold good, what makes it accepted, is simply the fact that it doesn't only weigh on us as a force that says no, but that it traverses and produces things, it induces pleasure, forms knowledge, produces discourse.[2]

By linking power and knowledge through their affirmative properties, Foucault argues that the modern subject invites power, in part, because of power's productive qualities, because power can "induce pleasure, form knowledge, and produce discourse."

The History of Sexuality was originally titled, in the French version, *La volonté de savoir* (The will to know). This distinction is significant beyond the semantic differences of what American and French publishers consider to be a more marketable name. The French title reminds us that, for Foucault, sexuality was not an object to analyze in and of itself but a reason to assess the productive and discursive nature of power—power realized through knowledge as well as power realized through the *desire* for knowledge. Moreover, for Foucault, sexuality also refers to manifestations and mutations of power. It is this sense of sexuality-as-power that we must retain in an analysis of institutionality and administration, particularly as they concern the American academy. Examining sexuality as an artifact of power and knowledge serves a way of assessing the forms of power elaborated by things academic in the current historical moment.

The critical scholarship on the contemporary university theorizes power as emanating from capital's encampment within the university and its culmination in administrative arrangements within university settings. According to Bill Readings, for instance, the crisis of the university can be seen in the increased ascendancy of the administrator and the resulting displacement of the scholar/professor. Applying Jacques Barzun's *The American University: How It Runs, Where It Is Going* as an unfortunately prophetic text, Readings states: "The central figure of the University is no longer the professor who is both scholar and teacher but the provost to whom both these apparatchiks and the professors are answerable."[3] Readings rightfully identifies the contemporary university as one that has prepared the way for the administrator who was once student and professor, this version of the liberal individual tailor-made for the academy's latest mode. In this narrative of maturation, the student becomes a professor who evolves into the administrator and assumes stewardship of the university in its most recent historical incarnation. In possessing a greater degree of influence, force, and power than the scholar, the administrator has the kind of managerial and economic profile appropriate for the contemporary moment of globalization. Readings thus addresses the rhetorical power of the category of "excellence" deployed by administrators as an institutional mode in the late twentieth century and beyond, a rhetorical power that allows administrators to situate the university within the international scene, within a global economy that gives more and more attention to administration to facilitate the union of market forces and knowledge.[4] In its latest iteration, the American academy confirms an observation that Weber once made. "Bureaucratization," he said, "is occasioned more by intensive and qualitative enlargement and internal deployment of the scope of administrative tasks than by their extensive and quantitative increase . . . In the modern state, the increasing demands for administration rest on the increasing complexity of civilization and push towards bureaucratization."[5]

While the American academy has always been influenced by market forces, the administrative transformation of the university, and the infiltration of administrative regimes into virtually all sectors of university life—both large and small, both structural and corporeal—is propelled by unprecedented social and economic processes.[6] As Sheila Slaughter and Larry Leslie argue in *Academic Capitalism: Politics, Policies, and the Entrepreneurial University,* "During the second half of the twentieth century, professors, like other professionals, gradually became more involved in the market . . . In the 1980's globalization accelerated the movement of faculty and universities toward the market."[7] Multinational corporations emerged in the 1970s and 1980s at the moment that industrialized countries began to lose market shares to Pacific Rim competitors.[8] To compensate for such losses, such corporations made more and more claims on public monies, diverting funds away from entitlement programs, social services, and public education. In addition, multinational corporations began to "devote more resources to the enhancement and management of innovation so that corporations and the nations in which they were headquartered could compete more successfully in the world markets."[9] As Slaughter and Leslie contend, a "quiet revolution . . . has taken place. Within public research universities, fewer and fewer funds are devoted to instruction and more and more to research and other endeavors that increase institutional ability to win external funds."[10] Hence, much of the research on the entrepreneurial transformation of the Western university corroborates Readings's analysis of the spread of an administrative ethos that nurtures market tendencies within the university.

As preceding chapters have illustrated, however, the production of new subjects and modes of difference required talents and functions not entirely possessed by capital. Turning a mode of difference like sexuality into a commodity depended on a system that would explore and elaborate sexuality as an object of inquiry. That system was the academy, and in the moments after the civil rights and liberation movements, the post–civil rights academy would become the presupposition of a mode of capital bent on working with and through minority difference.

This new partnership between the academy and global capital begs this question: In what ways has the modern university, as the sometimes sycophant but often instructor of contemporary globalization, attempted to negotiate, incorporate, and reflect the differences that it was trying to overcome? Put another way, how does global capital's commodification of difference and its promotion of administrative relations intersect with the management of difference in the contemporary university? The American academy intersects with corporate capital not only through maudlin, self-congratulatory categories such as "excellence" but also through the attempt to incorporate and thereby neutralize difference.

As the chapters leading up to this discussion suggest, sexuality's relationship to administrative power lies in the historic incorporation of institutionally anterior forms of difference. In a discussion of that history, Chandra Talpade Mohanty points out that black, ethnic, and women's studies programs came about through various sociohistorical factors—oppositional social movements that contested race- and gender-based discrimination, increases in black student enrollment in colleges and universities, and "broad-based [calls] for a transformation of a racist, Eurocentric curriculum."[11] Mohanty notes that the university responded to those factors in the eighties and nineties by rendering race and gender as individualized matters rather than as structural or institutional ones.

If contemporary globalization, as Stuart Hall argues, incorporates differences as a way to neutralize any ruptural possibilities, we might say that the administrative university unmarks and reabsorbs difference, one of the familiar imprints of globalization. As preceding chapters have suggested, we can think of this moment as unleashing a new mode of power, characterized generally by the commodification of difference as part of an emergent global capital, and denoted specifically through the university's own efforts to incorporate differences of race, disability, sexuality, and gender as objects of knowledge. We might even think of the institutional formations that Mohanty discusses as part of the moment in which—to use Hall's words—contemporary capital tries to "get hold of and neutralize difference." If neoliberalism, as Lisa Duggan defines it, represents the forcible curtailment of liberal, left-liberal, and leftist social movements of the sixties and seventies, then neoliberalism can be understood as part of those historic processes that attempt to "get hold of and neutralize difference."[12] Indeed, we might think of neoliberalism as the latest expression of contemporary globalization's effort to cannibalize difference and its potential for rupture. It is important to remember, though, that the precondition for this aspect of neoliberalism lies in the academy's transformation of minority cultures and differences into objects of institutional knowledge. In such a context, differences that were often articulated as critiques of the presumed benevolence of political and economic institutions become absorbed within an administrative ethos that recast those differences as testaments to the progress of the university and the resuscitation of a common national culture.

The historic arc that begins in the late 1960s signifies a profound change within modern institutions in the West. Administrative power had to restrict the collective, oppositional, and redistributive aims of difference at the same time that administrative power had to affirm difference to demonstrate institutional protocols and progress. We must read this affirmation as not simply a moment of construction but a moment of subjection. As power has negotiated and incorporated differences, it has also developed and deployed a calculus by which to determine the specific critical and ruptural capacities of those forms of difference. We may call this incorporation of modes of difference and the calculus that seeks to determine the properties and functions of those modes *as a will to institutionality*. The will to institutionality not only absorbs institutions and modern subjects; it is itself a mode of subjection as well. We might consider this rumination on administrative power in relation to Judith Butler's observation in *The Psychic Life of Power* that "'Subjection' signifies the process of becoming subordinated by power as well as the process of becoming a subject."[13]

Foucault discusses sexuality as a complex apparatus of truth-seeking and truth-producing practices:

> nearly one hundred and fifty years have gone into the making of a complex machinery for producing true discourses on sex: a deployment that spans a wide segment of history in that it connects the ancient injunction of confession to clinical listening methods. It is this deployment that enables something called "sexuality" to embody the truth of sex and its pleasures.[14]

As part of that "complex machinery for producing true discourses on sex," sexuality is thus a discursive effect. As the linchpin between "ancient injunctions of confession" and "clinical listening methods," sexuality accounts for the discursive outlines of practices geared toward extracting the truth of sex and gauging the pleasures presumably embodied in it. In other words, Foucault's revision of power exposes its affirmative rather than repressive itineraries. As such, this revision accounts not only for sexuality's embodiment in truth but its realization in institutionality and administration as well.

To Deviate from Deviance: The Affirmative and Sociological Roots of Hegemonic Sexuality

The relationship between sexuality as a claim of truth and sexuality as an artifact of institutionality implies a link between objects of knowledge and their institutional lives. If we were to trace the institutional life of sexuality, we might go back to those moments of the sixties and seventies when the sociology of deviance first promoted homosexuality as an object of inquiry and affirmation. Put another way, we might see the ways in which the genealogy of an administrative affirmation of queer sexuality lies partly in the affirming gestures of a social science. In "Queer-ing Sociology, Sociologizing Queer Theory: An Introduction," Steven Seidman situates a growing body of work on queer sexualities in the wake of the women's and gay liberation movements of the early seventies. Those movements, he says, "had fashioned elaborated social concepts of homosexuality that not only sought to normalize homoerotic desire and identities but also criticized the institutions of heterosexuality, marriage, and the family, and conventional gender roles."[15] Seidman shows that these movements also pressured and inspired sociology to address homosexuality in the late sixties and early seventies: "the growing national public awareness of homosexuality and the surfacing of social concepts of homosexuality prompted sociologists to conceive of homosexuality as within their domain of knowledge."[16] While sociologists were certainly concerned with how homosexuals negotiated a homophobic society, Seidman notes that "sociologists contributed to the public perception of the homosexual as a strange, exotic 'other' in contrast to the normal, respectable heterosexual." For Seidman and many other sociologists, the sociology of deviance stood as homosexuality's founding sympathizer and detractor.

We can see that sympathy not only in the content but also in the prose style of those texts from the post–civil rights period. For instance, the 1975 article by Martin Weinberg and Colin J. Williams "Gay Baths and the Social

Organization of Impersonal Sex" deploys a mostly descriptive rather than normative language to describe queer sex. Indeed, this Spartan prose works in the service of the article's sympathies toward homosexuality as it seeks to rhetorically alienate judgment and condemnation. For example, in a section describing how opportunities for sex are structured in gay baths, the authors state:

> As with any other behavior, in order to engage in impersonal sex one needs not only the motivation, but also the opportunity. The ideal opportunity structure is one where everyone is attractive and available at minimum expense. To a large degree, the baths are territories that provide such an opportunity structure. Their clienteles include many attractive men, with enough diversity in physical types to satisfy customers' varying notions of attractiveness.[17]

This sociological sympathy is sealed toward the end of the piece through symbolic-interactionist maneuvers that ask what the baths mean for their partakers:

> In addition, sociology traditionally conceptualizes impersonal relationships as superficial, tawdry, depressing, or pathological. This conception ignores the fact that such relationships may be defined as positive by the people involved. It ignores the fact that participants may interpret the impersonal experience as fun, enjoyable, or satisfactory, and that a market-type social organization may indeed be the best for facilitating such experiences.[18]

In a critical gesture, Williams and Weinberg frustrate the normative impulse of canonical sociology and the sociology of deviance. They strive to treat "deviance" as a rhetorical and discursive device rather than a transparent label. Taking this article as a representative piece, we can indeed say that Seidman and others are correct in their argument that sociology was first to affirm homosexuality, that is, long before the emergence of queer studies.

But affirmations possess complicated architectures. While the sociological work on sexuality from that era tended to uphold public sex and homosexuality, the parameters of its affirmations were narrow in relation to how many gay and lesbian grassroots organizations understood homosexuality's convergences with feminist and antiracist politics of the early 1970s. While sociological sympathizers observed homosexuality mainly, and often only in terms of sexuality, many gay and lesbian activists under stood homosexuality in relation to liberation struggles around race and gender. For instance, in her oral history *No Bath but Plenty of Bubbles: An Oral History of the Gay Liberation Front*, Gay Liberation Front (GLF) member Lisa Power notes the 1969 emergence of GLF within the context of liberation movements among women and African Americans. According to Power, one of the distinctive features of GLF was its abiding and often internally controversial interest in coalitional politics. Many who objected to GLF's coalitional politics "left to start the single-issue Gay Activists Alliance which, with its combination of an in-your-face manner and acceptance of male-identified formal organizing, was soon far more visibly successful than GLF."[19] We might contrast GLF's affirmation of homosexuality as a category that overlapped and intersected with other social formations, particularly race and gender, with a sociological and emergent political affirmation of homosexuality that understood it as removed from racial and gender difference.

Soon after the emergence of organizations like the Gay Liberation Front and in opposition to it, homosexuality was defined more and more as a single-issue mode of difference divorced from race and gender. This move would inaugurate the closing of a critical universe in which homosexuality was poised in competitive opposition to U.S. racial and imperial projects and to patriarchy. Homosexuality as the sign of a single-issue politics is significant because it became the grammar for institutional participation and belonging and the barricade against alternative forms of queerness. The single-issue affirmation that sociology installed would become the conventional way of writing about queer sexuality. This affirmation and the rhetorical convention that it inaugurated would work to conceal questions of intersectionality and histories of gay liberation's overlap with critiques of race, U.S. imperialism, and patriarchy. As sexuality was increasingly articulated apart from the critique of race, patriarchy, and U.S. nationalism, sexuality would become part of an institutional ethos that would affirm it as a mode of difference consistent with interest politics in liberal capitalist nation-states. As Foucault notes, sexuality has been as easily located in the religious arena of the church as it has been in the secular arena of modern epistemes. Now, we are in a moment in which sexuality finds itself—like other forms of minority difference—within the realm of administration.

Documenting Sexuality: The Domestic Partner Memo

As sexuality is articulated into administration, this mode of difference becomes a practice of documentation. To illustrate this point, we might examine the text of a memo written in 1997 by Richard Atkinson, then president of the University of California system, to the UC's Board of Regents on the topic of "limited domestic partner benefits." The memo begins by stating:

> The first prerequisite would be to meet the University's definition of domestic partner—an unmarried partner of the same sex as the University employee who is eligible for benefits. In addition, both partners must be at least 18 years of age; unmarried to any other person and uncommitted to any other domestic partner; not related by blood to a degree of closeness that would prohibit legal marriage in California; living together in a long-term relationship of indefinite duration with an exclusive mutual commitment similar to that of a marriage; and financially responsible for each other's well-being and for each other's debts to third parties.[20]

We can think of this section of the memo as emblematic of the ways in which sexuality is incorporated into the structural logic of the university. In the language of Gayle Rubin's 1984 essay "Thinking Sex: Notes for a Radical Theory of the Politics of Sexuality," those queers who can conform to the requirements of the memo "are rewarded with certified mental health, respectability, legality, social and physical mobility, institutional support, and material benefits."[21] That incorporation, that recognition, indexes the subjugation of a whole diversity of sexual practices and subjectivities—transsexuality, nonmonogamy, cross-generational intimacies, endogamous and nondomiciled relationships, to name but a few—to the privileges of normative and socially sanctioned domestic practices. As such, the memo works to marginalize the very queer subcultures that worked to alienate gender and sexual normativity in the first place.

The administrative memo also becomes a site for the emergence and recognition of homosexuality. Indeed, the second prerequisite requires would-be domestic partners to "sign and file with the University an affidavit declaring that the above-mentioned conditions have been met and that the partners have shared a common residence for at least twelve consecutive months. The third prerequisite would be to supply documentary proof of mutual financial support." With this documentary proof of mutual financial support, the legitimacy of domestic partnerships is determined according to their participation in market processes. The domestic partnership memo thus becomes a crucial element within the entrepreneurial and administrative ethos that characterizes contemporary Western universities. If, as legal scholar and anthropologist Annalise Riles argues, the history of documents in the modern West references "both a utopian modernist vision of world peace through transparency and information exchange,"[22] then the memo suggests that making queerness institutionally and administratively transparent and informative is an emergent criterion for social stability. Discussing the ways in which mainstreaming queer sexuality triggers social exclusions, Heather Love observes: "One may enter the mainstream on the condition that one breaks ties with all those who cannot make it—the nonwhite and the nonmonogamous, the poor and the gender deviant, the fat, the disabled, the unemployed, the infected and a host of unmentionable others."[23]

This desire for stability and legibility has its genealogy—to a large degree—in the promises of Western bureaucracy. For instance, Max Weber said this about the technical advantages of bureaucracy: "Bureaucratization offers above all the optimum possibility for carrying through the principle of specializing administrative functions according to purely objective considerations . . . The 'objective' discharge of business primarily means a discharge of business according to calculable rules and 'without regard for persons.'"[24] Bureaucracy promises predictability and thereby circumvents the vagaries of personal feelings and prejudice: "The peculiarity of modern culture, and specifically of its technical and economic basis, demands this very 'calculability' of results."[25] As a bureaucratic document, the memo uses sexuality to promote the calculability of not only administration but sexuality as well. In the context of minority difference, bureaucracy promises to transcend personal feelings and prejudice and to treat the minority in an objective manner. In the case of queer subjects, bureaucracy promises to transcend homophobic judgments and model objective and impersonal engagement. In doing so, bureaucracy sets itself up as the beacon of a posthomophobic—and, in other cases, a postracist and postsexist—social world.

For Weber, "Bureaucratic organization has usually come into power on the basis of a leveling of economic and social differences," but capital also presents itself as the basis for such a leveling. For example, Joe Scanlan's installation "The Massachusetts Wedding Bed" gets at the desire for permanence and legibility but connects it to the commercial sphere and its promises of stability, equality, and protection. In a fictional advertisement for the bed, Scanlan describes it as a "queen-sized bed that is made to order by hand in Wellfleet, Massachusetts, just twelve miles from where the pilgrims first landed in North America, and the first state in the United States to allow same-sex marriage." With this bit of information, Scanlon invokes gay rights discourses that posit same-sex marriage as the natural unfolding of the American promise. The bed is not fancy or ostentatious. It is made of a "matched-grain" headboard and footboard. It comes unfinished and can remain that way. Otherwise, the advertisement "recommends a 'clear varnish,' a low-lustre oil finish, or 'milk-paint,' a rich, flat and extremely durable paint used by the American shaker communities." The description of the materials subtly advertises the mainstream and agreeable nature of homosexuality. Although the bed is clearly made for a couple — "capable of providing a lifetime of rest and intimacy for a man and a woman or a woman and a woman or a man and man," capable of leveling social differences and sexual hierarchies — one image of the bed has two white men in matching blue pajamas in the bed and to their right is a black woman in white pajamas, sitting up on the end. We can read the presence of the black woman in bed with the two white gay men as a metaphor for a gay rights discourse that understands same-sex marriage as the inheritor of civil rights and feminist struggles.

In a section titled "Commerce Breeds Acceptance," the advertisement demonstrates how capital has absorbed and affirmed this interpretation of gay marriage and is working to incorporate minority difference into its maneuvers. The section invokes social movements as bringing difference and "issues to the attention of a wider public," provoking "frustration" and "anger." The advertisement argues that it is commerce that can transcend this ensuing chaos: "[After] the high ideals and lowdown nastiness have run their course, it is commerce that ultimately accomplishes what piety and aggression could not." The installation designates commercial culture with the "objective discharge of business," stating that although a majority of Americans are opposed to gay marriage, "[An] even greater majority — and one with a much deeper conviction — is for the profitable sale of shoes, gowns, tuxedos, rings, flowers, cakes, flatware, decorations, champagne, pajamas, hotel rooms, airline tickets, almonds, lace, and candles."

With this, the installation promotes a critical understanding of how the demand for gay rights has widened capital's capacity for identification and exchange and provides a critique of the conditions of homosexuality's affirmation.[26]

The Casualties of Affirmation

For some, domestic partnership and gay marriage are the culmination of the gay liberation movement's affirmation of sexuality. For them, they are proof of the unadulterated progress of gay rights. This narrative of progress figures queerness as the subject of rights and institutional representation within the American nation-state, as the latest installment in power's archive. In Mohan Sikka's short story "Ripe," we can observe what happens to sexual life within this new administrative ethos, the negotiations that sexuality undertakes in a chain of affirmations that began perhaps with a social science and ended with a memo. The story is about an affair that the main character has outside the bounds of a monogamous same-sex relationship. It begins with this characterization: "One day when I woke up the words 'dry marriage' and 'wet marriage' plum popped into my head. You know what mine is: some of each. I had a chance for something riper, but I lost it. That's the story. There's the pity."[27] We might imagine the setting of the short story as one installed by discourses and texts like the domestic partnership memo. The short story begins with the looming specter of sexual loss and raises it to the level of narrative theme. If the condition for sexuality's absorption into power's archive is the managing and disciplining of sexuality so that it conforms to institutional legibility, then the story allegorizes how various forms of sexual agency become the detritus of complex systems of intelligibility.

We might say that the passage from "Ripe" stands as the younger sibling of Gayle Rubin's now prophetic argument from 1984. Situating her remarks in the "sex conflicts of the last decade" and therefore evoking the gay liberation movement of the 1970s, Rubin said: "Unmarried couples living together, masturbation, and some forms of homosexuality are moving in the direction of respectability."[28] Rubin went on to say that homosexuality—while generally stigmatized—was beginning to achieve certain levels of recognition if coupled and monogamous. Against this respectable version, she argued: "Promiscuous homosexuality, sadomasochism, fetishism, transsexuality, and cross-generational encounters are still viewed as un-modulated horrors incapable of involving affection, love, free choice, kind-ness, or transcendence."[29] Here, Rubin identifies the emergence of power's new calculus for determining what forms and practices of sexuality will be admitted into the realms of institutional legitimacy and what formations will be excluded. The following passage from Sikka's "Ripe" narrates the main character's negotiation with this new calculus:

> I think I'm more open-minded than most. I've played with hundreds, young and old. Parks and gymnasiums and bathrooms and steamrooms are second homes to me. People think you have to be a regular closet case to crave such things. Wife and kids tucked away in bed; a blowjob in the Rambles. But *I* have a l-o-v-e-r, and *I* still want it. How to ex-plain?—It's different than the sheets. Trust me: get it while you can; the options fade quickly.[30]

The short story thus addresses the contemporary ethos around sexuality as one that requires a negotiation between seemingly residual sexual for-mations and an emergent one organized around respectability.

By the short story's end, the main character's "extramarital" affair is over and the now spurned lover threatens him with a reprisal of some sort. The narrator responds: "I laugh, hardly frightened at his antics now, not paying him heed anymore. All I can see through the falling steam and the harsh fluorescent light is my life come back and claim me."[31] The story therefore figures the end of the affair as the termination of prior sexual uni-verses that are laid to waste in a time of queer legitimacy.

As an appeal for recognition and legitimacy, we might situate the stip-ulations of the memo and the representations of the short story within what Martin Manalansan refers to as "gay and lesbian transnational pol-itics."[32] In his article "In the Shadows of Stonewall: Examining Gay Trans-national Politics and the Diasporic Dilemma," he discusses the ways in which international gay and lesbian social movements make appeals for recognition through constructions of gay and lesbian identity as "'out,' 'politicized,' [and] 'modern,'" a construction that racializes non-Western and subaltern queer practices and identities as premodern and backward.[33] As "In the Shadows of Stonewall" suggests, queer appeals for recognition and legitimacy are always articulated globally as well as nationally. Thus, we might understand the memo not simply as a local and national declaration of same-sex recognition, or the short story as a discrete critique of recognition, but as parts of a global constellation in which queerness seeks to attain status as a modern and normative mode of difference. In doing so, queerness becomes the engine for a series of exclusions and alienations, particularly around class, gender, and race.

The Will to Institutionality

To conceptualize sexuality as an institutional and administrative operation means that sexuality partakes in encounters that we have yet to theorize. In its performative stipulations, for instance, the memo resembles not so much the genre of the confession as the terms of the psychoanalytic encounter between analyst and analysand. Like these two encounters theorized in the first volume of *The History of Sexuality*, the Atkinson memo is a procedure for telling the "truth" of sexuality. But, unlike the confession and the psychoanalytic encounter, this declaration is not necessarily for the production of a *scientia sexualis* "geared to a form of knowledge/power" but for an *administrative sexualis* geared to a form of institutionality/power. This will to institutionality names the processes by which sexuality becomes claimed by administrative realms and protocols.

Such a claim is just one instantiation of contemporary globalization's ingestion of forms of difference. Again, as Stuart Hall argues, contemporary globalization cannot simply be grasped as a purely economic phenomenon but indeed as one that attempts to rule through culture and difference. As Hall and Chandra Talpade Mohanty suggest, we can also think of the historical moment in which difference became a commodity of capital and of the university as the moment in which a new type of academic subject came into being, one that spoke in terms of the institutionalization of difference. The reasons for that institutionalization varied, but most often it hinged on the promise of permanence. Modes of inquiry and histories of difference that were once threatened with extinction, existing only as ephemera, would now enjoy the consistency and reliability that the institutional form could presumably offer. The demand for the institutionalization of difference requires subjects that treat the administration as a matter of the libido. To paraphrase Nietzsche, we might say that the desire for institutionality has been "transformed among us into a passion which fears no sacrifice, which fears nothing but its own extinction."[34] This subject's agency depends on the very administrative forms of power that manage and discipline forms of difference.

This is the historical, political, and ideological context in which queerness enters the landscape of modern academic institutions. The administrative university adapts to modes of difference by attempting to normalize them. Inasmuch as the grammar for queerness's incorporation into the administrative university is derived from the university's incorporation of race and gender, understanding the procedures by which queerness is brought into the administrative ethos means that we have to both comprehend the administrative management of race and gender and theorize the relation of those forms of difference to queerness as an administrative object. This is the political economy that queerness—as a mode of embodiment and as a mode of critique—must negotiate. We are now in a moment in which we must analyze sexuality and other modes of difference as effects of a will to institutionality.

We might in fact read Foucault's early theorizations about discourses as theorizations about institutions and their exploitation of discourses. For instance, in "The Discourse on Language," a lecture that Foucault gave at the Collège de France on December 2, 1970, he begins by addressing the relationship between knowledge and institutions: "Inclination speaks out: 'I don't want to have to enter this risky world of discourse; I want nothing to do with it insofar as it is decisive and final; I would like to feel it all around me, calm and transparent, profound, infinitely open, with others responding to my expectations, and truth emerging, one by one.'"[35] Institutions, Foucault says, will arise to manage that risk, and to our anxious inclination

> Institutions reply: "But you have nothing to fear from launching out; we're here to show you discourse is within the established order of things, that we've waited a long time for its arrival, that a place has been set aside for it—a place which both honours and disarms it; and if it should happen to have a certain power, then it is we, and we alone, who give it that power." (216)

Foucault begins with the subject that is anxious about the unruly and disobedient nature of discourse, its penchant to steal away from human intentions. The subject desperately wishes for the innocence of discourse and for the promise of truth. The voice of comfort comes from the institution, telling the subject that discourse will bend to human agency and institutional protocols. Under the will to knowledge, the institution arises as that which will help the subject produce and tame discourse. And so we have the narrative of the rational and authoritative subject and the artifact known as truth—the dramatis personae and the central props that comprise the will to knowledge. As Foucault states, "This will to truth...relies on institutional support: it is both reinforced and accompanied by whole strata of practices such as pedagogy—naturally—the book system, publishing, libraries, such as the learned societies in the past, and laboratories today" (219).

Foucault contends that the will to truth and the will to knowledge depend on a distinction between reason and folly or evidence and falsehood. This distinction has several functions. First, it becomes the organizing principle of discourse—think here of the argument that sexuality constitutes the "ultimate" truth of the individual. The distinction also operates as a system of exclusion, admitting only those forms of knowledge that operate under a will to truth and excluding those subject and social formations marked as irrational. In addition, the division between truth and untruth works to conceal the very thing that it constitutes: "The will to truth, having imposed itself upon us for so long, is such that the truth it seeks to reveal cannot fail to mask it . . . thus only one truth appears before our eyes; wealth, fertility, and sweet strength in all its insidious universality. In contrast we are unaware of the prodigious machinery of the will to truth, with its vocation of exclusion" (220).

The will to truth was constituted in the eighteenth century, a historical moment organized around the discourses of universal humanism, homogeneity, and canonicity. But a new world has come into being in the era of feminist theory, ethnic studies, postcolonial studies, queer theory, and other forms of scholarship and activism engaged with the politics of identity and difference. One could argue that the will to institutionality among groups and communities associated with difference emerged precisely after the critical upheavals of race, gender, and sexuality of the post–civil rights era. We might say that the will to institutionality is founded on divisions between legitimacy and illegitimacy. For example, capital and the academy have to work through and with difference in the global moment if they can claim any integrity at all. The will to institutionality also seems to presume another distinction—between the promise of formality and the presumed ephemeral nature of informality. Formalizing certain forms of difference gives those forms permanence and institutional protection and will lift difference from the netherworld of marginalization and informal curiosity. The will to knowledge, according to Foucault, obliges discourse to truth. That obligation represents an engagement with institutionality as well. In "The Discourse on Language," Foucault states: "Education may be, as of right, the instrument whereby every individual, in a society like our own, can gain access to any kind of discourse. But we well know that in its distribution, in what it permits and in what it prevents, it follows the well-trodden battle-lines of social conflict. Every educational system is a political means of maintaining or of modifying the appropriation of a discourse, with the knowledge and the powers it carries with it" (227).

This will to institutionality suggests that minority difference can achieve effectiveness and agency by investing in dominant institutions, making institutionalization a historical necessity rather than one item on a menu of interventions, suggesting that minority difference can only be achieved through the forms that dominant institutions offer. Now is the time to pause and interrogate the subtle and silent transformations that knowledge and the subjects of knowledge have undergone. Now is the time to scrutinize this will to institutionality if we are to create alternative forms of agency and subjectivity not beholden to the logics of state, capital, and academy. We are now in a moment in which institutionalization is the standard of the evolved and developed critical subject.

If genealogy is a form of history that can account for the constitution of knowledges, discourses, domains of objects, now is the time to make genealogy into a form of history that can account for the institutionalization of knowledge, modes of difference, and critical agency. In doing so, we have to ask, By what counter-calculus can we maneuver difference for the purposes of rupture? Answering this question requires that queer intellectual, artistic, and social practices constantly engage power's apprehension of sexuality and other modes of minority difference. Whether as intellectuals, artists, or simply people trying to live examined lives, engaging minority difference today means that we must negotiate with and struggle against the steady closure of critical universes brokered in a time of affirmation.

CONCLUSION
CONLUCSION
COCLUNSION
COUNCOLSIN

An Alternative Currency of Difference

IN CEDRIC SMITH'S MIXED-MEDIA PIECE *Black Currency,* a photograph of the scientist and black history icon George Washington Carver appears on the obverse of a colorfully painted thousand-dollar bill. This bill differs from its 1934 counterpart, which features President Grover Cleveland and in which the Treasury seal reads "The Federal Reserve Bank of St. Louis Missouri." On Smith's bill, however, the Treasury Seal reads "Liberty Bank of Louisiana," one of the largest black-owned financial institutions in the United States, founded by Alden J. McDonald Jr., who Smith lists as Treasurer of the United States.

Black Currency summons the defining elements of this book: a minority intellectual and symbol of the injustices of racism—George Washington Carver—is reconfigured as representative of the nation and its currency, becoming the sign of a culturalist union between knowledge, state, and capital. The series date ("1972") and the name of this African American bank ("Liberty") invoke the strategic situation that this book has tried to detail as the period after the student movements—a network of power was constituted through the economic, political, and academic institutionalization of minority difference. The venerable face of the Black Leonardo graces the bill and is surrounded by an almost fauvist use of color in the piece—as if the blue, orange, red, yellow, purple, and green emphasize the changing nature of race in the moments after the 1960s and the hegemonic attempts to depict emergent and assertive meanings of racial difference as "values" consistent with institutions of power, a consistency that culminates in what Jodi Melamed calls "neoliberal multiculturalism." As a piece with certain archival qualities, *Black Currency* suggests that state and capital's articulation of and through minority difference was prepared long ago. Its archival

Cedric Smith, *Black Currency*, mixed medium on canvas. This painting reconfigures and reorders the $1,000 bill by featuring the scientist George Washington Carver on the obverse, making him the symbol of the nation-state and the economy. Courtesy of Cedric Smith.

and fauvist elements combined, *Black Currency* does not so much connote the primacy of blackness in this moment as convey the midwifery nature that the affirmation of blackness had on all forms of minority difference.

Liberty Bank's real-life narrative of itself corroborates the piece's observations about minority difference as simultaneously vernacular and dominant. As the bank's Web site attests, the bank focuses on "the traditionally under-served," advertises itself as having "deep roots in the community," and defines its origins through its belief that "education is the future for our young people."[1] The bank's value as both an economic and a social institution lies in its investment in "the people" and in the presumably salutary effects of knowledge: caring for the people becomes the basis for the bank's accumulation of profit, making the people a form of currency.

The piece also "dramatizes" the regulations of this affirmative practice: the iridescent colors and the visage of minority genius occlude the regulations and violence that occasion minority difference's hegemonic deployment. Carver's status as representative of the nation, its economy, and the hegemonic incorporation of minority knowledge strains against his position as racial outcast, as supposed castration victim, and as suspected homosexual—the unruly elements that a hegemonic valorization has to regulate.

As a depiction of an academic icon assimilated into state representation, the piece recalls Frederick Jackson Turner's understanding of the American university as an imperial site ready to discover and name new frontiers that the university might incorporate. Refuting the notion that the university is "the passive instrument of the State," Turner writes that the university exists to "create tendencies and to direct them."[2] Believing that the land and material resources that the United States could acquire in its manifested destiny would eventually come to an end, Turner turned toward the university as the domain that could produce the conditions for "the multiplication of motives for ambition and the opening of new lines of achievement for the strongest."[3] Constructing the American academy as the new vessel of manifest destiny, Turner wrote, "In place of old frontiers of wilderness, there are new frontiers of unwon fields of science, fruitful for the needs of the race; there are frontiers of better social domains yet unexplored."[4] Here, Turner identified the academy as an agent of a broadly conceived imperial power: "The [university] must awaken new demands and it must satisfy those demands by trained leaders with new motives, with new incentives to ambition, with higher and broader conception of what constitutes the prize in life, of what constitutes success."[5] But even Turner could not have imagined that minority difference would become one of the fields that the academy and other dominant institutions would attempt to win over.

As an institution that has attempted to mobilize knowledge formations for conquest, the university provides an explanation of power's strength, that power does not simply produce repression but that it "produces effects at the level of desire—and also at the level of knowledge."[6] Far from being an entity that is the reflection of capital or the impotent foundation of abstract ideas, the academy is—as this book has attempted to illustrate— part of the mechanisms of power that have functioned "outside, below, and alongside" apparatuses of state and capital.[7] As an entity that invests itself in motives, incentives, ambitions, and behaviors, the academy underlines the diffuse nature of institutionalization as a mode of hegemonic power. Summing up the diffuse strategies that comprise the academy's powers— that is, its simultaneous management of knowledge and subject formations—Turner wrote, "The University has to deal with both the soil and sifted seed in the agriculture of the human spirit."[8]

The post–civil rights academy represented the moment when the academy and other institutions of power would widen their "agricultural" horizons, tilling and harvesting forms of minority difference, preparing them for new horizons of success and attainment, culling those forms for the benefit of hegemony rather than the material well-being of disfranchised communities. This articulation of minority difference renders it into a good that bears the image of a minoritized subject but is too expensive to find itself in the hands of most minoritized people.

As an artwork that dramatizes the irony of a representation that is popular and a gradation of currency that is exclusive, *Black Currency* raises a question central to this book: Are there other ways to disseminate and circulate minority culture and difference that do not place them within dominant systems of value? What happens when the texts that engage minority difference disturb the expectations and systems of intelligibility put in place by disciplines and institutions? What happens if those texts are used to imagine how minoritized subjects and knowledge might inhabit institutional spaces in ways dominant institutions never intended?

We are now in the moment where it is crucial that we develop a critically agnostic relationship to minority difference and culture. If the history of minority difference and culture in the post–World War II moment, and after the student movements, bespeaks minority difference and culture's maneuverability by dominant systems of power, then we can no longer assume their radical alterity. In a period of hegemonic affirmation, the question for us has to be how best to maneuver an especially flexible social artifact to disrupt dominant forms of institutionality. If textual production is always a mode of institutional production, then how we read, write, and design minority difference and culture has everything to do with the kind of minority communities that we imagine and institutionalize and might become the very question of our reinvigorated interdisciplinary life.

Isn't this the moment to wrest minority difference away from specialization, away from "a set of authorities and canonical ideas,"[9] away from that mode of expertise that compels us to turn modes of difference into credentials that will put us in the employ of power? Isn't this the hour to define critical intellectual practice as the refusal to let minority difference be the functionary of institutions? Doesn't that task entail our constant attempt to make minority difference speak truth to a mode of power that claims to speak in our names? Isn't this the time to boldly confront the fact that resistance is not minority difference's taken-for-granted identity but is instead the redistributive practice that we devise under minority difference's various designations?

The well-being of interdisciplinary departments, centers, and programs has been debated and worried over, even more so since the current economic crisis. Departments, centers, and programs across the country have been downsized, merged, and dismantled, often with little to no deference to faculty governance. Given that those departments, centers, and programs have typically been the sites of experimentation and access in the American academy, preserving the best that they have to offer is a question and an effort that can never be retired. And yet we can't let the question of interdisciplinarity and power rest there. To do so would be to engage a repressive hypothesis that imagines relations of force and regulation as processes external to interdisciplinary formations, never wrestling with the fact that networks of power that align minority difference with institutional dominance constitute the day-to-day practices and formations of interdisciplinary venues; if left unattended and never brought to crisis, these networks will persist even if the programmatic structures are gone.

In the fifth century BC, philosophers of military maneuvers would travel China's central states, offering their insights about the tactics and strategies needed to wage war effectively. The most famous of those roving philosophers, Sun Tzu, observed: "[One's] victory in battle cannot be repeated — they take their form . . . in response to inexhaustibly changing circumstances."[10] Perhaps with Sun Tzu in mind, Foucault defined the intellectual as a surveyor and strategist of sorts: "What's effectively needed is a ramified, penetrative perception of the present, one that makes it possible to locate lines of weakness, strong points, positions where the instances of power have secured and implanted themselves."[11] In this day of institutionalized affirmations, the critical intellectual is that subject who understands that we determine lines of weakness and positions of strength in circumstances that are endlessly changing, the intellectual who is part of a group of strategists who will gather to make interdisciplinarity into a science of crisis and subversion.[12]

In terms of the stories handed down to us, we seem to have inherited a notion of crisis and subversion that takes the grandest structural efforts — the takeover of buildings and the inauguration of schools — as the only adventures worthy of our imagination and planning. But if power is "coextensive with the social body" and "interwoven with other kinds of relations," descriptive of strategic situations that are "dispersed, heteromorphous, and localised,"[13] then wouldn't it make sense to—at least partly—make those small and seemingly insignificant acts the basis of our alternatives?[14] After turning his attention to that small and insignificant thing called the body, Foucault argued that one "advantage of conducting a critique of relations existing at a minute level would be to render impossible the reproduction of the form of the State apparatus within revolutionary movements."[15] To undermine the reproduction of hegemony in those little acts of production— reading, writing, teaching, and advising—we might discover the revolutionary potential in such whatnots as an old woman's lemon tea and olive oil or a scholar's syllabus and research question, knowing full well that "power can retreat here, re-organise its forces, invest itself elsewhere . . . and so the battle continues."[16] A syllabus, a job ad, a recruitment strategy, a memo, a book, an artwork, a report, an organizational plan, a protest—such are the little things that we can deploy in order to imagine critical forms of community, forms in which minoritized subjects become the agents rather than the silent objects of knowledge formations and institutional practices. These little things represent the kind of work that can, should, and is taking place in institutions throughout our society, and they illustrate how imagination and institution come together to yield new types of peoples and communities. This is a different type of will to institutionality, one that searches for interpretative and institutional practices that will more likely protect and incite a dynamism around the meanings of minority culture and difference, a will to institutionality that honors that feeling that "this world is not enough."[17] In this moment in which minority difference can be used as an instrument of an archival mode of power that inscribes itself here and yonder, to "revolutionize" minority culture means to be less huddled around the herculean feat and more considered about the activation of minor details.

Notes

Introduction

1. Adrian Piper, *Self-Portrait 2000,* http://www.adrianpiper.com/art/g_self_2000.shtml, November 15, 2011; emphasis added.

2. Ibid.

3. Terry H. Anderson, *The Movement and the Sixties: Protest in America from Greensboro to Wounded Knee* (Oxford: Oxford University Press, 1995), 299.

4. Ibid., 299.

5. Ibid., 306.

6. See ibid. and Paul Chaat Smith and Robert Allen Warrior, *Like a Hurricane: The Indian Movement from Alcatraz to Wounded Knee* (New York: New Press, 1996).

7. Michel Foucault, *The History of Sexuality, Volume 1: An Introduction,* trans. Robert Hurley (New York: Vintage Books, 1990), 94.

8. Ibid., 94–95.

9. Ibid., 95.

10. Raymond Williams, *Marxism and Literature* (Oxford and New York: Oxford University Press, 1977), 113.

11. Foucault, *The History of Sexuality,* 95; emphasis added.

12. See Gayatri Chakravorty Spivak's chapter "More on Power/Knowledge" in *Outside in the Teaching Machine* (New York and London: Routledge, 1993), 26.

13. Michel Foucault, *Power/Knowledge: Selected Interviews and Other Writings 1972–1977,* ed. Colin Gordon (New York: Pantheon Books, 1980), 99, 186.

14. Foucault, *The History of Sexuality,* 142–43.

15. Ibid., 93.

16. Ibid.; emphasis added.

17. Ibid.

18. Jacques Derrida, *Eyes of the University: Right to Philosophy 2,* trans. Jan Plug (Stanford, Calif.: Stanford University Press, 2004), 85.

19. Ibid., 85–86; emphasis added.

20. Immanuel Kant, *The Conflict of the Faculties,* trans. Mary J. Gregor (Lincoln and London: University of Nebraska Press, 1979), 25.

21. Ibid., 27–29.

22. See Mary J. Gregor's "Translator's Introduction," in ibid.

23. Kant, *The Conflict of the Faculties,* 29.

24. Ibid., 45.

25. Jacques Derrida, *Archive Fever: A Freudian Impression,* trans. Eric Prenowitz (Chicago and London: University of Chicago Press, 1995), 7.

26. Derrida, *Eyes of the University,* 101.

27. Ibid.

28. Jacques Rancière, "Art of the Possible," interview by Fulvia Carnevale and John Kelsey, *Artforum* (March 2007): 264.

29. Ibid., 85.

30. Ibid., 83.

31. Williams, *Marxism and Literature,* 114.

1. The Birth of the Interdisciplines

1. Jacques Derrida, *Archive Fever: A Freudian Impression,* trans. Eric Prenowitz (Chicago and London: University of Chicago Press, 1998), 2.

2. Ibid.

3. Ibid., 3.

4. W. C. Harris, *E Pluribus Unum: Nineteenth-Century American Literature and the Constitutional Paradox* (Iowa City: University of Iowa Press, 2005), 12.

5. Ibid., 7.

6. Eqbal Ahmad, "Political Culture and Foreign Policy," in *The Selected Writings of Eqbal Ahmad,* ed. Carolee Bengelsdorf, Margaret Cerullo, and Yogesh Chandarani (New York: Columbia University Press, 2006), 206.

7. Ibid.

8. Kwame Nkrumah, *Neo-colonialism: The Last Stage of Imperialism* (New York: International Publishers, 1984), 239. Subsequent references are given in the text.

9. Ahmad, "Political Culture and Foreign Policy," 205.

10. See Greg Grandin, *Empire's Workshop: Latin America, the United States, and the Rise of New Imperialism* (New York: Owl Books, 2007).

11. Nkrumah, *Neo-colonialism,* 56.

12. Mary L. Dudziak, *Cold War Civil Rights: Race and the Image of American Democracy* (Princeton, N.J.: Princeton University Press, 2000).

13. Michael Hardt and Antonio Negri, *Empire* (Cambridge: Harvard University Press, 2000), 182.

14. Ibid.

15. Ibid., 172.

16. George Lipsitz, "Culture of War," *Critical Survey* 18:3 (2006): 83.

17. Michael Omi and Howard Winant, *Racial Formations in the United States, from the 1960s to the 1990s* (New York: Routledge, 1994), 96.

18. Ibid., 96–97.

19. Stuart Hall, "The Local and the Global," in *Dangerous Liaisons: Gender, Nation, and Postcolonial Perspectives,* ed. Anne McClintock, Aamir Mufti, and Ella Shohat (Minneapolis: University of Minnesota Press, 1997), 184.

20. Ibid., 181.

21. Omi and Winant, *Racial Formations in the United States,* 86; emphasis added.

22. Omi and Winant also point to strategies of "insulation" as one of the maneuvers that the state adopts in response to political pressures. But for purposes of this discussion of archontic power, I choose to focus more on absorption.

23. Omi and Winant, *Racial Formations in the United States,* 86.

24. *The Reorder of Things* is a rebuttal to Bill Reading's claim in *The University in Ruins* (Cambridge and London: Harvard University Press, 1996) that the American university released all claims on cultural regulation and articulation.

25. Omi and Winant, *Racial Formations in the United States,* 86.

26. Derrida, *Archive Fever,* 13.

27. See, for instance, Grace Hong, *The Ruptures of American Capital: Women of Color Feminism and the Culture of Immigrant Labor* (Minneapolis and London: University of Minnesota Press, 2006).

28. Michel Foucault, *The Order of Things: An Archaeology of the Human Sciences* (New York: Vintage Books, 1970), 308.

29. Ibid., 345.

30. Ibid.

31. Ibid, 351.

32. Michel Foucault, *Discipline and Punish: The Birth of the Prison,* trans. Alan Sheridan (New York: Vintage Books, 1979), 170.

33. Ibid., 170.

34. Mike Murase, "Ethnic Studies and Higher Education for Asian Americans," in *Counterpoint: Perspective on Asian America,* ed. Emma Gee et al. (Los Angeles: Regents of the University of California, 1976), 205.

35. Hall, "The Local and the Global," 184.

36. Foucault, *The History of Sexuality,* 140.

37. Ibid.

38. Ibid.

39. David Yamane, *Student Movements for Multiculturalism: Challenging the*

Curricular Color Line in Higher Education (Baltimore: Johns Hopkins University Press, 2002), 12.

40. Ibid.

41. Barbara Christian, "But What Do We Think We're Doing Anyway: The State of Black Feminist Criticism(s) or My Version of a Little Bit of History," in *Within the Circle: An Anthology of African American Literary Criticism from the Harlem Renaissance to the Present,* ed. Angelyn Mitchell (Durham, N.C., and London: Duke University Press, 1994), 509.

42. Ibid., 509–10.

43. Lisa Lowe, *Immigrant Acts: On Asian American Cultural Politics* (Durham, N.C., and London: Duke University Press, 1996), 41.

44. Stuart Hall, "Cultural Studies and Its Theoretical Legacies," in *Stuart Hall: Critical Dialogues in Cultural Studies,* ed. David Morley and Kuan-Hsing Chen (London and New York: Routledge, 1996), 273.

45. As Lisa Lowe argues, "While institutionalizing interdisciplinary study risks integrating into a system that threatens to appropriate what is most critical and oppositional about that study, the logic through which the university incorporates areas of interdisciplinarity provides for the possibility that these sites will remain oppositional forums, productively antagonistic to notions of autonomous culture and disciplinary regulation and to the interpellation of students as univocal subjects" (*Immigrant Acts,* 41).

46. Wahneema Lubiano, "Black Nationalism and Black Common Sense: Policing Ourselves," in *The House That Race Built,* ed. Wahneema Lubiano (New York: Vintage Books, 1998), 236.

47. Lisa Lowe and David Lloyd, "Introduction," in *The Politics of Culture in the Shadow of Capital,* ed. Lisa Lowe and David Lloyd (Durham, N.C., and London: Duke University Press, 1997), 9.

48. Ibid.

49. Norma Alarcón, "The Theoretical Subjects of *This Bridge Called My Back* and Anglo-American Feminism," in *Making Face, Making Soul/Haciendo Caras: Creative and Critical Perspectives by Women of Color,* ed. Gloria Anzaldúa (San Francisco: Aunt Lute Books, 1990), 357.

50. Barthes, *S/Z: An Essay,* trans. Richard Miller (New York: Hill and Wang, 1974), 4.

51. Ibid.

2. The Proliferation of Minority Difference

1. Liam Gillick, "The Difference Engine," *Artforum International,* May 2008, 322.

2. Anne Sa'adah, "Adieu: May '68 as End and Beginning," in *Protest in Paris 1968: Photographs by Serge Hambourg,* ed. Thomas Crow and Anne Sa'adah (Hanover, N.H.: Hood Museum of Art, 2006), 26.

3. Ibid.

4. See Paul Chaat Smith and Robert Allen Warrior, *Like a Hurricane: The Indian Movement from Alcatraz to Wounded Knee* (New York: New Press, 1996).

5. See George Mariscal, *Brown-Eyed Children of the Sun: Lessons from the Chicano Movement, 1965–1975* (Albuquerque: University of New Mexico Press, 2005).

6. Ibid., 223.

7. Angela Davis, *Angela Davis: An Autobiography* (New York: International Publishers, 2008), 196.

8. Ibid.

9. Paul Alexander Juutilainen, *Herbert's Hippopotamus* (New York: Cinema Guild, 1996).

10. Ibid.

11. Kristin Ross, *May '68 and Its Afterlives* (Chicago: University of Chicago Press, 2002), 25.

12. Antonio Negri, "A Revolutionary Process Never Ends: Sylvère Lotringer Talks with Antonio Negri," *Artforum International,* May 2008, 309.

13. Michel Foucault, *The Order of Things: An Archaeology of the Human Sciences* (New York: Vintage Books, 1970), xxiv.

14. Michel Foucault, *The Archaeology of Knowledge,* trans. A. M. Sheridan Smith (New York: Pantheon Books, 1972), 12.

15. Ibid.

16. Ibid.

17. Stuart Hall, "Europe's Other Self," *Marxism Today,* August 1991, 18.

18. Foucault, *The Order of Things,* 377.

19. Ibid., 378.

20. Ibid.; emphasis added.

21. Robert J. C. Young, *Postcolonialism: An Historical Introduction* (Oxford: Blackwell Publishers, 2001), 397.

22. Homi K. Bhabha, quoted in ibid.

23. Negri, "A Revolutionary Process Never Ends," 309.

24. Ross, *May '68 and Its Afterlives,* 8.

25. Ibid.

26. Ibid., 10.

27. Davis, *Angela Davis,* 152.

28. Wilson Smith and Thomas Bender, "Introduction," in *American Higher Education Transformed 1940–2005: Documenting the National Discourse,* ed. Wilson Smith and Thomas Bender (Baltimore: Johns Hopkins University Press, 2008), 2.

29. Ramón Gutiérrez, "Internal Colonialism: An American Theory of Race," *Du Bois Review: Social Science Research on Race* 1:2 (2004): 282.

30. Ibid.

31. Mariscal, *Brown-Eyes Children of the Sun*, 224.

32. Davis, *Angela Davis,* 196.

33. Lumumba-Zapata College in Robert Elliot Papers, Box 11, Folder 12, 3.

34. Ibid., 2.

35. Ibid., 7.

36. Mariscal, *Brown-Eyes Children of the Sun,* 229.

37. Ibid.

38. Foucault, *The Order of Things,* xvi.

39. Lumumba-Zapata College in Robert Elliot Papers, Box 11, Folder 12, 2.

40. Smith and Bender, "Introduction," 6.

41. Robert E. Weems Jr. and Lewis A. Randolph, "The Ideological Origins of Richard M. Nixon's 'Black Capitalism' Initiative," *Review of Black Political Economy* (summer 2001): 51. Subsequent references are given in the text.

42. Dean Kotlowski, "Black Power—Nixon Style: The Nixon Administration and Minority Business Enterprise," *Business History Review* 72 (autumn 1998): 412.

43. Ibid., 415.

44. Ibid., 421.

45. Ibid., 443.

46. Dean Kotlowski, "Alcatraz, Wounded Knee, and Beyond: The Nixon and Ford Administrations Respond to Native American Protest," *Pacific Historical Review* (2003): 202.

47. Ibid., 206.

48. Grace Hong, *The Ruptures of American Capital: Women of Color Feminism and the Culture of Immigrant Labor* (Minneapolis and London: University of Minnesota Press, 2006), 79.

49. Thomas Frank, *The Conquest of Cool: Business Culture, Counterculture, and the Rise of Hip Consumerism* (Chicago: University of Chicago Press, 1997), 9.

50. Ibid.

51. Ibid.

52. Ibid., 23.

53. Alfred P. Sloan, *My Years with General Motors* (New York: Doubleday, 1990), 389.

54. Robert Townsend, *Up the Organization: How to Stop the Corporation from Stifling People and Strangling Profits* (New York: Alfred A. Knopf, 1970), 10.

55. Ibid.

56. Ibid, 10–11.

57. Ibid., 142.

58. Ibid.

59. Frank, *The Conquest of the Cool,* 6.

60. Ibid., 35.

61. Stewart Alter, *Truth Well Told: McCann-Erickson and the Pioneering of Global Advertising* (McCann-Erickson Worldwide, 1995), 56–65, 88–93.

62. Stuart Hall, "The Local and the Global," in *Dangerous Liaisons: Gender, Nation, and Postcolonial Perspectives,* ed. Anne McClintock, Aamir Mufti, and Ella Shohat (Minneapolis: University of Minnesota Press, 1997), 181.

63. Alter, *Truth Well Told,* 187, 186.

64. Ibid., 188.

65. Hall, "The Local and the Global," 178.

66. Alter, *Truth Well Told,* 190.

67. http://memory.loc.gov/ammem/ccmphtml/colaadv.html; emphasis added.

68. Ibid.

69. http://www.thecoca-colacompany.com/heritage/cokelore_hilltop.html.

70. Ibid.; emphasis added.

71. http://memory.loc.gov/ammem/ccmphtml/colaadv.html.

72. http://www.thecoca-colacompany.com/heritage/cokelore_hilltop.html.

73. Hall, "The Local and the Global," 179.

74. Bernice Johnson Reagon, "The Song Culture of the Civil Rights Movement," in *Voices of the Civil Rights Movement: Black American Freedom Songs, 1960–1966* (Washington, D.C.: Smithsonian Folkways Recordings, 1997), 2.

75. Kobena Mercer, *Pop Art and Vernacular Cultures* (Cambridge: MIT Press, 2007), 11.

76. Suzanne E. Smith, *Dancing in the Street: Motown and the Cultural Politics of Detroit* (Cambridge and London: Harvard University Press, 2002), 7.

77. Kristen Marthe Lentz, "Quality versus Relevance: Feminism, Race, and the Politics of the Sign in 1970s Television," *Camera Obscura* 43, 15:1 (2000): 50.

78. Ibid., 60.

79. Hank Willis Thomas, "Hank Willis Thomas," in *After 1968: Contemporary Artists and the Civil Rights Legacy: Deborah Grant, Leslie Hewitt, Otabenga Jones and Associates, Adam Pendleton, Jefferson Pinder, Nadine Robinson, Hank Willis Thomas,* High Museum of Art (2008).

80. Roland Barthes, *Mythologies,* trans. Annette Lavers (New York: Hill and Wang, 1972), 132.

81. http://www.warholstars.org/articles/But%20Today%20We%20Collect%20Ads.html.

82. Ibid.

83. Mercer, *Pop Art and Vernacular Cultures,* 7.

84. Ibid., 15.

85. Hal Foster, "An Archival Impulse," *October* 110 (fall 2004): 5.

86. Tim Griffin, "Lessons of '68," *Artforum International* (May 2008): 71.

87. http://hankwillisthomas.com/#/2008/Unbranded%20/1/thumbs; accessed November 17, 2011.

88. Karl Marx, *Capital*, vol. 1, *A Critique of Political Economy*, trans. Ben Fawkes (London: Penguin Classics, 1990), 163–64.

89. Ibid., 164–77.

90. Ibid., 168.

91. See Raymond Williams, *Marxism and Literature* (Oxford and New York: Oxford University Press, 1977).

92. Mariscal, *Brown-Eyed Children of the Sun*, 232.

93. Ibid.

94. Ibid., 245.

95. Davis, *Angela Davis*, 197–98.

96. Clayborne Carson, "Foreword," in *The Black Panthers Speak*, ed. Philip S. Foner (New York: Da Capo Press, 1995), xiv.

97. See Smith and Warrior, *Like a Hurricane*.

98. See Ruth Wilson Gilmore, "Globalization and U.S. Prison Growth: From Military Keynesianism to Post-Keynesian Militarism," *Race and Class* 40:2/3 (October 1998–March 1999): 171–88.

3. *The Radical Genealogy of Excellence*

1. "Faculty for Action: Statement on the Five Demands," Five Demands Conflict Collection, City College Archives, City College, New York.

2. Lilian Jiménez, "Puerto Ricans and Educational Civil Rights: A History of the 1969 City College Takeover (An Interview with Five Participants)," *Centro Journal* 31:2 (fall 2009): 170–71.

3. http://www.aaup.org/AAUP/pubsres/academe/2003/JA/Feat/crai.htm.

4. Bill Readings, *The University in Ruins* (Cambridge: Harvard University Press, 1996), 29.

5. June Jordan, "Black Studies: Bringing Back the Person," in *Moving towards Home: Political Essays* (London: Virago, 1989), 20.

6. Ibid., 21.

7. Readings, *The University in Ruins*, 21, 22. Subsequent references are given in the text.

8. Raymond Williams, *Marxism and Literature* (Oxford and New York: Oxford University Press, 1977), 95.

9. Ibid.

10. Ibid., 104; emphasis added.

11. Ibid., 97.

12. John W. Gardner, *Excellence: Can We Be Equal and Excellent Too?* (New York: Harper and Row, 1961), 119–20.

13. Michel Foucault, "Governmentality," in *The Foucault Effect: Studies in Governmentality,* ed. Graham Burchell, Colin Gordon, and Peter Miller (Chicago: University of Chicago Press, 1991), 91.

14. Gardner, *Excellence,* 119–20.

15. Laurie Ouellette, *Viewers like You: How Public TV Failed the People* (New York: Columbia University Press, 2002), 74.

16. Gardner, *Excellence,* 92.

17. Ibid.

18. Ibid., 92–93.

19. Clark Kerr, *The Uses of the University,* 5th ed. (Cambridge and London: Harvard University Press, 2001), 100. Subsequent references are given in the text.

20. Christopher Newfield, *Ivy and Industry: Business and the Making of the American University, 1880–1980* (Durham, N.C., and London: Duke University Press, 2003), 26.

21. See "Morrill Act of 1890" by Charlene Clark, http://jschell.myweb.uga .edu/history/legis/morrill.htm; accessed November 18, 2011.

22. Immanuel Kant, *The Conflict of the Faculties,* trans. Mary J. Grego (Lincoln and London: University of Nebraska Press, 1979), 47–49. Subsequent references are given in the text.

23. Floyd B. McKissick, "Black Business Development with Social Commitment to Black Communities," in *Black Nationalism in America,* ed. John H. Bracey Jr., August Meier, and Elliot Rudwick (Indianapolis and New York: Bobbs-Merrill, 1970), 493.

24. Ibid., 494.

25. Jordan, "Black Studies," 21.

26. Ibid., 22.

27. Stephanie Smallwood, *Saltwater Slavery: A Middle Passage from Africa to American Diaspora* (Cambridge: Harvard University Press, 2008), 35.

28. Ibid., 35.

29. Jordan, "Black Studies," 22.

30. Eqbal Ahmad, "Political Culture and Foreign Policy," in *The Selected Writings of Eqbal Ahmad,* ed. Carolee Bengelsdorf, Margaret Cerullo, and Yogesh Chandarani (New York: Columbia University Press, 2006), 38.

31. Ibid., 39.

32. Ibid., 39–40.

33. Lisa Lowe, *Immigrant Acts: On Asian American Cultural Politics* (Durham, N.C., and London: Duke University Press, 1996), 18.

34. Laura Briggs, *Reproducing Empire: Race, Sex, Science, and U.S. Imperialism in Puerto Rico* (Berkeley: University of California Press, 2002), 166. Subsequent references are given in the text.

35. Jordan, "Black Studies," 20–21.

36. Ibid., 27.

37. Ibid., 27–28.

38. Ibid., 28.

39. Herbert Marcuse, "A Note on Dialectic," in *The Essential Frankfurt School Reader,* ed. Andrew Arato and Eike Gebhardt (New York: Continuum, 2000), 447.

40. W. J. T. Mitchell, *Picture Theory: Essays on Verbal and Visual Representation* (Chicago: University of Chicago Press, 1995), 5.

41. Readings, *The University in Ruins,* 91.

42. Pedro Cabán, "Black and Latino Studies and Social Capital Theory," *SAGE Race Relations Abstracts* (2007): 6.

43. Quoted in "Faculty for Action: Statement of the Five Demands."

44. Ibid.

45. Zygmunt Bauman, *Intimations of Postmodernity* (London and New York: Routledge, 1992), 70.

46. Ibid., 71.

47. Curtis Stokes, Bill E. Lawson, and Geneva Smitherman, "The Language of Affirmative Action: History, Public Policy, and Liberalism," *Black Scholar* 33:3–4 (fall/winter 2003): 15.

48. Judith Butler, "An Affirmative View," in *Race and Representation: Affirmative Action* (Cambridge: Zone, 1998), 163.

49. Ibid.

50. Ibid., 164.

51. Ibid.

52. Newfield, *Ivy and Industry,* 27.

53. Jordan "Black Studies," 24.

54. As Jordan puts it in relation to African Americans, "Education has paralleled the history of our black lives" (ibid.).

55. Ibid., 26.

56. Marcuse, "A Note on Dialectic," 450.

57. As Marcuse argued, "[When] Marxian theory takes shape as a critique of Hegel's philosophy, it does so in the name of Reason. It is consonant with the innermost effort of Hegel's thought if his own philosophy is 'cancelled,' not by substituting for Reason some extrarational standards, but by driving Reason itself to recognize the extent to which it is still unreasonable, blind, the victim of unmastered forces. Reason, as the developing and applied knowledge of man—as 'free thought'—was instrumental in creating the world we live in" (ibid.).

58. Butler, "An Affirmative View," 165.

59. Marcuse, "A Note on Dialectic," 449.

4. The Reproduction of Things Academic

1. Manning Marable, "Introduction: Black Studies and the Racial Mountain," in *Dispatches from the Ebony Tower: Intellectuals Confront the African American Experience,* ed. Manning Marable (New York: Columbia University Press, 2000), 6.

2. Ibid.

3. Ibid.

4. See, for example, Donna Jean Murch, *Living for the City: Migration, Education, and the Rise of the Black Panther Party in Oakland, California* (Chapel Hill: University of North Carolina Press, 2010).

5. Jacques Derrida, *Eyes of the University: Right to Philosophy 2,* trans. Jan Plug (Stanford, Calif.: Stanford University Press, 2004), 86.

6. Jane Rhodes, *Framing the Black Panthers: The Spectacular Rise of a Black Power Icon* (New York: New Press, 2007), 93.

7. Ibid., 97.

8. Ibid., 105.

9. See Chris Brancaccio, "*Negro Digest* and *Black World:* Exploring the Archive 1961–1975," http://www.looks-like-freedom.com/negro_digest.php.

10. Toni Cade Bambara, "My Man Bovanne," in *Gorilla, My Love* (New York: Vintage Books, 1981), 4.

11. http://www.aiga.org/visualizing-a-revolution-emory-douglas-and-the-black-panther-new/.

12. http://bad.eserver.org/issues/2004/65/gaiter.html.

13. Ibid.

14. Jacques Rancière, *The Names of History: On the Poetics of Knowledge* (Minneapolis and London: University of Minnesota Press, 1994), 50.

15. Ibid., 11.

16. Richard A. Etlin, "Architecture and the Festival of Federation, Paris, 1790," *Architectural History* 18 (1975): 23.

17. Roland Barthes, *S/Z: An Essay,* trans. Richard Miller (New York: Hill and Wang, 1974), 9.

18. Bambara, "My Man Bovanne," 4–5.

19. Michel de Certeau, *The Writing of History,* trans. Tom Conley (New York: Columbia University Press, 1988), 2, 3.

20. Bambara, "My Man Bovanne," 8.

21. Rancière, *The Names of History,* 46.

22. Ibid.

23. Jacques Rancière, "The Emancipated Spectator," *Artforum* (March 2007): 275.

24. Ibid.

25. Bambara, "My Man Bovanne," 6.

26. Jacques Rancière, *The Ignorant Schoolmaster: Five Lessons in Intellectual Emancipation,* trans. Kristin Ross (Stanford, Calif.: Stanford University Press, 1991), 5.

27. Bambara, "My Man Bovanne," 8.

28. Marable, "Introduction," 10.

29. Paula Giddings, *When and Where I Enter: The Impact of Black Women on Race and Sex in America* (New York: William Morrow and Company, 1984), 315.

30. Ibid.

31. Ibid., 316.

32. Bambara, "My Man Bovanne," 6.

33. Rhodes, *Framing the Black Panthers,* 107.

34. Ibid.

35. Friedrich Nietzsche, *Daybreak: Thoughts on the Prejudices of Morality,* trans. R. J. Hollingdale (Cambridge: Cambridge University Press, 1982), 2.

36. Nathan Hare, "A Radical Perspective on Social Science Curricula," in *Black Studies in the University* (New Haven and London: Yale University Press), 111.

37. Rancière, *The Ignorant Schoolmaster,* 7.

38. Stuart Hall, "An Interview with Stuart Hall, December 2007" interview by Colin McCabe, *Critical Quarterly* 50, no. 1–2 (Spring–Summer 2008) 15. Subsequent references are given in the text.

39. Bambara, "My Man Bovanne," 5; emphasis added.

40. Derrida, *Eyes of the University,* 2.

41. Gayatri Chakravorty Spivak, "Criticism, Feminism, and the Institution," interview with Elizabeth Grosz, in *The Post-Colonial Critic: Interviews, Strategies, Dialogues: Gayatri Chakravorty Spivak,* ed. Sarah Harasym (New York: Routledge, 1990), 5.

42. Ibid., 43. John H. Bracey Jr., August Meier, and Elliott Rudwick, eds., *Black Nationalism in America* (Indianapolis and New York: Bobbs-Merrill, 1970), lii; emphasis added.

44. Ibid., lix.

45. Kay Lindsey, "Poem," in *The Black Woman: An Anthology,* ed. Toni Cade Bambara (Signet: New York, 1970), 17.

46. Derrida, *Eyes of the University* 102.

47. For instance, in an interview with Claudia Tate, Bambara stated, "I'm a nationalist; I'm a feminist, at least that. That's clear, I'm sure in the work" (*Black Women Writers at Work,* ed. Claudia Tate [New York: Continuum, 1983], 14).

48. James P. Garrett, "Black/Africana/Pan-African Studies: From Radical to

Reaction to Reform?—Its Role and Relevance in the Era of Global Capitalism in the New Millennium," *Journal of Pan African Studies* 1:1 (fall–winter 1998–99): 160–62.

49. *The Harvard Report on General Education,* in *American Higher Education Transformed 1940–2005: Documenting the National Discourse,* ed. Wilson Smith and Thomas Bender (Baltimore: Johns Hopkins University Press, 2008), 13.

50. Ibid., 15.

51. Ibid.

52. Immanuel Kant, *The Conflict of the Faculties,* trans. Mary J. Gregor (Lincoln and London: University of Nebraska Press, 1979), 11; emphasis added.

53. For a discussion of Kant's importance for the modern university, see Bill Readings, *The University in Ruins* (Cambridge: Harvard University Press, 1996), particularly the chapter titled "The University within the Limits of Reason."

54. Derrida, *Eyes of the University,* 83.

55. Thaddeus Russell, "The Color of Discipline: Civil Rights and Black Sexuality," *American Quarterly* (March 2008): 113.

56. Ibid., 116.

57. Ibid., 117.

58. Barbara Smith, *The Truth That Never Hurts: Writings on Race, Gender, and Freedom* (New Brunswick, N.J., and London: Rutgers University Press, 1998), 89.

59. Ibid.

60. Maulana Karenga, "The Black Community and the University: A Community Organizer's Perspective," in *Black Studies in the University: A Symposium,* ed. Amstead L. Robinson, Craig C. Foster, and Donald H. Ogilvie (New Haven and London: Yale University Press), 45.

61. Bambara, "My Man Bovanne," 9–10.

62. Michel Foucault, *Power/Knowledge: Selected Interviews and Other Writings 1972–1977,* ed. Colin Gordon (New York: Pantheon Books, 1980), 82.

63. Rancière, *The Ignorant Schoolmaster,* 17.

64. Ibid., 71.

65. Ibid., 107.

66. Bambara, "My Man Bovanne," 10; emphasis added.

67. Douglas C. Baynton, "Disability and the Justification of Inequality in American History," in *The New Disability History: American Perspectives,* ed. Paul K. Longmore and Lauri Umanksy (New York and London: New York University Press, 2001), 33.

68. Ibid.

69. Ibid.

70. Ibid., 34.

71. Robert McRuer, *Crip Theory: Cultural Signs of Queerness and Disability* (New York: New York University Press, 2006), 2.

72. Bambara, "My Man Bovanne," 6.

73. Baynton, "Disability and the Justification of Inequality in American History," 34.

74. Frederick Douglass, *Woman's Rights Conventions: Seneca Falls and Rochester, 1848* (New York: Arno Press, 1969), 4–6, quoted in ibid., 44.

75. Bambara, "My Man Bovanne,"5.

76. Michel Foucault, *The History of Sexuality, Volume 1: An Introduction,* trans. Robert Hurley (New York: Vintage Books, 1990), 100.

77. Karl Marx, *Capital,* vol. 1, *A Critique of Political Economy,* trans. Ben Fawkes (London: Penguin Classics, 1990), 270.

78. Ibid.

79. Gayatri Chakravorty Spivak, "Marginality in the Teaching Machine," in *Outside in the Teaching Machine* (New York and London: Routledge, 1993), 62.

80. Ibid.

81. See the chapter "Something Else to Be: *Sula, The Moynihan Report,* and the Negations of Black Lesbian Feminism" in Roderick A. Ferguson, *Aberrations in Black: Toward a Queer of Color Critique* (Minneapolis: University of Minnesota Press, 2004).

82. Douglas Massey, *Categorically Unequal: The American Stratification System* (New York: Russell Sage Foundation, 2007), 35.

83. Ibid., 38.

84. See Ruth Wilson Gilmore, *Golden Gulag: Prisons, Surplus, Crisis, and Opposition in Globalizing California* (Berkeley: University of California Press, 2007), and ibid.

5. Immigration and the Drama of Affirmation

1. The pioneering work that Lisa Lowe has conducted has made Asian American studies perhaps one of the few exceptions, if not the only exception, to this observation.

2. Kandice Chuh, *Imagine Otherwise: On Asian Americanist Critique* (Durham, N.C., and London: Duke University Press, 2003), 9.

3. Paul A. Kramer, "Is the World Our Campus? International Students and U.S. Global Power in the Long Twentieth Century," *Diplomatic History* 33:5 (November 2009): 792.

4. Ibid.

5. Ibid., 799.

6. Walter Lippmann, "Today and Tomorrow: Wanton Carelessness," *Washington Post and Times Herald,* May 27, 1954, 17, quoted in ibid.; emphasis added. Subsequent references are given in the text.

7. Susan Choi, *The Foreign Student: A Novel* (New York: HarperPerennial, 1999), 34.

8. Ibid., 53.

9. Ibid., 67.

10. Tejaswini Niranjana, *Siting Translation: History, Post-Structuralism, and the Colonial Context* (Berkeley and Los Angeles: University of California Press, 1992), 2.

11. Ibid., 3.

12. Ibid., 2.

13. Choi, *The Foreign Student,* 52.

14. Gayatri Chakravorty Spivak, *Outside in the Teaching Machine* (New York and London: Routledge, 1993), 181.

15. Ibid., 182.

16. Nirañjana, *Siting Translation,* 2.

17. Dong Choon Kim, "Forgotten War, Forgotten Massacres—the Korean War (1950–1953) as Licensed Mass Killings," *Journal of Genocide Research* 6:4 (December 2004): 532.

18. Ibid., 530.

19. Ibid., 529.

20. Kramer, "Is the World Our Campus?" 794.

21. Ibid.

22. Lisa Lowe, *Immigrant Acts: On Asian American Cultural Politics* (Durham, N.C., and London: Duke University Press, 1996), 15.

23. Ibid., 17.

24. Choi, *The Foreign Student,* 84.

25. Nicholas Cull, *The Cold War and the United States Information Agency: American Propaganda and Public Diplomacy, 1945–1989* (Cambridge: Cambridge University Press, 2008), 108.

26. Ibid., 101.

27. Penny M. von Eschen, *Satchmo Blows Up the World: Jazz Ambassadors Play the Cold War* (Cambridge and London: Harvard University Press, 2004), 7.

28. Cull, *The Cold War and the United States Information Agency,* 115, 116.

29. Roland Barthes, *Mythologies,* trans. Richard Howard and Annette Lavers (New York: Hill and Wang, 2012), 196.

30. Edward M. Kennedy, "The Immigration Act of 1965," *Annals of the American Academy of Political and Social Science* 367 (September 1966): 138.

31. Ibid., 141.

32. Ibid., 139.

33. See Vijay Prashad, *The Karma of Brown Folk* (Minneapolis and London: University of Minnesota Press, 2000), 74.

34. Ibid., 75.

35. Sucheng Chan, *Asian Americans: An Interpretive History* (New York: Twayne Publishers, 1991), 142.

36. Lowe, *Immigrant Acts,* 7.

37. Ibid.

38. Ibid.

39. Eqbal Ahmad, "Political Culture and Foreign Policy," in *The Selected Writings of Eqbal Ahmad,* ed. Carolee Bengelsdorf, Margaret Cerullo, and Yogesh Chandarani (New York: Columbia University Press, 2006), 215.

40. Aihwa Ong, *Neoliberalism as Exception: Mutations in Citizenship and Sovereignty* (Durham, N.C.: Duke University Press, 2006), 140 .

41. Mike Murase, "Ethnic Studies and Higher Education for Asian Americans," in *Counterpoint: Perspective on Asian America,* ed. Emma Gee et al. (Los Angeles: Regents of the University of California, 1976), 205.

42. Jhumpa Lahiri, *The Namesake: A Novel* (New York: First Mariner Books, 2003), 25–26; emphasis added. Subsequent references are given in the text.

43. Lowe, *Immigrant Acts,* 23.

44. Michael Omi and Howard Winant, *Racial Formations in the United States, from the 1960s to the 1990s* (New York: Routledge, 1994), 105.

45. Lowe, *Immigrant Acts,* 23–24.

46. For a discussion of the limits of the state as a site of appeal and resolution in minority demands, see "Angela Davis: Reflections on Race, Class, and Gender in the U.S.A.," in *The Politics of Culture in the Shadow of Capital,* ed. Lisa Lowe and David Lloyd (Durham, N.C., and London: Duke University Press, 1997).

47. Kimberlé Crenshaw, Neil Gotanda, Gary Peller, and Kendall Thomas, eds., *Critical Race Theory: The Key Writings That Formed the Movement* (New York: New Press, 1996), xiv.

48. Omi and Winant, *Racial Formations in the United States,* 97.

49. Karl Marx, "On the Jewish Question," in *The Marx-Engels Reader,* ed. Robert C. Tucker (New York: W. W. Norton, 1978), 31.

50. Ibid., 32.

51. Ibid., 31.

52. Ibid., 42.

53. Lahiri, *The Namesake,* 118.

54. Jenny Sharpe, "Postcolonial Studies in the House of U.S. Multiculturalism," in *A Companion to Postcolonial Studies,* ed. Henry Schwarz and Sangeeta Ray (Malden, Mass.: Blackwell, 2007), 114.

55. Ibid., 120.

56. Ibid., 115.

57. Spivak, *Outside in the Teaching Machine,* 55.

58. Prashad, *The Karma of Brown Folk,* 77–80.

59. Randall Williams, *The Divided World: Human Rights and Its Violence* (Minneapolis and London: University of Minnesota Press, 2010), xvi.

60. Lahiri, *The Namesake,* 288.

61. Choi, *The Foreign Student,* 247.

62. Ibid, 246.

63. Chuh, *Imagine Otherwise,* 9.

64. Max Weber, *From Max Weber: Essays in Sociology,* trans. and ed. H. H. Gerth and C. Wright Mills (New York: Oxford University Press, 1946), 240.

65. Roland Barthes, *S/Z: An Essay,* trans. Richard Miller (New York: Hill and Wang, 1974), 10–11.

66. Lahiri, *The Namesake,* 291.

6. *The Golden Era of Instructed Minorities*

1. Jacques Rancière, *The Politics of Aesthetics: The Distribution of the Sensible,* trans. Gabriel Rockhill (London and New York: Continuum, 2006), 13.

2. Brett Benjamin, *Invested Interests: Capital, Culture, and the World Bank* (Minneapolis and London: University of Minnesota Press, 2007), 92. I thank Rosemary Hennessy for this reference.

3. Ibid., 93.

4. Wilson Smith and Thomas Bender, "Disciplines and Interdisciplinarity," in *American Higher Education Transformed 1940–2005: Documenting the National Discourse,* ed. Wilson Smith and Thomas Bender (Baltimore: Johns Hopkins University Press, 2008), 239.

5. Ibid.

6. See Grace Hong, "The Future of Our Worlds: Black Feminism and the Politics of Knowledge under Globalization," *Meridians: Feminism, Race, Transnationalism* 8:2 (2008): 95–115.

7. See Christopher Newfield, *Unmaking the Public University: The Forty-Year Assault on the Middle Class* (Cambridge: Harvard University Press, 2008), 3.

8. Ibid., 2.

9. Ibid., 3, 4.

10. Ibid., 4.

11. John Stuart Mill, *On Liberty and Considerations of Representative Government,* ed. R. B. McCallum (Oxford: Basil and Blackwell, 1946), 190.

12. Ibid., 155–56.

13. Ibid., 156.

14. David Lloyd, "Genet's Genealogies: European Minorities and the Ends of the Canon," in *The Nature and Context of Minority Discourse,* ed. Abdul R. JanMohamed and David Lloyd (New York: Oxford University Press, 1990), 372.

15. Mill, *On Liberty and Considerations of Representative Government,* 291.

16. Lloyd, "Genet's Genealogies," 377. Subsequent references are given in the text.

17. Rancière, *The Politics of the Aesthetics,* 12.

18. Ibid.

19. Michael Denning, *Culture in the Age of Three Worlds* (London: Verso, 2004), 2.

20. Hong, "The Future of Our Worlds," 100.

21. Benjamin, *Invested Interests,* 115. Subsequent references are given in the text.

22. Cynthia Tolentino, *America's Experts: Race and the Fictions of Sociology* (Minneapolis and London: University of Minnesota Press, 2009), x.

23. Jodi Melamed, *Represent and Destroy: Rationalizing Violence in the New Racial Capitalism* (Minneapolis and London: University of Minnesota Press, 2011), xvi.

24. Ibid., 27.

25. Avery F. Gordon and Christopher Newfield, "Introduction," in *Mapping Multiculturalism,* ed. Avery F. Gordon and Christopher Newfield (Minneapolis and London: University of Minnesota Press, 1996), 4.

26. Ibid., 3.

27. Jacques Derrida, *Archive Fever: A Freudian Impression,* trans. Eric Prenowitz (Chicago and London: University of Chicago Press, 1995), 2.

28. See Sheila Slaughter and Larry L. Leslie, *Academic Capitalism: Politics, Policies, and the Entrepreneurial University* (Baltimore and London: Johns Hopkins University Press, 1997), 5–22.

29. Lisa Duggan, *The Twilight of Equality: Neoliberalism, Cultural Politics, and the Attack on Democracy* (Boston: Beacon Press, 2003), 9–10.

30. Ibid., xii.

31. Ibid., 10.

32. Zadie Smith, *On Beauty: A Novel* (New York: Penguin Press, 2005), 4–5.

33. See Herbert Marcuse, *One-Dimensional Man: Studies in the Ideology of Advanced Industrial Society* (London and New York: Routledge, 2002).

34. Smith, *On Beauty,* 117–18.

35. Michel Foucault, *The Order of Things: An Archaeology of the Human Sciences* (New York: Vintage Books, 1970), xxiii.

36. Kimberlé Crenshaw, Neil Gotanda, Gary Peller, and Kendall Thomas, eds., *Critical Race Theory: The Key Writings That Formed the Movement* (New York: New Press, 1996), xvi.

37. Howard Winant, *The New Politics of Race: Globalism, Difference, Justice* (Minneapolis and London: University of Minnesota Press, 2004), xiv; emphasis added.

38. James Baldwin, "Disturber of the Peace: James Baldwin—An Interview," in *Conversations with James Baldwin,* ed. Fred L. Stanley and Louis H. Pratt (Jackson and London: University of Mississippi Press, 1989), 64–65.

39. Saidiya V. Hartman, *Scenes of Subjection: Terror, Slavery, and Self-Making in Nineteenth-Century America* (Oxford and London: Oxford University Press, 1997), 18.

40. Ibid.

41. Crenshaw et al., *Critical Race Theory,* xvi.

42. Judith Butler, "An Affirmative View," in *Race and Representation: Affirmative Action* (Cambridge: Zone, 1998), 168–69.

43. Ibid., 169.

44. Crenshaw et al., *Critical Race Theory,* xv.

45. Lloyd, "Genet's Genealogy," 382.

46. Ibid.

47. Wilhelm von Humboldt, *Humanist without a Portfolio: An Anthology of the Writings of Wilhelm von Humboldt,* trans. Marianne Cowan (Detroit: Wayne State University Press, 1963), 126.

48. Smith, *On Beauty,* 261.

49. Ibid.

50. See Christopher Newfield's chapters 5 ("From Affirmative Action to the New Economy") and 6 ("The Battle for Meritocracy") in *Unmaking the Public University: The Forty-Year Assault on the Middle Class* (Cambridge: Harvard University Press, 2011).

51. Ibid., 87.

52. Smith, *On Beauty,* 227.

53. M. Jacqui Alexander, *Pedagogies of Crossing: Meditations on Feminism, Sexual Politics, Memory, and the Sacred* (Durham, N.C.: Duke University Press, 2005), 133.

54. Hong, "The Future of Our Worlds," 102.

55. Ibid., 102–3.

56. Ibid., 103.

57. Marcuse, *One-Dimensional Man,* 7.

58. Ibid., xii.

59. Smith, *On Beauty,* 177.

60. Audre Lorde, *Sister Outsider: Essays and Speeches* (New York: Quality Paperback Book Club, 1993), 57.

61. Ibid., 53.

62. Hong, "The Future of Our Worlds," 106.

63. Newfield, *The Unmaking of the Public University,* 4.

7. *Administering Sexuality; or, The Will to Institutionality*

1. Jacques Derrida, *Archive Fever: A Freudian Impression,* trans. Eric Prenowitz (Chicago and London: University of Chicago Press, 1995), 2.

2. Michel Foucault, *Power/Knowledge: Selected Interviews and Writings 1972–1977,* ed. Colin Gordon (New York: Pantheon Books, 1980), 119.

3. Bill Readings, *The University in Ruins* (Cambridge: Harvard University Press, 1996), 8.

4. Ibid., 30.

5. Max Weber, *From Max Weber: Essays in Sociology,* trans. and ed. H. H. Gerth and C. Wright Mills (New York: Oxford University Press, 1946), 212.

6. See, for instance, Christopher Newfield's deeply insightful book *Ivy and Industry: Business and the Making of the American University, 1880–1980* (Durham, N.C., and London: Duke University Press, 2003).

7. Sheila Slaughter and Larry Leslie, *Academic Capitalism: Politics, Policies, and the Entrepreneurial University* (Baltimore and London: Johns Hopkins University Press, 1997), 5.

8. Ibid., 6.

9. Ibid., 7.

10. Ibid., 12.

11. Chandra Talpade Mohanty, "On Race and Voice: Challenges for Liberal Education in the 1990s," in *Beyond a Dream Deferred: Multicultural Education and the Politics of Excellence,* ed. Becky Thompson and Sangeeta Tyagi (Minneapolis: University of Minnesota Press, 1993), 46.

12. See Lisa Duggan, *The Twilight of Equality: Neoliberalism, Cultural Politics, and the Attack on Democracy* (Boston: Beacon Press, 2003).

13. Judith Butler, *The Psychic Life of Power: Theories in Subjection* (Stanford, Calif.: Stanford University Press, 1997), 2.

14. Michel Foucault, *The History of Sexuality, Volume 1: An Introduction,* trans. Robert Hurley (New York: Vintage Books, 1990), 68.

15. Steven Seidman, "Queer-ing Sociology, Sociologizing Queer Theory: An Introduction," *Sociological Theory* 12:2 (July 1994): 169.

16. Ibid., 170.

17. Martin Weinberg and Colin J. Williams, "Gay Baths and the Social Organization of Impersonal Sex," *Social Problems* 23:2 (December 1975): 129.

18. Ibid., 134–35.

19. Lisa Power, *No Bath but Plenty of Bubbles: An Oral History of the Gay Liberation Front* (London: Cassell, 1995), 3.

20. http://psychology.ucdavis.edu/rainbow/html/dp-atkinson.html.

21. Gayle S. Rubin, "Thinking Sex: Notes for a Radical Theory of the Politics

of Sexuality," in *The Lesbian and Gay Studies Reader,* ed. Henry Abelove, Michèle Aina Barale, and David M. Halperin (New York and London: Routledge, 1993), 12.

22. Annalise Riles, "Introduction: In Response," in *Documents: Artifacts of Modern Knowledge,* ed. Annalise Riles (Ann Arbor: University of Michigan Press, 2006), 6.

23. Heather Love, *Feeling Backward: Loss and the Politics of Queer History* (Cambridge and London: Harvard University Press, 2007), 10.

24. Weber, *From Max Weber,* 215.

25. Ibid.

26. www.thingsthatfall.com/sleep.php; accessed February 28, 2010.

27. Mohan Sikka, "Ripe," unpublished manuscript.

28. Rubin "Thinking Sex," 15.

29. Ibid.

30. Sikka, "Ripe."

31. Ibid.

32. Martin F. Manalansan, "In the Shadows of Stonewall: Examining Gay Transnational Politics and the Gay Diasporic Dilemma," in *The Politics of Culture in the Shadow of Capital,* ed. Lisa Lowe and David Lloyd (Durham, N.C., and London: Duke University Press, 1997), 486.

33. Ibid., 487.

34. Friedrich Nietzsche, *Daybreak: Thoughts on the Prejudices of Morality,* trans. R. J. Hollingdale (Cambridge: Cambridge University Press, 1982), 184.

35. Michel Foucault, *The Archaeology of Knowledge and The Discourse on Language,* trans. A. M. Sheridan Smith (New York: Pantheon Books, 1972), 215–16. Subsequent references are given in the text.

Conclusion

1. http://www.libertybank.net/about/history.cfm; accessed September 3, 2011.

2. Frederick Jackson Turner, *The Frontier in American History* (New York: H. Holt and Company, 1920), 291.

3. Ibid., 309.

4. Ibid., 300.

5. Ibid., 292.

6. Michel Foucault, *Power/Knowledge: Selected Interviews and Other Writings 1972–1977,* ed. Colin Gordon (New York: Pantheon Books, 1980), 59.

7. Ibid., 60.

8. Turner, *The Frontier in American History,* 292.

9. Edward W. Said, *Representations of the Intellectual* (New York: Vintage Books, 1994), 76.

10. Sun Tzu, *The Art of Warfare,* trans. Roger Ames (New York: Ballantine Books, 1993), 126.

11. Foucault, *Power/Knowledge,* 62.

12. This designation of a theory of critical interdisciplinarity is taken from Antonio Negri's theorization of marxism in *Marx beyond Marx: Lessons on the Grundrisse* (London: Autonomedia, 1991).

13. Foucault, *Power/Knowledge,* 142.

14. For an analogous discussion, see Judith Halberstam, "Queer Temporality and Postmodern Geographies," in *In a Queer Time and Place: Transgender Bodies, Subcultural Lives* (New York and London: New York University Press, 2005).

15. Ibid., 61.

16. Foucault, *Power/Knowledge,* 56.

17. José Esteban Muñoz, *Cruising Utopia: The Then and There of Queer Futurity* (New York and London: New York University Press, 2009), 1.

Index

abolitionists: Hartman's analysis of white, 196–97

absorption, policies of, 27; assistance of academy with, 27–29. *See also* affirmation; recognition

Academic Capitalism: Politics, Policies, and the Entrepreneurial University (Slaughter and Leslie), 212

academy: as archiving institution, 12, 14–15; as both object of critique and instrument of alternatives, 108–9; as conduit for conveying forms of political economy to state and capital, 8; excellence as unifying principle of, 80; materialist critique and relocation of, 8–18, 145–46; new configuration of power within, 4–5; as primary articulator of state and civil society, Kant on, 11; read as derivation of capitalist economic formations, 8–9, 18; as site for articulating representation and welfare of people, 87–88

academy, American: absorption of local culture and difference through, 27–29; affirmative action, dismantling of, 198–99,

202–3; affirmative action, factoring race for, 104–9; alternatives to evaluative systems of, 177–79; ascendancy of administrator and displacement of scholar/professor in university, crisis of, 211–12; closure of critical universes and, 206, 207–8; as contradictory site, 190; diffuse strategies comprising powers of, 229; as domain of minority opportunity and diminishment, 207; eco-nomic character of, 12; as embodiment of Kant's lower faculty, 88; epistemological propositions of post–civil rights, 143–46; flow of influence, student movements as contradiction of, 9; historic task of representing national culture, 27; identified as writerly vs. readerly by student movements, 38–39; inclusion and regulation of Asian labor, 163–64; incorporation of black literature within, 34–35; institutional discourse of diversity shaping life within, 203–5; lack of redistributive practices in, 174; liberal arts vs. managerial training, debate in

Roderick A. Ferguson is professor of race and critical theory in the Department of American Studies at the University of Minnesota, Twin Cities. He is author of *Aberrations in Black: Toward a Queer of Color Critique* (Minnesota, 2003) and coeditor, with Grace Hong, of *Strange Affinities: The Gender and Sexual Politics of Comparative Racialization.*